*Religion, politics and violence in
nineteenth-century Belfast*

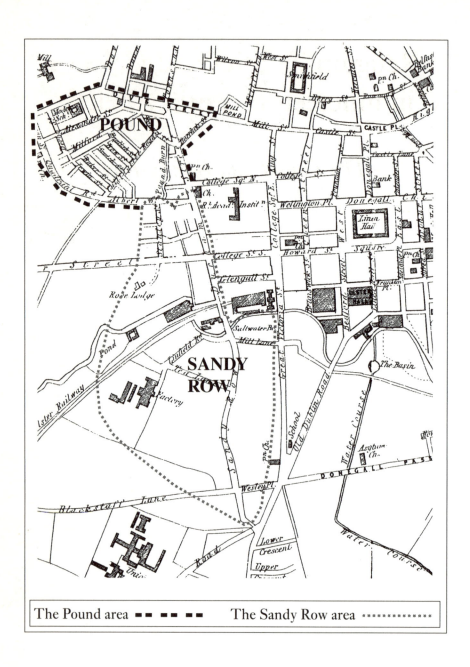

The Pound and Sandy Row districts

Religion, politics and violence in nineteenth-century Belfast

The Pound and Sandy Row

❖

Catherine Hirst

FOUR COURTS PRESS

Set in 10.5 on 12.5 point Ehrhardt for
FOUR COURTS PRESS LTD
Fumbally Lane, Dublin 8, Ireland
e-mail: info@four-courts-press.ie
http://www.four-courts-press.ie
and in North America
FOUR COURTS PRESS
c/o ISBS, 5824 N.E. Hassalo Street, Portland, OR 97213.

A catalogue record for this title
is available from the British Library.

ISBN 1–85182–651–3

Printed in Great Britain
by MPG Books, Bodmin, Cornwall

For Mark

Contents

Acknowledgments

I would like to thank, firstly, Professor Sean Connolly and Dr Alvin Jackson, for their invaluable assistance, dedication and encouragement when supervising my PhD research at Queen's University, Belfast, on which this book is based. I am particularly grateful to Professor Connolly for advice about publication.

I would like to express my gratitude to the Commonwealth Scholarship Commission and the British Council for their financial support.

I wish to thank the staff of the following institutions: Queen's University library; the Public Records Office of Northern Ireland, the Linen Hall library; the Central Library, Belfast; the House of Orange, Belfast; the Ulster Museum; the Ulster Folk and Transport Museum; and the National Archives of Ireland.

I would like to thank my parents, John and Christine Hirst, for reading draft chapters and for all their support during my years of study. I would like to thank my grandma, Nancy Hirst, for giving me my computer. I would also like to thank my friends from Queen's, Jill Baisinger, Gill McIntosh, Diane Urquhart, Rosemary Richey, Marc Mulholland and Noel and Patricia Armour for their encouragement and for welcoming us so warmly to Belfast. I would like to thank all our relatives who travelled from Australia to visit us in Belfast, John and Christine Hirst, Dave Jaques, Anne and Jane Rawson, Christina and Kyle Fazari, Lois Pollock, Louise and Michael Andrew, Betty Penberthy, Marj Orford and Karen Orford. I would like to especially thank Patricia Horton for proof reading and Simone Wöhst for her friendship and encouragement during the final stages of writing.

Finally, I would like to thank Mark Orford for all his support and encouragement, for proof reading draft chapters and for coming to live in Belfast for three years.

Introduction

This book challenges the current assumptions about the development of Belfast politics in the nineteenth century. The historical consensus at the present time is that Belfast politics could have developed into something other than a unionist/nationalist divide before the 1880s. This argument rests on the assumption that Belfast Catholics only became nationalist in the 1880s after the home rule movement had been imported into Ulster from the south of Ireland. The unionism of working-class Protestants is considered to have originated during the same period and is often seen as a reflection of the Protestant domination of the skilled trades from the 1860s onwards. The arguments of the historians who subscribe to these views are outlined below. Their findings will be examined in the body of this work in the light of new evidence uncovered during my research.

A.C. Hepburn argues that 'until the last decade of the nineteenth century, ... the minority in Belfast was defined fairly narrowly by its Catholic religion, was under clerical leadership in social and political as well as spiritual life, and had more in common with Irish migrant groups in British and overseas cities than with the rest of Ireland ... In particular, the popular nationalism of the late nineteenth century was developed entirely in the south and subsequently imported into the north.' Hepburn maintains that until the 1890s, there was some possibility of Belfast Catholics developing a regional identity. He points to the fact that for part of the 1890s, Bishop Henry of Down and Connor succeeded, in opposition to the local Irish National League, in running candidates to represent Catholic interests in local elections. In this rejection of nationalism at the local level, Hepburn sees the seeds of a potential development of a regional identity based on accommodation of local Catholic interests.[1]

Brian Walker also maintains that a political division other than unionism or nationalism could have developed prior to the 1880s. A division between Ulster, Catholic and Protestant, and the rest of Ireland could have developed based on the division between an industrial society and an agricultural society and a liberal/conservative or a labour/conservative division could have been the defining feature of Ulster politics. Walker points to the increase in literacy, the resolution of the land question, the growth of Belfast and the strengthening of religious identities which occurred during this period as assisting the development of unionism and nationalism. He adds that 'possibly a more sensitive and effective government reaction to the situation in Ireland in the early 1870s could have undermined home rule and nationalist demands.'[2]

Peter Gibbon in his *Origins of Ulster unionism* sees the Protestant working-class's commitment to the union as originating in their domination of skilled trades in Belfast from the 1860s onwards. These Protestant skilled tradesmen realised that their prosperity depended on the continual success of heavy industry in Belfast which could have been put in jeopardy by an end to the British link. Gibbon considers the manifestations of sectarianism prior to the 1860s to be the product of local rivalry rather than evidence of an 'ethnic' conflict. Before the development of heavy industry in the 1860s, Protestants had an 'Orange' outlook, according to Gibbon, because of loyalty to 'Orange patrons' responsible for jobs and housing. The riots during this period did not, he argues, represent an understanding of wider Catholic and Protestant interests.[3]

Frank Wright in his *Two lands on one soil* takes a longer term view of the development of unionism and nationalism than other historians.[4] However, as the book covers Ulster as a whole, the development of unionism and nationalism among the working class in Belfast has not been as fully researched as it could have been in a study devoted entirely to Belfast. In particular, the importance of the Repeal Association and the Fenian society among Belfast Catholics has been missed in Wright's analysis.

Apart from Wright's study, not much work has been done on Belfast politics prior to 1886. By examining the evidence of police and magisterial reports sent to Dublin Castle concerning the Ribbon society, the Repeal Association, the Fenian society and the Home Rule Association, this book challenges the argument that the politics of Belfast Catholics only became nationalist in the 1880s. In addition, articles in the Catholic newspapers in Belfast are analysed to illuminate the development of politics among the Catholic population. Magisterial reports, as well as Belfast newspapers, are also examined in order to test the thesis that unionism developed relatively late among Protestant workers. The importance of economic advantage in working-class Protestants' commitment to the union is also assessed.

The decision to study two working-class areas in particular was taken in order to obtain a better understanding of the causes of sectarian conflict and the development of unionism and nationalism among the Belfast working classes. If sectarian conflict in Belfast is only examined in the light of the social and economic positions of Catholics and Protestants as a whole, the relevance of Protestant economic advantage cannot be properly assessed. The Catholic Pound and Protestant Sandy Row districts were the logical choices for this study as their inhabitants were the main combatants in sectarian riots throughout the nineteenth century. In order to fully understand the causes of sectarian conflict, it is necessary to examine the social and economic composition of these districts. The baptismal records of the Protestant churches, the 1852 census of Church of Ireland members in the Christ Church district, the 1837 and 1860 land valuations, the Belfast street directories, the 1901 census and contemporary descriptions of the two districts have been used to try to reconstruct the social and economic composition of the Pound and Sandy Row.

Many assumptions have been made about the causes and nature of rioting in Belfast but no thorough study of the topic has been made. This book looks at the reports of the riot commissioners who investigated the riots of 1857, 1864 and 1886, police and magisterial reports as well as newspaper reports in an attempt to produce a comprehensive analysis of rioting in Belfast. An understanding of the nature of rioting in Belfast is essential for constructing an analysis of the wider problem of the development of sectarian politics among the Catholic and Protestant working class. The literature on British riots is also referred to in order to establish whether any comparisons can be made which could be helpful for understanding the dynamics of Belfast rioting.

Catholic and Protestant working-class Belfast: the Pound and Sandy Row, 1820-50

The most violent districts of Belfast in the nineteenth century were the Catholic Pound and the Protestant Sandy Row. This book focuses on these two communities in order to gain a better understanding of the causes of sectarian conflict and the development of unionism and nationalism among the working class in Belfast. This chapter examines the social and economic composition of the Sandy Row and Pound districts to establish whether there were substantial differences between the two areas which could have contributed to sectarian conflict.

The Pound, a Catholic district, was centred around the old cattle pound in Pound Street about half a mile west of the city centre; it was bordered by Divis Street and the lower Falls Road on the north and west, Barrack Street and Durham Street on the east and Albert Street on the south. Catholics, and unskilled Protestants, migrating to Belfast in the first half of the nineteenth century were attracted to the Pound area because of its proximity to the town's linen and cotton mills. Catholics also favoured the Pound because it was not far from St Mary's chapel and it was within walking distance of St Patrick's, the only other Catholic church in Belfast until 1844. There was also the security of living among one's own kind. The Pound bordered the district of Castle Street, Mill Street and Smithfield, an area with a traditionally high Catholic population, being just outside the old town walls where Catholics were allowed to settle in the seventeenth century.[1]

Although the Pound is first mentioned as a Catholic stronghold in the press in 1835, its links with the Catholic community went back to the 1820s. Many of the Pound's streets were developed by Catholic investors who owned or leased the land from the marquis of Donegall. The older streets of the Pound appearing in the 1820 Belfast street directory, such as Hamill Street and Lettuce Hill, later John Street, were built by the Catholic businessman John Hamill after whom they were named, and the newer streets, such as Albert Street, Quadrant Street and Brooke Street, were built by a Catholic investor, William Watson, in the early 1850s.[2] The evidence submitted to the commissioners of Irish education shows that there were three small schools run by Catholic teachers in Lettuce Hill and Barrack Street with a majority of Catholic pupils in the mid 1820s.[3]

According to the Belfast street directories, the majority of the Pound's population in the early to mid nineteenth century were unskilled labourers, mill workers, weavers and artisans. Publicans, shopkeepers, dealers and cow keepers also lived in the district as well as more substantial shopkeepers in Barrack Street.[4]

The origin of the people who migrated to the Pound from 1820 to 1850 is difficult to pin down. The account of John Burrow, a traveller to Ireland in 1835, is often used to describe the origins of Belfast Catholics. He recorded that 'some 4–5000 raw, uneducated Catholic labourers from the south' had 'poured into the city'.[5] If Burrow is not referring to the south of Ulster but to the south of Ireland, the census figures contradict him. The 1841 census shows that 84.8% of the town's population were born in Antrim, Down or Belfast, 10.5% elsewhere in Ulster and only 2.1% in the rest of Ireland.[6] It seems clear from these figures that the majority of the Pound population probably originated from Ulster. Due to the Catholic majority in the outlying parts of Ulster and the Protestant majority in Antrim and Down, Catholics probably formed the majority of the Ulster migrants from areas other than Antrim and Down. However, the distinction was not clear cut. Protestants also migrated from these areas and, conversely, many Catholics originally came from Antrim and Down.[7]

In the first half of the nineteenth century there was a not-insignificant number of Protestants, both Presbyterian and Episcopalian, living in the Pound district. A few of these Protestants were well off such as the merchant and the distiller mentioned in the Christ Church baptismal register as living in Barrack Street in 1837 and the mill manager recorded as living in Albert Street in 1844. However, the vast majority of Protestants living in the Pound were labourers, mill workers, weavers or artisans just like their Catholic neighbours.[8] Obviously the church records only tell of those Protestants who actually attended church and had their children baptised. The number of nominal Protestants was probably higher. The Christ Church census of 1852 gives the exact numbers of all Episcopalians in the Pound, whether nominal or church-going. There are only four Episcopalian families left in Barrack Street and, although there are not equivalent Presbyterian statistics, this seems to indicate a decline in the Protestant population resulting from the deterioration of community relations and increased sectarian rioting. Surprisingly there are nine Episcopalian families, mainly mill workers and labourers, recorded as living in Pound Street itself in 1852 and most of these had at least some church-going members. Although the Protestant population of the old streets of the Pound appears to have declined during the late 1840s, some Protestants continued to live in the very heart of this Catholic ghetto despite the riots of the 1830s and 1840s.[9]

Apart from the more prosperous thoroughfares, such as Barrack Street, the area was one of cramped terrace housing, often without yards, piped water, private privies or even back doors. The dwellings were often shared by more than one family. Part of the district was subject to flooding whenever the

'Blackstaff nuisance' broke its banks and the people suffered greatly during cholera and fever epidemics. The slovenly thatched cottages recorded in the 1837 valuation on wasteland between the terraced housing would have heightened the impression of a slum area. After 1845 when regulations were introduced, the standard of housing improved as rooms had to be a certain size and thatch was made illegal.[10] Despite this miserable description of the district, the housing was actually slightly better than that in Protestant Sandy Row so it was by no means only the Catholic working class who suffered appalling housing conditions in Belfast.[11]

The Protestant district of Sandy Row bordered the Pound to the south. The district centred around Sandy Row, the old road leading out of Belfast to Lisburn, and for the purposes of this study all the intersecting streets and their lanes and entries west of Great Victoria Street and north of the present train line near Donegall Road will be included. From very early times, Sandy Row had an industrial, working-class character. The Blackstaff river which runs through the area is a good source of sleech, a type of clay used to make bricks. Situated conveniently just outside Belfast, Sandy Row began as a brick-making centre for the town. A map of Belfast in 1783 shows a road leading off Sandy Row 'to the Brickfield'.[12] This road became known as Tea Lane, later Rowland Street, apparently because the brickfield workers would throw their tea dregs into the street in their tea breaks.[13] In the early 1800s, the establishment of cotton and linen mills in nearby Durham Street, Tea Lane and Linfield Road consolidated the industrial nature of the area and made it the destination of numerous migrants from the countryside. Unlike the Pound district, there were no incentives for migrants settling in Sandy Row other than proximity to the mills. There were no churches or schools in the area until the 1830s and it was not a haven for any particular group in the way that the Pound was due to its proximity to St Mary's and the older Catholic area around Mill Street.

The early character of Sandy Row was, at least nominally, Protestant and possibly mainly Presbyterian. In the 1780s, Belfast was a mainly Presbyterian town and the few Catholics generally resided in the Mill Street/Smithfield area. In the late 1820s, the researchers of the interdenominational Belfast town mission described the inhabitants of Sandy Row as generally being Protestant, the majority of whom were Presbyterian.[14] However, by 1852 the two denominations' numbers were roughly equal according to the Christ Church census, suggesting that the migration of the rural poor from Episcopalian parts of Ulster may have exceeded that of Presbyterians.[15] In common with Belfast as a whole, the majority of people migrating to Sandy Row probably came from Antrim and Down; but the heavy flow of Episcopalian migrants suggests a disproportionate number came from Down and other Episcopalian regions of Ulster such as parts of Armagh and Fermanagh. The limited records available suggest a small Methodist presence in Sandy Row from as early as 1820.[16] These people probably came from the insecure outlying parts of Ulster, such as the Lough Erne area, or areas of high sectarian tension, such as the 'linen triangle' between Lisburn, Dungannon and Armagh, where Methodism made most of its converts among Episcopalians.[17]

It is difficult to estimate the number of Catholics who lived in Sandy Row in the early to mid nineteenth century. Some undoubtedly would have been attracted to the area by the proximity of the mills despite the disadvantages of living in an area without a traditionally strong Catholic presence. However, the numbers of Catholics in Sandy Row were probably lower than the numbers of Protestants in the Pound. In addition to the disadvantages mentioned above, Sandy Row acquired a reputation for intimidation at an early stage. As early as 1825, a Catholic was beaten in a sectarian attack in Sandy Row.[18] Still, a few Catholics did live there as there are accounts of their houses being burned in riots in 1843 and there are reports of further burnings and expulsions during the 1857 riots.[19] Catholics probably lived on the outskirts of the district as the expulsions during riots occurred in border streets such as Combermere Street near Shaftesbury Square and Stanley Street near the Pound.[20]

The people of Sandy Row were mainly weavers and labourers. Weavers form a majority of those appearing on the limited school and baptismal records while labourers are the largest occupation group listed in the Belfast Street Directory. The numbers of weavers and labourers were undoubtedly higher than the street directory suggests, since many of them would have occupied the poorest houses which were not included in the directories. The other common occupations were mill workers, such as warpers and flax dressers, and tradesmen, such as shoemakers, carpenters and bricklayers, as well as publicans and small shopkeepers.[21]

The housing in the Sandy Row district was very poor, poorer in fact than that of the main streets of the Pound. A typical second-class row house was let for £5 5s per annum compared to £6 to £8 per annum in the Pound. Some houses in Sandy Row itself were classified as third-class whereas the houses in Pound Street were nearly always given a second-class rating. The housing in lanes and entries was extremely poor. In Tea Lane, for example, 38 houses were too poor to be valued for rates purposes and the valuation records the existence of 'six small cabbins very small and bad paying 0/10d a week'.[22] The district also suffered from the flooding of the Blackstaff river and severe fever and cholera outbreaks. The Christ Church baptismal register testifies to the extent of death and disease with many children in the 1830s being baptised 'in a dying state'.[23]

It has often been assumed that the mill owners owned the bulk of the houses in Sandy Row.[24] In fact they owned only a small number of houses. The only mill owner land lord mentioned in the 1837 valuation, Conway Grimshaw of Murphy and Grimshaw's Linfield Mill, only owned ten houses in Tea Lane, including one substantial house occupied by the mill foreman. As in the Pound, some of the housing was owned by developers who built themselves houses in the area whereas other developers lived outside the district.[25] The importance of mill owners in this area has been overstated and consequently their role in influencing the politics of the inhabitants has also been exaggerated.

Apart from being predominantly Protestant and Catholic respectively, the Sandy Row and Pound districts were similar in socio-economic terms. The inhabitants were generally weavers and unskilled workers while a few were tradesmen. Although a description of the two districts in 1857 given by the resident magistrate suggests that there were more labourers in the Pound district, the two districts were still said to be populated with 'people from much the same class ... tradesmen, operatives and people connected with mills and factories'.[26] If Sandy Row had fewer labourers, this advantage was cancelled out by a poorer standard of housing as shown in the 1837 and 1860 valuations. The population of both areas came overwhelmingly from Ulster and although more Catholics than Protestants probably came from the outlying areas of Ulster, the high numbers of Church of Ireland migrants to Sandy Row suggest that many of these migrants also came from areas other than Antrim and Down. In any case, the difference in origins of the migrants in the two districts was not stark enough to be reflected in different customs. The similar nature of the two districts suggests that the origins of sectarianism cannot be found in any economic advantages enjoyed by the Protestants or in suspicion caused by the practice of different customs.

Sectarian conflict, 1813–34

In this period, the inhabitants of Sandy Row and the Pound had little contact with ministers, priests or middle-class Belfast. The sectarianism of these districts during this period was due to the importation of conflict from the Ulster countryside. Districts like Sandy Row began to develop in the 1820s, a time of heightened tension in rural Ulster. Migrants from the Ulster countryside brought with them their sectarian fears and hatreds and this was reflected in the establishment and growth of the Orange and Ribbon societies in Belfast. The most sectarian working-class areas, particularly Protestant districts, coincided with the main handloom weaver residential areas suggesting that the peculiar social and economic situation of weavers is also relevant to an understanding of the development of sectarianism in Belfast. As in much of Ulster, sectarian tension increased in the wake of the successful campaign for Catholic emancipation in 1829, resulting in numerous riots in the early 1830s.

It is not my intention to analyse in depth the origins of sectarianism in Ulster or the reasons for the spread of sectarianism in the early nineteenth century but rather to examine how this ethnic conflict was transferred to Belfast.[1] I would accept the thesis outlined by A.T.Q. Stewart, David Miller and Frank Wright that sectarianism had its origins in the colonial settlement and Protestant fears of Catholic attack.[2] Frank Wright's explanation is more comprehensive in that he demonstrates the effect Catholic organisation and self-defence had on moderate Protestant opinion. Wright maintains that, in colonial settlements, a point is reached when the colonial elite feel secure enough not to favour the 'plebeian' settlers if it is not economically advantageous. Moreover, privileges of status are no longer the exclusive property of the 'settler' population. In the 1780s in Armagh, the local Protestant elite allowed Catholics to join the Volunteers, this outraged plebeian settlers who both feared the arming of Catholics and resented the loss of status to themselves that this entailed. The 'plebeian' Protestants began to raid Catholic homes for weapons. At first the local elite sympathised with the Catholics, and some landlords even distributed arms to their Catholic tenants. However, once Catholics were no longer simply the victims and began to militarily oppose these Protestant gangs such as the Peep O Day boys, the fears of moderate Protestants were heightened to such an extent that they began to accept pan-Protestant defence organisations such as the Orange Order.[3]

Other parts of Ulster, particularly Antrim and north Down, experienced a different political development in the late eighteenth century. In these predominantly Presbyterian districts, there was significant support for the Society of United Irishmen, a radical revolutionary movement for Irish independence inspired by the democratic ideals of the American and French revolutions. As the Presbyterians were, like Roman Catholics, excluded from government office up to 1780 and forced to pay tithes to the Church of Ireland, they felt a strong sense of grievance towards the government which was not tempered by fears of the Catholic population who were, in these districts, few in number and non-threatening. Although many Presbyterians would have distrusted and disliked the Roman Catholic Church, they were able to feel empathy with the situation of Catholics under siege from the Orange Order in Co. Armagh. Wright emphasises that they had the necessary 'space' and distance from the sharp edge of colonial settlement to empathise with the Catholics and indeed some of the prominent United Irishmen from these areas defended Armagh Catholics in court.[4]

The State of the Country papers and newspaper reports suggest that sectarian hostility in the Ulster countryside increased between 1812 and 1815 to such an extent that 'party' (i.e., sectarian) riots began to occur in areas such as Ballynahinch which had previously been United Irish strongholds. Sectarian clashes were also reported for the first time in Belfast in 1813, reflecting the increasing tension of rural Ulster. As there is no social history of the Ulster countryside in this period, it is not easy to ascertain the causes of increasing sectarianism between 1812 and 1815. Unfortunately, the reports in the State of the Country papers suggest no reason for the increasing tension except mutual fear. In this period weavers and factory workers did experience a sharp decline in their living standards as the price of food rose. There were economically motivated riots in Belfast, Bangor and Antrim. This economic distress may have exacerbated sectarian tension.

In the same decade, the sectarian hostility of parts of the Ulster countryside was transferred to Belfast by settlers from Down, Armagh, Derry and the Ulster border counties. The first riot in Belfast between Orangemen and Catholics in North Street on the Twelfth of July 1813 was similar to orange and green encounters in agrarian areas. Orangemen returning from Lisburn on the evening of the Twelfth were attacked by Catholics with brick bats outside a public house used by the Orangemen as a lodge. Some of the Orangemen fired shots at the Catholic crowd. Two people were killed and four were severely injured.[5] This tradition of conflict was carried on into the 1830s and beyond but its significance has been overlooked by historians such as Maguire. He describes the 1813 riot as being agrarian in nature and not typical of early nineteenth-century Belfast.[6] A close examination of newspapers and the State of the Country papers reveals how frequent such encounters were. In January 1814, a yeoman's funeral procession played orange tunes which led a group of Catholics to dig up the yeoman's coffin and leave it exposed on the Ormeau bridge.[7] In August 1814, an attack took place on the public house of an Orangeman in North Street who had been at the centre of the 1813 riot. In June 1815, another riot took place in North Street when Catholics prevented a group of Protestants from leaving for the Shankill after they had been yelling insults and making threats.[8]

In the early 1820s, there was a general upsurge in sectarian tension throughout Ulster which was again reflected in rioting in Belfast. The 'Second Reformation', the unprecedented attempt by Protestant missionaries and voluntary societies to convert the Catholic population, is generally seen as the cause of the increased tension of the 1820s. Hempton and Hill also emphasise the impact on Protestant fears of the general resurgence of Irish Catholicism in the early nineteenth century. The number of chapels in Ulster increased significantly, church administration was improved as was discipline and pastoral care. The number of priests in Ulster increased by 52% between 1800 and 1835. Societies such as the Catholic Bible Society, established in 1813, and the Irish Catholic Society for the Diffusion of Religious Knowledge, established in 1823, helped counteract the proselytising efforts of the Protestant voluntary societies and increased Catholic confidence. Catholic confidence was also increased by the development of a Catholic middle-class who could provide leadership in the battle against Protestant proselytisers, produce Catholic newspapers and generally demonstrate that Catholics were capable of taking their rightful place in society.[9]

The second reformation's attempt to eliminate Catholicism coincided with the circulation of a pamphlet called *Pastorini's prophecies* among the Catholics of Ulster which predicted the downfall of Protestantism on Christmas Day 1824. This millenarianism was probably a symptom rather than a cause of conflict; however, the prophecies did, in turn, increase the fears of rural communities. Evangelical missionaries claimed that the prophecies, based on the writings of a Catholic bishop, Walmsley, in 1771, encouraged Catholics to 'cut off heresy, that is, exterminate all Protestants and overturn the present government'.[10] Although the Catholic hierarchy declared that Walmsley's writings had been misinterpreted, fears were not allayed among Protestants in rural Ulster. An example of the threats facing communities in Ulster can be seen in a notice displayed near Tandragee in 1819 warning that all Protestants would shortly be massacred.[11] Regardless of the true origin of this threatening notice, Protestant peasants were afraid and applied to their landlord for protection. The government also took it seriously enough to order extra troops to the area.

This excitement and fear encouraged Protestant and Catholic peasants to band together for protection. Many Protestants joined the Orange Order particularly in areas with a finely balanced sectarian divide. Catholics banded together in the secret society known as the Ribbon society which had as its objects the defeat of Orangeism and Protestantism and a commitment to an

Irish Republic hazily defined as the separation of Ireland from England. An informer at a Ribbonmen trial in Dublin in 1822 declared that 'their intention was to rebel, to separate themselves from the English government, and put down the Protestant religion'. Their catechism included such lines as 'What are your intentions? – To regain all lost rights since the Reformation. Where are your intentions? – In my head, under my hat in an ivory box locked with a golden key. Where is the golden key? – In the ocean of eternity.' The Ribbon society had no effective military plan for an uprising beyond the notion of them all rising together throughout Ireland at a given moment. They also appeared to be waiting for middle-class Catholics to take the lead in any uprising but they were sorely disappointed when O'Connell failed to give them any such encouragement. After the 1820s, the emphasis on insurrection declined and the Ribbon society's main objectives were to resist the Orange Order and to provide mutual aid to their members.[12]

Clashes between Orangemen and Ribbonmen occurred in many parts of Ulster in the early 1820s. Sectarian hostility was particularly strong in counties Londonderry, Tyrone, Down, Armagh, Cavan and Monaghan and took the form of riots at fairs or on the Twelfth of July, house burning and military drilling at night.[13] In 1825, the inspector general of police described the state of the Ulster countryside in a report to the lord lieutenant, 'Throughout almost the whole of the province, the lower orders of the Protestants and Catholics appear to be pitted at each other and the slightest commencement of hostilities on either side would ... be attended with the loss of many lives. Great alarm and terror ... has for some time past existed, the Protestants fully satisfied that an attempt would be made to assassinate and exterminate them and the Catholics ... equally convinced that the Orangemen mediated an attack on the lives of all their persuasion. In many places, both parties stay up at night with dread but this has much abated, although confidence is far from being restored.'[14]

The fact that the Ribbon and Orange societies were introduced into Belfast in the early decades of the nineteenth century shows the extent to which sectarian tension had been imported into the town. The existence of these societies then helped to perpetuate sectarianism in Belfast. Sectarian tension in Belfast did not increase solely because the Catholic population was increasing as A.T.Q. Stewart has argued.[15] Increasing Catholic migration would have increased Protestant anxieties but the fact that the new Protestant and Catholic migrants came from an environment of sectarian tension greatly exacerbated the situation.

A description of the state of Ribbonism submitted to Dublin Castle by a Catholic barrister in the 1830s testifies to the organisation's strength in Belfast: 'As to Antrim, it is extremely odd that the system prevails to a greater extent in Belfast than in any other town in the kingdom. On this point, my information is above suspicion. There are 53 companies of Ribbonmen in that town, and the number in each individual company can be accurately ascertained [the rule was 36]. The entire body is very large as shown by gatherings at the funerals of its members on several occasions – They have regular meetings, dances etc. but they have never committed any crimes … They consist of the poorer classes, tradesmen and servants, with many publicans at their head, who … find their support worth something.' The Belfast Ribbonmen take 'no oath and profess to be united with the view of resisting the Orangemen. Great efforts have been made to break up the association by many of the Catholic clergy but, so far, vainly.'[16] Ribbonism in Belfast, and in other northern and eastern towns, made most of its converts among the lower classes (but not among the destitute) and many of its leaders were publicans who profited from the society's meetings which took place in public houses.[17] In 1839, a number of suspected Ribbon leaders were arrested in Belfast including two publicans and one tile manufacturer from the Pound. John Houston, a publican from Divis Street, was accused of being a county delegate and the other two were alleged to be lodge masters. Other leaders mentioned by informers included a shoemaker and an iron dealer from Smithfield and a chandler from Carrick Hill.[18] In the 1840s, the society was still strong in Belfast with an estimated 1000 members.[19]

There is little information on the Orange Order in Belfast in the first half of the nineteenth century. The Select Committee inquiry into the Orange Order hardly mentions Belfast and the Orange Order records are fairly sparse. The Grand Lodge registry of warrants lists 10 lodges in Belfast in 1823, 27 in 1828-9 and 42 in 1856.[20] The number of lodges was not particularly large but, judging by newspaper reports, they were concentrated in the weaving districts of Sandy Row, Brown's Square and Ballymaccarret so in these districts the number of Orangemen could have been quite substantial.[21] Some friendly societies which met in public houses also tended to have an Orange character so it was not just the Orange Order proper which brought together working-class Protestants in a sectarian organisation. The Orangemen had only limited middle-class support in the early nineteenth century, particularly during the institution's dissolution between 1836 and 1845. Its local leaders, like those of the Ribbonmen, were mainly publicans and others from within the working-class communities.[22]

The existence of secret sectarian societies in Belfast was encouraged by the absence of an impartial system of law and order. Prior to the establishment of the system of centrally appointed magistrates in 1835-6, the administration of justice rested with local landlords,[23] whose sympathies were often conservative and Orange. Although the Orange Order lacked widespread support among the Belfast middle-class in the 1820s and 1830s, they had the sympathy of the local authorities in the event of any clashes with Catholic crowds. For example, in 1825, the police arrested 23 Catholics for rioting whereas no Orangemen were charged with any acts of violence or for parading illegally. In 1832, two local magistrates and the deputy lord lieutenant for Co. Down attended the funeral of an Orangeman who had been murdered. The next day, a Catholic was murdered in retaliation. The magistrates offered a reward for the capture of the Orangeman's murderer but not for the capture of the Catholic's murderer. In 1833, a group of special constables alleged that instead of removing an Orange arch in Brown Square, four local magistrates and the town police were actually protecting it. A group of Orangemen who had erected it were forcing passers by to lift their hats as they passed under it.[24] The sympathy of the local magistrates and police made Orange crowds bolder in their actions while the absence of any reliable protection from the state against the Orangemen made the Ribbon society seem even more essential within working-class Catholic districts. It should be stressed, however, that the authorities did not deliberately encourage sectarian clashes and on the occasions when they attempted to enforce government proclamations against Orange parades, there were violent clashes between Orangemen and the local authorities.

Sectarianism took on a more uncompromising form in the environment of an industrial town. The relatively stable and familial relationships of the countryside which to some extent could regulate sectarianism were absent in the town. Although Catholics and Protestants lived in mutual fear in parts of the Ulster countryside, it was often Catholics or Protestants in general they feared rather than all their neighbours of the opposite persuasion. Witnesses to government enquiries, such as the Orange convert, the Revd Mortimer O'Sullivan, commented that it was not necessarily Protestant or Catholic neighbours that were feared but the wider Orange and Ribbon conspiracies. In the event of a massacre launched by either of these societies, it was assumed that some untrustworthy locals would willingly join in but others would be forced to participate.[25] The Tandragee landlord who brought a massacre warning to the attention of the government in 1819 stated that it was not the local Catholics who the Protestants feared but the Ribbonmen in the next county.[26]

If neighbours were not generally feared, then it can be assumed that at some level relations were civil. More recent studies of sectarianism in rural areas, such as Rosemary Harris' *Prejudice and tolerance in Ulster*, reveal that relations between Catholics and Protestants are neighbourly, civil and even friendly despite there being a general fear of and prejudice towards the other group. These civil relationships are based on shared, long-standing family connections in the locality and shared interests in farming. In Harris' study, an Orangeman regards his Catholic neighbour's farm as a bench mark for good farming, a relationship of mutual respect stretching back over generations. Catholic and Protestant farmers socialise at the local fair and attend each other's wakes. At the same time there are accepted conventions regulating the behaviour between members of the different communities. Harris describes how it was considered natural for Protestants and Catholics to sell their land only to co-religionists and to shop only in establishments run by members of their own community.

Intermarriage was considered taboo by both communities.[27] Today in some mixed rural areas of Co. Antrim, it is considered natural for an Orangeman to attend a deceased Catholic's wake but not to enter the chapel at the funeral. This behaviour, apparently, does not cause offence. Although farmers of such diverse political persuasions as supporters of the Orange Order and violent republicanism can visit each other and chat about farming, if their children were to marry they would be disowned. Even the farmer's wife who lives on the property where the Orange Order was first established in Co. Armagh emphasised to me the neighbourly relations they have with the Catholic family who live across the field where the 'battle of the Diamond' was fought. This contrasts with the expression unfortunately often heard in urban working-class areas, 'I have nothing against Catholics but I wouldn't want them living next door to me.' Sectarian conflict in industrial towns does not seem amenable to the sort of regulation which allows people to co-exist at some level in the countryside. When sectarianism was imported into Belfast, it was not subjected to the restraints imposed in the countryside and co-existence was managed by ever increasing segregation.

The fact that the ethnic groups in Ulster and Belfast were defined by religion, instead of language, also contributed to the segregated nature of the town. A.C. Hepburn has pointed out that when religion is welded to an ethnic identity, integration of two or more groups is more difficult to achieve than in cases where groups are defined by language alone. In his study of Trieste, Hepburn shows that up until the late nineteenth century, Slovenes migrating to the mainly Italian city would quickly discard their language in order to advance their place in society. They would then become integrated into the majority community. In Belfast, religion was not so easily discarded and co-existence was managed by segregation.[28]

Some historians maintain that job competition between Catholics and Protestants was an important cause of sectarianism in Belfast.[29] Catholic navvies used the Ribbon society to exclude Protestants from public works labouring in the 1840s.[30] In 1843, the Belfast Protestant Operatives' Association discussed a report on exclusive dealing and the exclusive employment of tradesmen and labourers.[31] However, these attempts to introduce exclusive practises were the result of existing ethnic divisions rather than their cause. There is also little evidence of job competition in the 1820s and 1830s when sectarianism was entrenching itself in areas like Sandy Row and the Pound. The only evidence of job competition provoking sectarian hostility in this period is in Whiteabbey, a village on the northern outskirts of Belfast. In 1835, a flax store was burnt down and the assumption was that 'it might have been done on account of party feeling. A number of men employed in the mill nearby [were] Catholics' and 'persons of a different persuasion [were] not pleased at their being employed'.[32] However, there are no such reports from Belfast proper. There is evidence of one case of a Catholic building worker being attacked while working on a house with two other workmen in Sandy Row in 1837. Three local men attacked the Catholic worker declaring, 'No Papist should work here'. The worker took refuge in a Protestant house but the three locals 'forced open the door and violently assaulted [the occupier] and his wife'.[33] The motivating factor here, however, appears to be territorial (i.e. Sandy Row is Protestant and no Catholic should be working in the district) rather than competition for jobs. Apart from paucity of evidence in the 1820s and 1830s, the job competition theory does not take account of the fact that many Sandy Row men, some of the Pound men and many of those in other Orange districts, such as Ballymaccarret and Brown's Square,[34] were independent weavers, not employees in the strict sense of the term.

The social and economic decline of the independent weaving class probably had some impact on the development of sectarianism in Belfast. The majority of weavers in the 1820s and 1830s wove at home and were not in direct competition with each other for work. There was enough work but often at such low rates that it was not enough to maintain a weaver and his family. Increasingly, many cotton weavers became linen weavers which involved working in factories rather than at home. The weavers disliked the factories which they called 'lock-ups' and even alleged that employers had on occasions prevented workers from leaving their employment. The report on the condition of hand loom weavers rejected these allegations and maintained that 'the restraint and regular hours of a factory are the real cause of the dislike'.[35] In newly industrialising areas throughout Britain, workers who had previously had more flexible employment on farms or at the loom found factory discipline and the innovation of working between set times particularly oppressive.[36] In Belfast in the 1820s and 1830s, the weavers' survival and independence were threatened and this may have exacerbated the sectarian feelings which they had brought with them from the countryside.

Paradoxically, weavers were also involved in occasional cross-community industrial action as well as sectarian riots. As in Britain, Belfast weavers were involved in industrial action and violent protest in an attempt to avoid the slide into destitution after the Napoleonic wars. In 1814 and 1815, Belfast weavers tried to enforce minimum pay rates by returning unfinished webs to employers and refusing to work below a certain rate. The weavers smashed the webs of other weavers from the countryside as they walked into Sandy Row from the countryside. The sovereign and the magistrates unsuccessfully remonstrated with them and took five of them into custody. They were 'subsequently rescued by the rest and the magistrates received considerable abuse' before six others were finally captured and put in the 'Black Hole', the Belfast lock-up. Unfortunately for the weavers, their actions only resulted in prosecution for combination and assault.[37]

In March 1815, a 'mob of apprentice lads, boys and women' assembled to protest against the expected increase in the price of food which they believed would result from the passage of the corn laws. The crowd paraded with two poles, on one there was a large loaf of bread and on the other a sign with the inscription 'King and Constitution' and 'No Corn Bill'. This is a remarkable imitation of British food rioters who often carried some display of loyalty as well as bread on a pole dipped in blood or wrapped in black paper. They marched to Ormeau to see the marquis of Donegall and, on being told that he was at the theatre, proceeded there only to be told he was not there either. They then rampaged through the town, smashing windows until the military managed to disperse them, having taken twelve of them prisoner. Riots also occurred in April 1815 when people convicted of rioting in Antrim against the corn laws were flogged in the streets of Belfast. The prisoners from Antrim were stripped, tied to a cart and conveyed through the streets of Belfast 'followed by the executioner, flogging as they went'. 'A very tumultuous mob of the lower orders' began to throw brick-bats, stones, etc. at the sheriff, the soldiers guarding the procession and the executioner. After the prisoners were returned to the exchange to put on their clothes and the procession headed off to Carrickfergus jail, 'the mob became exceedingly furious. They stopped a cart loaded with bricks, which they emptied in a few minutes, and attacked the sheriff, the military and the executioner in the most violent manner.' The sheriff was struck and had to take refuge in a house which was then set upon by the crowd. Military reinforcements were required to disperse the crowd and five rioters were taken prisoner.[38]

In 1825, Belfast weavers were involved in a riot of obscure origins against one of their colleagues. The newspaper report of the resulting court case revealed only that a weaver, McGowan, had made himself obnoxious to his colleagues 'by having been supposed to carry injurious tidings from the weavers to the agent of a Manufacturing house in town.' A crowd, 'principally weavers,' assembled riotously outside his house on a Monday morning. They produced an effigy of the man and paraded it through the main streets around Brown's Square. They then took the effigy to an enclosure called 'Major's field' where 'with some ceremony, they decapitated the figure and having stripped it of its more valuable habiliments, they stuffed it into a tar barrel, which was kindled and the procession returned to the front of McGowan's house ... Here the mob increased and stones were thrown into McGowan's windows while a ballad singer attended for the purpose of commemorating in verse, the achievements of the day.' The effigy's coat was then auctioned ominously for the benefit of McGowan's widow. The next day, a summons server visited the houses of some of the eight men charged with rioting. One of the leaders gave a cheer when the process server arrived at his door and a huge crowd instantly gathered and attacked the process server. In the court room (which was 'literally crammed with crowds of weavers') at the opening of the subsequent trial, the judge declared that he was surprised that 'persons of their apparent respectability (the prisoners were all clean, hale-looking and well clothed) ...

should have been in any degree implicated in conduct that ... would lead to very alarming and ruinous consequences to manufacturers.'[39]

The Belfast weavers continued to be obsessed with the repeal of the corn laws and they were still regarded by the middle-classes as potentially dangerous in the 1830s. Maurice Cross, the secretary of the Frederick Street School, declared in 1838 that they were unable 'to form a correct and enlightened view of their own position in society. They are victims of delusion in all matters affecting their real interests. They do not understand the principle of sound legislation; they have formed erroneous opinions of the relations of employers and labourers, of masters and servants; hence it is that they look to legislative enactments as a panacea for the evils under which they labour. To save them from the consequences of these chimeras, they must be educated upon comprehensive and sound principles; not the education which begins and ends with the elementary branches of learning, but which will have an effect upon their conduct in every relation of life, as citizens, husbands and fathers.'[40]

The Sandy Row weavers were not 'Orange' because of any paternalistic relations with employers as Peter Gibbon has argued. Gibbon claims that the Sandy Row population had no sense of 'ethnic' Protestant loyalty and instead displayed a localised Orange identity arising from a dependency on 'Orange patrons' for employment and housing.[41] The weavers did not view their relationship with mill owners in a paternalistic light. The linen weavers' representative, Samuel McKenny, declared in 1838, 'As the producers of wealth, we should have a fair share of the profits of the wealth we create. As it is, it all goes to the manufacturer; if prices fall, he reduces the weaver so as not to diminish his profits; if they rise he pockets all.'[42] The extent of the weavers' and mill workers' dependency upon mill owners for housing has also been exaggerated as, in the first half of the nineteenth century, only a minority of housing in Sandy Row was owned by mill owners. In any case, the majority of mill owners voted Liberal in the 1830s and the biggest employer in Sandy Row, Mr Murphy of Murphy and Grimshaw's mill, was a Liberal-voting Quaker.[43]

Despite displaying signs of class consciousness, the sectarian divisions among the weavers hindered effective industrial action or campaigns against the corn laws. Samuel McKenny declared to the commissioners on the state of hand loom weavers that 'next to the repeal of those bad laws (i.e. the corn laws), would be the abolition of those party ebullitions, such as celebrating the anniversaries of great butchers, like William the Conqueror [William of Orange ?], or falsely called Saints such as St Patrick; these promote disunion among the people ... We would soon repeal the corn laws had we unanimity, but we are divided by religious animosities, which impair the strength of the community.'[44] Class conflict obviously co-existed with sectarianism in the early nineteenth century (although its effectiveness was reduced by it) just as Henry Patterson has demonstrated that it did in the latter part of the century.[45]

The fact that the main Orange districts were weaving areas suggests that the weavers' origins and peculiar social and economic situation are of relevance in explaining the development of sectarianism in Belfast. The weavers' sectarianism was exacerbated by the decline in their standard of living and independence. This frustration then erupted on occasions of political controversy. The Sandy Row weavers were not 'Orange' because of any paternalistic relations with their employers. The contemporary descriptions of the weavers and the statements of their representative suggest they viewed employers with a degree of antagonism. Indeed, on the twelfth of July 1825, a mob of 'the lowest class of the Orange party' on their way to Carrickfergus stopped outside 'the demesnes of Mr Lannigan, Mr Boomer (a Falls Road mill owner) and other gentlemen' where they 'huzzaed with great vehemence, and in a most irritating and clamorous manner'.[46]

From 1818 to 1821, Orange lodges paraded in Belfast on the twelfth without any riots ensuing.[47] However, in 1822, 1824 and 1825, riots broke out on the twelfth reflecting the heightened sectarian tension of the Ulster countryside which had been transferred to Belfast. The rioting in 1825 was particularly severe. The government had issued a proclamation banning processions and the leaders of the Orange Order had requested that the Orangemen observe the government's wishes. The Belfast magistrate accepted the verbal assurances of the Orange district master that there would be no parades. When some lodges assembled at a public house in Smithfield, the magistrate did not have sufficient policemen to enforce the law. The magistrate and police tried to seize the Orangemen's banners but they resisted and marched off to Carrickfergus in triumph. On their return, 'the effects of drunkenness operated as fuel to the flames of party animosity.' In York Street, there was a skirmish between Orange and Green factions 'who were goaded to madness and were unsparing in their taunts and revilings.' At 3 p.m., an Orangeman who was out buying cloth was attacked in High Street. The resulting riot lasted for some time. However, Smithfield and its neighbourhood were the main scenes of battle. There was intermittent fighting there throughout the evening. McClure's public house, where the Orangemen had assembled that morning, was attacked and the Orangemen repelled the attack with swords. In the evening, two crowds in Brown's Square and Millfield attacked each other with stones before being dispersed by the police. At 8 p.m. in Sandy Row, a 16-year-old boy was beaten by a mob on his way to the Malone turnpike. In dealing with the disturbances, the bias of the magistrate and the police was revealed by the fact that 23 Catholics were charged with assaulting the Orangeman in High Street and attacking McClure's pub whilst no Orangemen were charged with any acts of violence or parading illegally.[48]

The magistrates' tougher line on Orange parades and better police preparation ensured relatively quiet twelfths in 1826, 1827 and 1828.[49] However, the excitement of the early 1820s had hardly subsided when sectarian tensions were raised again by the campaign for Catholic emancipation. The Catholic emancipation campaign, led by 'the Liberator' Daniel O'Connell, resulted in the abolition of laws that discriminated against Catholics by convincing the British government that Ireland would be ungovernable if this reform were not granted. The hostility surrounding emancipation was important for Belfast's development as it not only effected Protestant-Catholic relations in the town itself but also soured community relationships in rural Ulster which was to provide Belfast's immigrants of the 1830s and 1840s.

The nation-wide display of Catholic power evident in the 'monster meetings' of the emancipation campaign produced a Protestant reaction, particularly in Ulster. Lawless, O'Connell's northern representative, was prevented from entering Armagh with his procession of supporters to collect the Catholic 'rent' by a large mob of armed Protestants. He was forced to retreat from Ulster having only managed to collect the rent in Co. Monaghan. In other parts of Ulster, such as Co. Down, there was great excitement and tension at the prospect of Lawless entering the district. According to the state of the country reports, this excitement took a long time to decline.[50] Even in counties far from the Lawless confrontation, the emancipation campaign fuelled sectarian hostility. In Co. Antrim, it was reported that 'party spirit ... runs very high throughout the greater part of the county from the well known causes of excitement which have latterly so much agitated the public mind.'[51] In Co. Tyrone, 'party spirit' was reported to 'prevail very much and the great body of the population of both persuasions appear to be in the utmost alarm and dread of attacks from each other and both evince much anxiety to provide themselves with arms for their own defence'.[52] In Co. Londonderry, Brunswick Clubs were established in the main towns and 'the minds of all classes in every part of the county' were declared to be 'much agitated by party feeling which becomes more inveterate every day ...' This hostility usually took the form of affrays and waylaying at fairs and markets although there were occasionally more unusual manifestations. A riot in Kilrea, Co. Londonderry, demonstrates the extent of hostility between the two communities. A group of Protestants alleged that a Protestant woman had been 'carried off' and married to a Catholic. In the court house where the case was being heard, 'the parties attacked each other in the most furious manner and several sustained severe injury. The police with difficulty dispersed them and secured the ring-leaders.'[53] Throughout much of Ulster the spectre of Catholic power evoked by the emancipation campaign, increased Protestants' fears of Catholics which encouraged Protestants to band together which in turn provoked a similar reaction from Ulster Catholics. Belfast could not escape this upsurge in sectarian hostility and continued to feel its effects as migrants from these districts flooded into the town over subsequent decades.

Although the Catholic workers of Belfast were not mobilised in support of the emancipation campaign (which in Belfast remained a mixed, middle-class affair), relations between Protestant and Catholic workers appear to have been soured by the tension created in Ulster by the campaign. The triumph of Catholic emancipation increased the determination of Belfast Orangemen to march on the Twelfth. In the previous three years, Orangemen had not paraded in Belfast and instead celebrated the Twelfth in their lodgerooms. This was due to the banning of processions by the town authorities, the deployment of the police and the advice of their leaders not to challenge the ban.[54] In 1829 a similar situation existed but the Orangemen defied their leaders and the authorities and marched as they wanted to show their strength in the wake of Catholic emancipation. As the under-secretary at Dublin Castle feared, 'nothing will prevent the Orangemen of the North from walking in procession on the twelfth of July. The persons of rank who formerly had influence over them have lost it and they are in the hands of inferior men, who are as violent as the lowest of their order.'[55] After the procession in Belfast, Catholics attacked Orangemen's houses in Brown's Square and a serious riot ensued. According to the *Belfast Newsletter*, 'the vigour of the attack was met by a proportionally vigorous defence in which persons of all ages, and of both sexes, indiscriminately engaged. A man whose house was attacked, fired at the crowd and a man fell severely, although not mortally wounded.' The magistrate and the police eventually dispersed the rioters. The violence was typical of Ulster in the wake of Catholic emancipation 'which in some places amounted almost to a civil war'.[56]

The increase in tension following Catholic emancipation is shown not only by the determination of the Orangemen to parade but by new manifestations of violence such as sectarian murders, St Patrick's day disturbances and funeral riots. The tendency of many scholars to only consider the 1813 riot and then those after the December 1832 election (when people actually died) obscures the extent to which the sectarian rivalry of the countryside was reproduced in Belfast and the effect of Catholic emancipation in exacerbating tension.[57] In 1830, serious disturbances occurred on St Patrick's day. According to the *Northern Whig*, the celebrations began peacefully. A crowd marched through the main streets of the town 'playing the national air of Patrick's Day.' They 'halted opposite to the houses of a number of individuals for whom they appeared to entertain sentiments of peculiar respect and gave many a loud and hearty cheer'. However, later in the day, 'a considerable mob' emerged from the public houses and proceeded to smash windows in Brown's Square. They were provoked, according to the *Whig*, by 'a notorious partyman' opposite whose house they had halted and groaned. The 'partyman' fired into the crowd but his gun only 'flashed in the pan'. In retaliation, the crowd wrecked his house and nine or ten others belonging to those 'supposed to be of Brunswick or Orange principles'. An hour after the incident began, the magistrate and police arrived and they arrested sixteen Catholic rioters, all 'of the very lowest order' and 'probably mostly strangers in Belfast, at least not residents of any duration'.[58]

Funeral processions became another occasion for rioting in the early 1830s. In April 1832, the master of an Orange lodge was murdered by four men at Newtownbreda. His funeral was attended by the Orangemen of Belfast and the surrounding countryside as well as such local notables as Sir Robert Bateson Bart, MP, JP and deputy lord lieutenant for Co. Down, another JP and one of the proprietors of the pro-Orange Belfast newspaper, the *Guardian*. To the astonishment and amusement of the *Northern Whig*, Sir Robert rode up and down the procession, 'condescendingly saluting the various lodges as they fell in; repeatedly taking off his hat and bowing to them and constantly observing "I am extremely glad to see so many *respectable* men assembled here".'[59] Some rioting occurred when the Orangemen returned to Belfast but it was quickly suppressed by the authorities. The day after the Orangeman's death, a Catholic cooper, 'a quiet, well behaved man', was stabbed to death in Millfield by a Protestant coal carter after refusing to fight with him and his four friends. According to the *Northern Whig*, the cooper's funeral was 'orderly, sober and quiet' and the Catholic bishop, Dr Crolly, succeeded in preventing any party exhibition. The only colours displayed were the white scarves of 'the trades' which were worn by Protestants and Catholics and were customary on such occasions. However, on the way back into town, the procession was attacked by 'a band of young ruffians sent out … from Sandy Row' with stones and 'the most insulting and abusive epithets of party rage … But for the exertions of a number of respectable people in the funeral party, aided by Dr Crolly' there would have been a terrible riot.[60] A few days later, the *Whig* declared that 'throughout the entire town and its vicinity … a spirit of hatred and distrust is greatly on the increase between certain portions of the Protestant and Catholic community' due to 'the violent declamations and harangues of the lordly leaders of the Orange faction.' The 'drumming and shouting and vociferating of party denunciations from Sandy Row keep the whole neighbourhood in a constant state of alarm and fear. The keepers of the Malone toll bar are even annoyed in their business by these disturbers of the public peace.' The *Northern Whig* proprietor himself was 'assailed with the vilest abuse' by the Sandy Row mob at the turnpike.[61] In fact, the funeral riots caused such concern that a number of 'respectable' Belfast citizens of all religious persuasions presented a memorial to the lord lieutenant outlining the recent sectarian clashes and requesting (unsuccessfully) a judicial inquiry into the causes of the unfortunate state of Belfast society.[62]

The question of the reform of the House of Commons also sparked clashes between Orangemen and 'Reformers' in May 1832. Orangemen were opposed to an increase in the franchise as they feared it would increase the power of the Whigs or Liberals who were softer on Catholics. The arrival of the Dublin mail coach with the news of the recall of the Whig administration was eagerly awaited in Belfast. The Belfast middle-class was still liberal enough for this news to be greeted with general satisfaction. The chief constable reported that 'the greatest satisfaction and rejoicing were exhibited generally throughout the town and some hundred persons soon collecting paraded the streets with blazing tar barrels'. However, the Orangemen and their allies at the *Guardian* newspaper were strong enough for a serious riot to ensue when Michael Andrews, a linen merchant, addressed a crowd of reformers opposite the offices of the *Northern Whig*. The reformers attacked the town police and the Orange party with stones and then proceeded to wreck the *Guardian* office and an Orange public house in Ann Street. Shots were fired from the pub and one boy was killed and two were wounded.[63] Unfortunately, no description is given of the 'reformer' crowd so its religious composition is not clear. Given that the Liberal crowd which did battle with the Orange Tory crowd at the subsequent elections was composed chiefly of Catholics and that the boy shot while attacking the pub was Catholic, there is a strong possibility that this reforming crowd was mainly Catholic.

On St Patrick's day, 1833, there was another serious funeral riot. According to the *Belfast Newsletter*, there were groups of drunken men loitering around different parts of the town throughout the day. In the afternoon, there was 'considerable rioting' in Brown's Square and many windows were broken. There were rumours that Sandy Row would be attacked in a similar way and 'some excitement consequently prevailed'. Late in the afternoon, a Catholic funeral was attacked by a crowd from Sandy Row at the Dublin bridge. The procession managed to continue and when it reached a public house used for Orange gatherings, some of the funeral party attacked the pub with stones. Orangemen inside the pub fired shots at the funeral party. 'A regular battle ensued between the parties and several individuals were seriously wounded,' including six who were injured by bullets. Some of the funeral party continued to Friar's Bush for the service. The police were unable to disperse the rioters. The military were sent for 'before whose charge the rioters instantly fled'. The magistrate entered the public house, seized guns and arrested fourteen of the men inside. The *Newsletter* lamented that 'occurrences of this kind have of late been frequent and the authorities must take rigorous measures for their future prevention ... It is perfectly out of all character that funerals which ought to be scenes of solemnity ..., should be regularly turned into occasions of outrage.'[64]

By the early 1830s, sectarianism was well entrenched in working-class districts like the Pound and Sandy Row. The flourishing state of the Orange and Ribbon societies bears testament to the importation of sectarian conflict from rural Ulster, particularly after the campaign for Catholic emancipation. The sectarianism of the inhabitants was not implanted by ministers or priests or by middle-class mill owners. The districts, being on the whole without schools and churches, had little contact with institutionalised religion. The weavers were not 'Orange' due to any paternalistic relationships with mill owners. The relationship between weavers and mill owners was not paternalistic and the mill owners' politics were generally liberal in the 1830s. The Orange and Ribbon societies were generally led by men from within working-class communities such as publicans and shopkeepers and the local Orange societies often acted independently of the more cautious aristocratic county leaders. Sectarianism was a working-class phenomenon, fostered to some extent by the Orange bias of the local authorities.

Political and religious conflict, 1835-50

During this period, working-class Catholics and Protestants acquired an ideological legitimacy for their sectarian beliefs and their conflict became more clearly a political one. The conflict was not based on any differences in customs or economic advantage. The Protestants of Sandy Row had no economic advantage over the Catholics of the Pound (see chapter one) and to a great extent the two groups shared a common culture, united by working class tastes. Although the influence of the churches from the 1830s onwards resulted in increasing segregation in education, leisure time and possibly marriage, this common culture persisted even as the political divisions developed. In the 1830s and 1840s, the sectarian views of Protestant workers were legitimised by evangelical Protestantism and that of the Catholics by Irish nationalism. The serious riots of 1835 occurred after evangelical ministers had given special Twelfth of July sermons for the first time, reflecting the importance of the influence of these ministers in the growth of sectarianism. In the 1840s, Catholic workers from districts like the Pound came under the influence of the Repeal Association where their sectarianism was given a political expression in the form of Irish nationalism. At the same time, Protestant workers were mobilised by ministers such as Cooke and the Belfast Protestant Operatives Association in an anti-repeal campaign resulting in the political division among the Protestant and Catholic working class. The new political nature of the conflict led to serious rioting during O'Connell's visit to Belfast in 1841 and particularly during July of the 'repeal year', 1843.

THE SHARED CULTURE OF PROTESTANT AND CATHOLIC WORKERS AND THE INCREASING INFLUENCE OF THE CHURCHES

After 1830, the churches increased their influence among the working class in the Pound and Sandy Row through the establishment of schools, churches and voluntary organisations. Although this led to an increase in divisions in society, working class habits still united most of the Protestant and Catholic working class in some sense. Apart from specifically religious practices, there were no discernible differences in the customs of working-class Catholics and Protestants. Their diet, clothing and housing were identical within the same occupational group. In the evidence presented to the select committee on the state of the poorer classes by such diverse witnesses as Revd Henry Cooke and the Catholic bishop William Crolly, there is no religious distinction made when discussing the state of various classes of workers.[1] Witnesses to the committee reporting on rural areas and country towns in Ulster also failed to make religious distinctions when discussing the morals and the condition of the people within the same class in particular regions.[2] The difference in religious customs in Belfast would not have been as obvious to allow one to judge which religion someone was by superficial observation. Catholic devotional practices were not as rich and as widespread as they were to become later. Although the increase in evangelical churches in Belfast from the 1830s resulted in a heightened awareness among Protestants of the differences between Protestantism and Catholicism, this did not lead in most cases to the adoption of an evangelical way of life and the lifestyles of both groups remained similar. The Revd McIntyre, a Presbyterian missionary who recorded his impressions of the Belfast poor in his diary, found the Sandy Row inhabitants in 1854 to be very proud of their Protestant identity but lacking in any real biblical knowledge. Moreover, he found the behaviour of some connected to churches to be no better than the rest of the inhabitants. Upon observing two young women from Dr Drew's Christ Church Sunday school sitting on the ground 'bulking marbles' and 'in other ways conducting themselves rudely', he asked a local woman, 'Are they Protestants?'[3]

Working-class Protestants and Catholics shared many customs and beliefs which were condemned by the middle class, both Catholic and Protestant. In the early to mid nineteenth century, the custom of wakes for the dead was still practised by working-class Catholics and Protestants in Belfast. A wake was like a party for the dead person which involved dancing, drinking and games thought to be pre-Christian in origin. The deceased was laid out on or under a table around which the older people drank whiskey, smoked, talked, told stories and played cards. Sometimes the deceased was given a hand of cards or even dragged up for a dance. The young people danced and played games designed to pair them off into couples. The generally strict sexual morality was relaxed on these occasions and men and women played miming games together such as 'making the ship'. These suggestive games are thought to have a pre-Christian origin and may have been designed to instil confidence in life and reproduction in the face of death. Another aspect of wake games involved poking fun at Catholic priests by having a fake priest perform marriage ceremonies on all the couples present.[4] This evidence concerning wakes comes from accounts in Catholic rural areas and the extent to which it applied to Belfast is questionable. However, Bishop Crolly's condemnation of wakes in 1835 due to drunkenness and the ruin of young women in unguarded moments suggests that at least some of these aspects which the Catholic hierarchy declared to be immoral had been imported into Belfast. It is also apparent that Protestants attended wakes. In 1835, Dr Crolly declared he was willing to join with the *clergy of other denominations* in an attempt to wipe out the custom of wakes in

Belfast.[5] As late as the 1950s, Rosemary Harris found wakes, although of a more subdued character, being held by Protestants and Catholics in the poorer, hilly part of the townland she studied near the border. In some parts of Ulster, such as the rural area near Kells, Co. Antrim, practices such as wakes which are often considered to be 'Irish' and therefore Catholic, are still carried on today by both communities.[6] The fact that Catholics and Protestants within the same economic class share, to some extent, a common culture renders the evidence of common customs in early nineteenth century Belfast believable.

The Protestant and Catholic lower classes in Belfast believed in fairies like their rural counterparts to the astonishment of the middle classes. In the countryside, the deeds of fairies were used to explain sickness in cattle and children, and problems with milking and butter churning. The 'wee folk' were thought to be particularly active on certain days and protective measures had to be taken to appease them. In 1853, a Congregational minister, the Revd O'Hanlon, in his walks along Sandy Row was surprised to find among some of the people a belief in magic spells and fairies. He found people who 'retain the elder faith on these subjects' and 'night after night and month after month, in the midnight hour, Oberon and Titania, Puck, Peasblossom, Robin good fellow and all the rest of those little gentry whom Shakespeare had immortalised in his 'Dream' have found willing followers in this neighbourhood and led them a mystic dance for gold to Cave Hill'. The gold is said to be in chests on the summit of Cave Hill. It was left there by the Danes when they had to make a hasty retreat. The people, who had been digging there for the past two to three years at least, maintained that on more than one occasion they had found the iron chests but at that moment 'the propitious influence was absent and a kind of mysterious darkness and confusion fell upon their eyes. However, the people believed that the chests were still where the Danes left them and they were looking for 'the seventh son of a seventh son gifted with the second sight and with the power to take the spell off the gold'. The Revd O'Hanlon goes on to condemn these people as they had 'abjured religion and their family members who know aught of Christianity are considered a hindrance as "the spirits of the vasty deep cannot come so freely where these are". They themselves are tossed and agitated in mind by day and night, feverish and dissatisfied with a life of ordinary industry and toil.'[7] In 1854, a Presbyterian missionary found the same beliefs still prevalent in the district. In his diary he recorded that 'the people here seem to be under some kind of enchantment about ghost stories, finding money and the like'. A 'respectable woman' told the minister that an old man continually torments her husband, a carpenter, 'to go with him and take his tools and he will show him where a large treasure of gold is to be found which the "wee folks" have been keeping for him this long time'. The minister recorded that he had heard 'many other strange tales'.[8]

The belief in fairies indicates the extent to which the Sandy Row district was an autonomous community with its own beliefs which the outside middle class world had failed to penetrate completely. Despite the increase in churches, Sunday schools and day schools, all of which would have condemned belief in fairies, the notion that there were 'wee folk' with gold on Cave Hill persisted. The obsession with finding gold may have played the same psychological role as the lottery does today with the working classes who are the keenest players. Some of the Sandy Row workers saw in the elusive gold the only hope of ever being well-off, but like the lottery in Orwell's *Nineteen eighty-four* no-one ever won it.

Popular entertainment in the first half of the nineteenth century also reflected sections of the working class's immunity to evangelical and middle class influence. For men, the most common form of entertainment was drinking in the pub or spirit shop. The temptations to lure people into the pubs were strong, bemoaned missionaries in their reports, 'especially the Sunday band parades which had the effect of collecting crowds, and keeping young people away from the Sabbath schools'.[9] Also popular were the music saloons where singers and actors entertained the customers, who in return had to buy a large number of drinks. Many of these saloons were in Smithfield, within easy reach of the Pound and Sandy Row. In 1825, the *Northern Whig* condemned the 'vulgar shows in Smithfield and Hammond's Court near Castle Street where showmen bang drums and pickpockets are rife'.[10] Others were situated in the city centre and had 'snugs' for gentlemen as they would have been ridiculed by the main audience if they were seen.[11] These music saloons were condemned by evangelical clergy and respectable citizens alike but continued to operate until the 1870s at least.[12]

The Protestant and Catholic working classes also shared a liking for cockfighting. This 'sport' became less popular as the century progressed due to clerical and middle-class opposition. In 1847, the Catholic *Vindicator* praised the Society for the Prevention of Cruelty to Animals for offering a ten pound reward to any person who could secure a conviction against people for 'the inhuman and disgusting practice of cockfighting'. They expected that 'the local authorities will also direct a vigilant eye to the abettors of such cruel sports and not suffer Belfast to be disgraced by them'.[13] The minister of Christ Church, Drew, claimed that the practice was rife in Sandy Row before he managed to stamp it out in the late 1830s.[14]

A great tradition of the working class, both Catholic and Protestant, was the celebration on Cave Hill on Easter Monday. Huge crowds gathered on the hill to drink, dance and go courting. They were entertained by fiddlers and bag-pipers. Special tents were set up with stalls selling drinks and food such as cockles and mussels. There was much gambling and playing of games and in the evening a blind harper accompanied the crowds down the hill. By the 1840s this festival was coming under attack from evangelical churchmen who considered courting sinful and condemned the drunkenness associated with the festival which often led to fights and accidents. Despite this condemnation,

20,000 people still attended the celebration in 1845. Although the Easter celebrations became more organised and respectable in the mid nineteenth century when they were transferred to Queen's Island and then the Botanic Gardens, as late as 1861, the *Northern Whig* described Easter as a 'drunken festival'.[15]

Between 1830 and 1850, the influence of churches increased the divisions among the working class. Education became increasingly segregated and mixed marriages probably became rarer. The churches also made some inroads into popular entertainment. Despite the increase in church influence, the working class habits which united the poor Catholics and Protestants of Sandy Row and the Pound were not eradicated. They continued to interact in the workplace and to some extent during leisure time. However, the increasing influence of the churches made contacts between working-class Catholics and Protestants less frequent and more fraught.

Mixed marriages probably came under more pressure as the churches, particularly the Protestant denominations, attempted to increase church and school attendance between 1830 and 1850. Although comparisons are difficult due to the lack of figures for the early nineteenth century, it seems reasonable to suppose that the increasing influence of the churches made mixed marriages more difficult. In any case, it can be stated that mixed marriages were rare in the mid nineteenth century. In the entire Christ Church district there were only 26 mixed marriages out of approximately 600 Church of Ireland families in 1852. The difficulties of mixed marriages were compounded by the lack of any custom relating to the upbringing of the children of such unions. The Christ Church census shows that none of the couples practised the custom of bringing up daughters in the mother's religion and sons in the father's religion. The children were either all Protestant or all Catholic. There was also no practice of one of the spouses, such as the Catholic partner today, determining the children's religion. Of the six families in the Pound who chose to rear their children as Protestants, three had a Protestant mother and three had a Protestant father. There does seem to be a tendency for mixed marriage couples in the Sandy Row to bring their children up as Protestants, perhaps due to the orange nature of the district. In the Pound, however, of the eight mixed marriage couples with children, six chose to rear their children as Protestants despite the Catholic nature of the district. Only two couples recorded in the census coped with the problem by the Catholic partner converting to Protestantism.[16] The fact that there was no generally acceptable solution to the rearing of children in mixed marriages would have made these unions more difficult, especially as opportunities for integrated education were diminishing and the churches were attempting to increase attendance at public worship. Increasing residential segregation and increasing sectarian animosity presumably also made mixed marriages more difficult.

In the 1820s, the small number of school children from the Sandy Row and

Pound districts attended schools which were thoroughly mixed. By 1850, schooling was almost entirely segregated and any opportunity of integrating society through schooling disappeared. In 1826, there were no schools in Sandy Row and three small private schools in the Pound. These three schools, two in Lettuce Hill and one in Barrack Street, were run by Catholic teachers but the pupils were evenly divided along religious lines. It is not clear what arrangements were made, if any, for religious instruction in these schools but at similar schools in the countryside the teacher would instruct all the children in their respective catechisms. The only other schools that children from these areas could have attended were the larger schools run by committees of Catholics and Protestants which were sustained by public subscriptions and were also mixed. In these schools, religious instruction was confined to general aspects upon which all denominations could agree and the respective catechisms were taught.[17]

The upsurge of evangelicalism in Belfast in the late 1820s and 1830s signalled the beginning of the collapse of mixed education. Evangelical ministers were eager to promote education among the poor but the education they envisaged included the elements of their particular creed, not a general form of Christianity or separate religious instruction which would be acceptable to Catholics. For the first time, schools were established which were attached to particular churches such as those connected with the Fisherwick Place Presbyterian church and Christ Church. In 1853, there were only 2 Catholics in the Christ Church boys school compared to 54 Dissenters and 241 Church of Ireland members. The girls' school had 7 Catholic pupils, 67 Dissenters and 150 Church of Ireland members on its books.[18] The controversy surrounding the use of the Catholic Douay version of the Bible by Catholic pupils in the Brown Street Sunday School showed that the tide was turning against mixed education. When the parish priest, the Revd William Crolly, was refused permission by the committee to distribute the Douay version of the Bible, he withdrew the Catholic pupils from the school and established his own school next to the chapel in Donegall Street.[19] Even though the Donegall Street school joined the National system of education in 1832 and therefore had separate secular and religious instruction, in 1837 there were only 2 Protestant boys enrolled compared to 377 Catholics and of the 303 girls none were Protestants.[20] In the early 1850s, Catholic operated national schools were established in the Pound district in Cullingtree Road and Alexander Street West and although no figures are available, the availability of Protestant education probably ensured that few Protestants attended.[21]

When national schools were established by Presbyterians to serve the Sandy Row/Pound area, there was a tendency to try to evade the rules of the national education board which were designed to ensure a non-denominational environment. The minister of Townsend Street Presbyterian Church, the Revd Josias Wilson, founded a school in Tea Lane, in the heart of Sandy Row, in 1841. In 1848, the school inspector discovered that 'the one room on one evening in each week is used as a preaching station in connection with the Town Mission of the General Assembly' and the National Board threatened to withdraw the school's grant. A similar situation was discovered at the Birch Street School, also managed by the Townsend Street minister.[22]

From the 1830s onwards, the churches began to play a role in the leisure time activities of some working-class Catholics and Protestants. Sunday school outings and processions were common especially on festival days or when new schools or churches were opened. On Queen Victoria's coronation day in 1838, Christ Church, the Episcopalian church which served the Sandy Row, organised the laying of the foundation stones of two school houses, one for infants behind Christ Church and one at Whiterock. The children, accompanied by many friends, marched in procession to Whiterock, led by a teacher carrying a flag with the inscription 'Feed my lambs' and a picture of a crown and a sceptre laid upon a bible. From 1834, Rev. Dr Drew of Christ Church organised processions on Easter Mondays of all the children from the schools connected with Christ Church. Some of the adults of the district were also involved in the pageantry of the day. 'Many of the parents of the children had expected their return and as the procession reached Sandy Row, hundreds of the inhabitants were ready to greet them. The large flag was now moved to the front, and amid the welcomes and blessings of old and young, the long line of Sandy Row and Durham Street was traversed.'[23]

Other Protestant churches are mentioned as having followed the example of processions and picnics set by Christ Church[24] although detailed records of these do not exist. Catholic churches also began to organise social events during this period although the evidence is not as abundant as for Christ Church. Activities were organised for the children of the Donegall Street school on Easter Monday mirroring Drew's attempts to alter the traditional celebrations associated with the holiday. On Easter Monday 1846, the children of the Donegall Street national school were treated to a public breakfast by the school patrons. The Catholic Bishop, Dr Denvir, and all the Belfast clergy were present. On the previous morning 'the choirs and the young men attending at the altars numbering about eighty were entertained by his Lordship at the same place'.[25]

A new form of popular entertainment introduced in the 1830s and 1840s were the temperance soirees organised by the temperance and teetotal societies of Belfast. These 'soirees' were dances held in the evening where the refreshment consisted of tea, coffee and cakes rather than alcohol. Although Protestant and Catholic societies co-operated to build a temperance hall in which 'inculcating peculiar views of politics or religion shall disentitle the society or branch society so acting to the use of said hall',[26] the division of the temperance movement along religious lines ensured that this area of popular entertainment was increasingly segregated. The division in the temperance movement was so stark that by the late 1840s, the Catholic Teetotal Society was regarded by working-class Protestants as a front for the Ribbonmen. The Protestant Association, a front for the Orange Order, threatened a counter demonstration against a Catholic Teetotal procession to Cave Hill in 1842. A violent encounter between the two sides was only averted when the resident magistrate convinced the teetotal leaders to call off the parade and the Orangemen promised in turn to call off their counter demonstration. In 1852, Orangemen attacked a party of teetotalers returning from a railway excursion as 'their music gave offence and they were set down as Ribbonmen and sympathisers'.[27]

By the mid-nineteenth century, churches had made some impact on popular entertainment although drinking, music saloons and Easter celebrations on Cave hill and later on Queen's Island continued to be popular. The intrusion of the churches into the recreation of the working class, meant that for those involved another aspect of their lives was segregated from those of the opposite religion. Events such as school processions and temperance parades not only led to increasing segregation of social life but increased the opportunities for conflict as such processions could sometimes cause offence to those of the opposite religion.

Although integrated education, and possibly mixed marriages, were becoming less common between 1830 and 1850 and the churches had made inroads into popular entertainment, Catholics and Protestants still interacted in other situations, particularly in the work place and their residential areas, but it is difficult to generalise about what their everyday relationships were like. The events which were reported in the press such as the Sandy Row crowd accosting everyone passing through the district and Protestants being beaten up as they returned to their homes in the Pound after church do not seem to indicate friendly relations. However, acts of civility, decency and kindness are not generally reported but may have been more numerous than acts of intimidation. Witnesses to the 1857 riots commission gave contradictory evidence about community relations in the mills. One Catholic victim forced to leave Stanley Street maintained that relations in the mills were friendly but other evidence was submitted suggesting that there was a group of Protestant girls in the Linfield mill who were trying to force the Catholics out. Instances of kindness were recorded during the residential intimidation which accompanied the 1857 riots. Protestants defended their Catholic lodgers from angry mobs and people were often warned by sympathetic neighbours of impending attacks.[28] Many people may not have felt any hostility towards those of the opposite faith but could not stand up to the mob. In 1855, a town missionary, the Revd McIntyre, was told by a Catholic woman in the Pound district that 'even quiet decent people who wished to live in peace can scarcely keep from getting mixed up with such scenes as frequently take place here'.[29] In segregated areas today, many older people have fond memories of living, visiting relatives or drinking in mixed working-class areas before 1969. Others may have held a general prejudice against those who 'dug with the wrong foot' but could not bear to see their own neighbour, whom they considered to be a good man despite his religion, being attacked and so forewarned him. Again there are parallels with the recent 'Troubles'. Gerry Fitt is remembered in Protestant ghettos for his kindness in helping to re-house Protestants burnt out of the Broadway area and the IRA's attack on him is thought to be due to him 'helping the Prods'. The commission's report on the 1857 riots accepted that community relations were generally friendly except around the twelfth of July although this conclusion may have been reached in order to support their argument as to the cause of disturbances.[30] Parades and outdoor preaching were often the immediate causes for rioting but they could not occur without the existence of a general, under-lying hostility which, if not shared by all the inhabitants to the same degree, was widespread enough to submerge the civility and decency of the rest of the population of these areas.

THE POLITICAL INFLUENCE OF EVANGELICAL MINISTERS

Evangelical ministers were not responsible for the creation of sectarian division in Belfast. However, their evangelising campaigns and attempts to recruit Protestant workers for their political causes in the 1830s and 1840s gave added legitimacy to existing sectarianism and fostered its further development. By mobilising Protestant workers against repeal, these ministers helped turn the sectarian division into a political one.

Until the late 1820s or early 1830s, the Protestant working classes of Belfast were almost completely isolated from the effects of evangelical Protestantism. Before the establishment of Christ Church in 1833 and outposts of the Town Mission in 1829, there were no churches specifically for working-class Protestants in Belfast. However, by the early 1830s, attempts were being made to increase church attendance and Protestant workers were being informed about the challenges facing Protestantism in Ireland.

The Protestant churches established in the 1830s which served the Sandy Row district offered the working-class benefits such as cheap or free education for their children, occasional help with clothing and medicine and a sense of belonging. The churches serving Sandy Row, such as Christ Church, Fisherwick Place Presbyterian Church and Townsend Street Presbyterian Church, were all evangelical.[31] Evangelical Protestantism laid great stress on the conversion experience and the need to find salvation only through Jesus. Evangelical ministers regarded tolerance of other faiths as a betrayal of their duty to convert as many people as possible who otherwise would not be saved. By its very nature, evangelical Protestantism was hostile towards the Catholic Church and this hostility provided an ideological legitimacy for the sectarianism of the Protestant working class.

Dr Drew, the popular minister of Christ Church in Sandy Row, ensured that Sandy Row and Belfast as a whole were made aware of battles being fought against the perceived increase in power of the Catholic Church. He frequently arranged special lectures for his congregation, given by clerics such as the convert Mortimer O'Sullivan who described the oppression of priests and the threats facing Protestants in the south. Drew frequently clashed with his bishop over the establishment of evangelising societies and his use of controversial guest preachers. He personally visited the west of Ireland in the early 1850s to report on the progress of conversion campaigns. He returned and informed his congregation and general audiences in Belfast of the persecution suffered by Protestants in Galway.[32] This undoubtedly heightened the fears of some Protestants already concerned about the rise of Ultramontanism, the doctrine of absolute papal supremacy, within the Catholic Church in Ireland.

Drew recognised the value of the uncompromising Protestantism of his parishioners when he established the Christ Church Protestant Association in 1854 which demanded the reversal of Catholic emancipation (as 'the Romanists ... have proven themselves by many acts utterly unworthy to have any share in legislation which affects our lives, religion and liberty'), the abolition of nunneries, the enforcement of the rules relating to the assumption by Catholic bishops of ecclesiastical titles, and the withdrawal of all grants to Maynooth seminary. Middle-class people outside the Christ Church district could only be associate members as previous Protestant associations had become inoperative due to the suppression of certain topics in order to keep more moderate or important parties involved. Drew revealed that he had made the association's principles 'so plain, so uncompromising, so scriptural as would at once serve to repel the false, the double-minded, the nominal Protestant with whom we were not desirous to associate; and invite ... those honest and true men who, however humble, were like minded with ourselves in veneration for the Word of God and in attachment to those glorious civil and religious liberties which were acquired and bequeathed to us by our Protestant forefathers ...' The association also held quarterly meetings on special topics for the general public which were well attended.[33] Drew managed to maintain the purity of the organisation and at the same time influence the opinion of the wider Protestant community in Belfast.

Drew's great influence in the Sandy Row district is shown by the 75% church attendance rate for Church of Ireland members in the Sandy Row district recorded in the 1852 Christ Church census.[34] Even if the church attendance figure in the census is exaggerated (and it appears to be attempting to portray a genuine picture of the district with notations of illegitimate children, drunkards and wife beating), it is still remarkable when compared to the very low attendance figures for English workers in the same period. In a study of the English religious census, Inglis has argued that the deep class divisions in English churches discouraged workers from attending.[35] These divisions also existed in Christ Church. There were rented pews although the great majority of the seats were free. The church was not attended solely by workers and their families. Local notables, such as the architect Charles Lanyon, were also members of the church. Drew probably lessened the impact of the class divisions by his appreciation of workers as the vanguard in the defence of Protestantism. Drew's anti-Catholicism was successful in wooing Sandy Row Protestants who had already developed a fierce rivalry with their Catholic neighbours. The high rate of church attendance for men (compared to Britain where women were much more likely to be church attendees)[36] was probably due to Drew's prominent position as a defender of Protestantism. At twelfth of July celebrations he was cheered by workers as the 'Sandy Row hero',[37] a relationship very different from that between minister and workers in England. The religious divide in Belfast, while not completely subsuming class conflict, must have somewhat blunted it. The bond between Protestants was strong enough to ensure workers were not treated with quite the same degree of social disdain as in England and the workers themselves did not see church attendance as in any way betraying their class. Their main battle was with the Catholics, not the middle class.

The Protestant Operatives Association, established in April 1843, was an important organisation in Sandy Row. It was founded by the Revd Tresham Gregg, a Dublin evangelical preacher, based on his own organisation in Dublin.[38] Its membership was reported to consist of the working-class Protestants of Sandy Row and Ballymaccarret. The society's secretary, Sam Tierney, was a grocer from Durham Street (the continuation of Sandy Row) and another prominent member David Alderdice was a publican from Durham Street who had a police record for sectarian rioting offences.[39] Church of Ireland ministers and another gentleman, presumably a minister, referred to as the 'Protestant Gun' and occasionally the Revd Dr Cooke led the discussion at the meetings on topics such as 'Is the Church of Rome immutable, unchanged and unchangeable?; Are the laws still unrepealed under the influence of which 20 million of human beings were most barbarously slaughtered in a few years simply for being Protestants?; How many Protestants were slaughtered in Ireland on the night of the 23rd of October 1641?; Can a Papist consistently with the principles of his church be a good member of society or a loyal subject in a Protestant state ... or a good husband to a Protestant wife or can a Papist woman be a good wife to a Protestant husband ... ?' The organisation also held a public meeting against the repeal of the Union attended by 2-3000 Protestant workers and collected 17,000 signatures on a petition opposing the scheme.[40]

On the Twelfth of July 1835, rioting erupted between Sandy Row and Pound crowds and between both sides and the police. Two people were killed and many more were injured. The serious nature of the 1835 riots is probably attributable to the increasing influence of evangelical ministers and the expansion of the Pound district. For the first time in Belfast, special church services for the Orangemen were held in Christ Church and St Anne's.[41] Drew's sermons were infamous for their violent hostility towards Catholicism and he undoubtedly provided the Orangemen with an inspiring sermon for the twelfth. The fact that the Pound district had expanded so that the Catholic population could see the Orange arches of Sandy Row also meant that Orange celebrations in that district were less likely to go unnoticed or unchallenged. However, it should be remembered that the violence of 1835 followed six years of determined parading by Orangemen since Catholic emancipation. The tensions could not be contained once the Orangemen were challenged by the developing Catholic area adjoining them, particularly after a night of heavy drinking (the twelfth fell on a Sunday and Saturday night was traditionally a night of heavy drinking) and a rousing sermon from Dr Drew.

During the evening of the Twelfth of July 1835, the Pound Catholics erected a green arch in opposition to the orange arch erected by the Sandy Row crowd on the border between the two districts. '... A regular series of engagements with stones and other missiles was kept up between the two parties during which several individuals were severely injured.' The police had to send for the military who destroyed the green arch but in attempting to pull down the orange one, encountered 'severe and protracted resistance' from the crowd of between 200 and 500 people. An unknown gentleman attempted to use his influence with some of the Sandy Row crowd to have the arch removed. He managed to convince some of the men 'but a number of women came up and would not permit it. The women appeared to be the officers of the day.' The military then charged but were assailed by stones from the street which 'having been newly paved were abundant and considerable injury was done'. This form of warfare, stone throwing, should not be underestimated. A police witness to the subsequent court case declared that 'the macadamised stones were sufficient to disable any man whom they hit' and there was 'not one boy in the crowd who was not able to kill a man with a stone'. The police magistrate and many soldiers were wounded by stones. The Riot Act was read and the military fired at the crowd, killing a woman from the Pound (who was visiting a friend in Sandy Row and was not involved in the riot) and an Orangeman defending the arch who died later as a result of his injuries.[42]

While the military and the Orange crowd were fighting in Sandy Row, a Catholic procession entered Millfield from the direction of Mill Street. Many in the procession carried green branches and they were led by a man with a green flag who used it to indicate the houses to be attacked. Many windows were smashed, shutters were torn off and some houses were completely wrecked. Orangemen's houses were not the only targets. A spirit dealer's house was attacked even though, according to the *Belfast Newsletter*, he had never taken part in politics. 'The mob drank as much whiskey as possible', spilled the rest on the floor and stole goods as well as £20. 'There were a number of women in the crowd who were the foremost in leading the attack upon the houses.' The following day, a crowd of 100 from Sandy Row attempted to attack the Pound from behind and fighting ensued in King Street and Mill Street. Fifteen people from both sides were arrested over the two days for stone throwing and all were fined 40s. each or two months in jail.[43]

The 1835 riot between Sandy Row and the Pound was the first to be clearly between two areas. At this time there appears to be a shift towards increasing, though far from complete, residential segregation. Riots are more clearly *between* areas rather than *within* areas. The descriptions in the press of the Twelfth in the 1820s suggest that Smithfield, North Street, Millfield, Brown's Square and Barrack Street were to varying degrees mixed. In 1824 and 1825, Orangemen assembled in public houses in Smithfield which is considered to be a traditionally Catholic area. In 1825, trouble erupted between Orange and Green factions within Smithfield. On the Twelfth of July 1824, Orangemen assembled at a public house in Barrack Street which was one of the main streets of the Pound with a substantial Catholic population. Crowds are mentioned as attacking each other in Millfield and Brown's Square as early as 1822. However, it is not clear whether the two groups hailed from the respective districts or not. By 1829, Brown's Square was considered to be an Orange area but Millfield was described as a somewhat Orange district as late as 1843 because, according to the *Vindicator*, 'the ——— of Brown's Square' drank there.[44] In the late 1820s and early 1830s, there was probably some shift towards increasing segregation in some of the areas which had been home to rival factions. After 1825, there is no further mention in the press of Orange lodges in Smithfield (although, in 1835, there were still Orangemen living in the streets off Smithfield)[45] or Barrack Street in the Pound. It is likely that these Orangemen relocated to more heavily Protestant areas such as Sandy Row and Brown's Square which by 1829 was described as 'an area chiefly inhabited by Orangemen'.[46]

The 1835 riot increased the segregation of the Pound and Sandy Row districts. Although house wrecking of non-political Catholics and Protestants was still rare and some Catholics continued to live in Sandy Row and some Protestants continued to live in the Pound, life in the 'wrong' district was becoming increasingly precarious. Shortly after the riots, a Protestant was attacked in Barrack Street after attending Christ Church and a number of gentlemen complained that 'no person except a recognised party man could pass through Sandy Row without being assaulted'.[47]

Between 1836 and 1842, the authorities took precautions that generally succeeded in preventing a repeat of the 1835 riots on the Twelfth of July. The reforming Dublin Castle administration under the direction of Thomas Drummond appointed stipendiary magistrates who were more independent than local justices of the peace who often, as in the case of Belfast, favoured the Orange party. These stipendiary magistrates held higher rank than the local magistrates and had a police force at their disposal which was more disciplined than the yeomanry. However, in Belfast, the stipendiary magistrates still had to endure the biased and inefficient town police as the primary force of law and order and were only able to use the Constabulary as reinforcements. Nevertheless, the innovation of the stipendiary magistrates ensured that the ban on Orange processions was enforced. This was also a period of weakness for the Orange Order which had dissolved itself in 1836 after parliament released its damning Select Committee report. During the Drummond era, there were also very few reports of Ribbon disturbances on St Patrick's day. There were none in Belfast and very few elsewhere in Ulster. In Belfast, the higher risk of arrest and the prompt removal of provocative arches resulted in relatively peaceful Twelfths in 1836, 1837, 1839 and 1840.[48]

In 1838, there was no Orange parade or 'party exhibition' during the day in Belfast. However, during the evening, there was extensive rioting in Sandy Row, Great George's Street, York Street and Donegall Street. Dr Denvir, the Catholic bishop of Down and Connor, had his house attacked and all the windows broken. Houses in Great George's Street and York Street were also attacked. A policeman was struck in the head and severely injured by a brick thrown by a retreating Protestant crowd. A stipendiary magistrate was also struck. The cause of this outbreak of violence is not readily apparent although the *Northern Whig* blamed the inactivity of the town watch and the laziness of some of the magistrates who did not come into town and deal with the problem. In 1842, there was no Orange procession but two crowds of about 2000 each assailed each other with stones. The authorities managed to separate them 'with the greatest difficulty' and the dragoons had to be called out to disperse the crowds.[49]

Although the weakness of the Orange Order and the tough policy of the magistrates generally prevented processions and their accompanying violence on the twelfth between 1836 and 1842, sectarian hostility still erupted on other occasions. In 1837, the resident magistrate was concerned by the 'several attempts ... made to excite party feeling in the town' particularly the planned funeral of 'a leader on the Roman Catholic side of those who disturb the peace on party anniversaries'. The magistrate enlisted the bishop's help to try to get this leader buried on Saturday rather than Sunday to avoid huge turnouts on both sides. Despite the efforts of the bishop and his clergy, the man was buried on Sunday and it was only 'with the greatest difficulty' that the magistrate 'succeeded in keeping the parties asunder, the crowds having far exceeded anything [he] could have anticipated'.[50] In 1838, a wedding turned into a riot on the Falls Road when a tar barrel was lit and party expressions used.[51] An Orange dance in a publican's house in 1840 ended violently when police tried to break it up and seized the flags illegally on display.[52] In 1843, two meetings held to establish a branch of the Protestant Operative Association ended in riots between Protestants and Catholics who had attended to prevent the organisation being established.[53]

Despite the ban on the Ribbon society, the Orange Order and party processions, Orangemen and Ribbonmen continued to operate in other guises. The teetotal society was considered by the magistrates to be a possible front for the Ribbonmen and the self styled 'Protestant Association', to be a front for the Orange Order. When it became known in 1842 that the teetotal society was going to parade with band and banners up Cave Hill on Easter Monday, the Protestant Association threatened a counter demonstration. The resident magistrate informed Dublin Castle that the teetotal plan 'has given great offence to the Orange party' who believe that 'under the cloak of teetotalism, it is intended as an offensive demonstration of physical force on the part of the Ribbon society' and they will assemble in great numbers to prevent it. Anonymous letters were received insisting that the 'Ribbon procession' be banned and observing that 'the last government put down Orangeism' and 'broke the yeomanry' and concluded defiantly 'No Pope in Sandy Row'. The magistrates, fearing trouble on a grand scale and having no power to ban a purely temperance procession, eventually convinced the leaders of the teetotal society to call off the parade and in return the 'Protestant Association' called off its counter parade.[54]

The continuation of the Orange/Ribbon rivalry, despite the ban on the Orange Order and party processions, and the clashes at funerals, weddings and political occasions demonstrate the virulence and tenacity of sectarian rivalry. This also suggests that the Orange Order itself was a symptom rather than a cause of sectarianism during this period.

The effect of national politics on communal relations is clearly seen in the terrible riots of 1841 and 1843. In both cases, the challenge of the campaign for the repeal of the Union between Great Britain and Ireland prompted violence by the Sandy Row Protestants. For these Protestants, repeal of the Union with Britain meant a Catholic ascendancy and the elevation of their hereditary enemies. Their tradition of sectarian rivalry ensured that they would probably view repeal in this manner. Ministers, such as the Revd Dr Cooke and Revd Dr Drew, reinforced Protestant working-class hostility to repeal by declaring that it would inevitably lead to Catholic ascendancy and the subjugation of Protestants. The subsequent espousal of Catholic causes by the Belfast Repeal Association would have confirmed Protestant workers in their opposition to repeal. Although there was no organised 'unionist' movement, apart from the banned Orange lodges and the Belfast Protestant Operatives Association, working-class unionism clearly dates from this period. In the early 1840s, Protestant workers displayed their conviction that the union was necessary to safeguard their position in Ireland.

In January 1841, Daniel O'Connell visited Belfast to promote the repeal of the union. As many liberal Protestants had been insulted by his criticism of them due to their opposition to repeal, he was not warmly welcomed outside the Catholic community.[55] O'Connell also declined an invitation by the Rev. Dr

Cooke to publicly debate the issue of repeal. This decision was criticised by liberal Protestants and Conservatives.[56]

It is not clear whether the working-class Catholics of Belfast had a real understanding of what repeal actually meant at this stage as regular public meetings and educational campaigns had not yet taken place. Ballads about repeal sung throughout Ireland suggest Catholic peasants and workers envisaged repeal as bringing defeat for Protestantism and a land of plenty for the people.[57] This ballad recorded in a contemporary anti-repeal pamphlet is given as an example of the ballads sung in rural Ulster and 'the Barrack Street tap rooms':

The Blessin's of Repale

No tithes nor taxes 'ud be to vex us
Likewise no rints as yees soon shall hear …
… When back the Parliament again we'll bring
An' whin nixt saison, we will be raisin'
The great O'Connell for to be our King
May the Virgin Mary who lives in glory
Grant unto us that we nivir fail
An' may Saint Patrick ether be our directhur
An' thin by gorra, we will have Repale![58]

Whilst in Belfast, O'Connell spent most of his time in his hotel. The Repeal meeting he was to address was moved at the last minute from a large pavilion to the outside of his hotel. Conservative sources suggest that the pavilion was abandoned as when a green banner was unfurled, only about half the crowd cheered. The audience who had paid their 6*d.* admission did not receive a refund and had to join the crowd of curious onlookers on the street beneath O'Connell's hotel balcony. The cheering of the repeal supporters and the hooting of the opponents, whose anger had increased as a result of losing their ticket money, drowned out O'Connell's speech.[59]

Throughout the evening serious rioting occurred in many parts of Belfast. A Protestant crowd went on the rampage yelling 'Down with rebellious repeal' and 'To hell with the big beggarman and his tail!'. They attacked the Royal Hotel where O'Connell was staying, the diocesan seminary, the Ulster Railway Tavern in Durham Street and the houses of priests and prominent repealers. The Music Hall where the repealers were holding a soiree was also attacked. A rival Catholic crowd joined in the battle and threw stones at the windows of many houses, including one belonging to a 'respectable lady' in Dr Cooke's congregation.[60] O'Connell was escorted out of town the next morning by the police for his own protection to the delight of the Orange inhabitants from Sandy Row, Brown's Square and Ballymaccarret who celebrated the occasion in song:

> ... The armed police by his coach did ride,
> Which nobody can deny.
> Below the bridge did Lagan glide,
> While the tollman flung the gates so wide,
> For they said a prisoner was inside,
> Which nobody can deny,
> Which nobody can deny.[61]

THE BELFAST REPEAL ASSOCIATION

The repeal campaign, launched in late 1842, had a decisive impact on the political development of the Pound. It gave the sectarianism of Pound Catholics the ideological legitimacy of nationalism just as evangelical Protestantism legitimised the sectarianism of Sandy Row Protestants. The weekly meetings of the Belfast Repeal Association which commenced in late 1842 gave the people of the Pound a wider understanding of the envisaged benefits of repeal and some sense of Irish nationhood which transcended their simpler sectarian outlook. However, this politicisation was accompanied by an increased awareness and involvement in specifically Catholic issues which reinforced their sectarian views.

In October 1842, Daniel O'Connell sent his 'chief pacificator' Thomas Steele to Belfast and the north of Ireland to organise the repeal movement there. The Belfast repeal leaders assured him that repeal was popular among the working classes but a lack of organisation meant they had no opportunity to express their support. The five repeal 'wardens' were each given an area of Belfast for which they would be responsible for collecting the repeal 'rent' and attendance at weekly meetings was to be encouraged. The reorganisation of the repeal movement in Belfast suffered an initial set back when a public meeting in Batty's Circus at which Tom Steele was to speak was abandoned on O'Connell's orders after Orangemen threatened to hold a counter demonstration. However, by early 1843, the regular weekly meetings of the association were so crowded that they had to be moved from the room in Chapel Lane to Byrne's 'large rooms' in Berry Street. Funds were raised for the establishment of larger premises in Chapel Lane and by June 1843, the weekly meetings in the new repeal rooms were attended by between 2000 and 2500 people.[62] Often the meetings were so crowded that large numbers of people spilled out onto the street outside. In 1844 twelve repeal wardens and numerous assistants were appointed and the town was divided into smaller wards named after repeal leaders such as the 'Liberator ward' and 'O'Brien ward' to ensure the maximum amount of rent was collected. The amounts collected in Belfast were not large (the rent usually ranged from £8 to £18 per week in 1843, peaking at £62 in the week O'Connell was arrested for conspiracy)[63] compared to the national figure but there was only a small

Catholic middle class in Belfast and not all of them supported repeal. Members of the Repeal Association had to subscribe one pound per annum and associates one shilling. The Belfast Repeal Association introduced a penny a month scheme to enable poorer people to join. In one week in September 1844, 443 one penny subscriptions were collected in Belfast. 'Honour to Belfast!' declared the delighted *Vindicator*.[64]

The success of the Belfast Repeal Association in mobilising the Catholics of Belfast was assisted by the support of the parish priests and the approval of some middle-class Catholics. Despite the disapproval of both Dr William Crolly, archbishop of Armagh, and Dr Cornelius Denvir, bishop of Down and Connor, four priests in Belfast were members of the Belfast Repeal Association.[65] Although they did not take an active part in its proceedings, their support for the cause may have encouraged others to join. A number of middle-class Catholics supported the Repeal Association but generally they did not take an active part in the ordinary business of the organisation such as collecting rent or attending the weekly meetings. They supported the cause financially and attended social functions such as the St Patrick's Day dinner but only attended the repeal meetings en masse when there was something of great importance to discuss such as O'Connell's imprisonment or the denunciation of the Young Irelanders.

The success of the Belfast Repeal Association in mobilising the Catholics of Belfast has not been recognised in the literature. This is partly due to the practice of looking at the low amount of rent collected in Ulster as a whole. The exertions of the Belfast repeal wardens in collecting penny a month subscriptions from poor working-class Catholics is lost in the overall view. The fact that no monster meetings were held in Belfast during the 'repeal year' of 1843 is also put forward to demonstrate the weakness of the repeal movement in Belfast.[66] However, the reason why no outdoor rallies or 'monster meetings' were held in Belfast is that O'Connell would not have approved of them being held. O'Connell strongly disapproved of anything likely to lead to sectarian strife and riotous behaviour on the part of repeal supporters. This would alienate the Orangemen, whom he had some hopes of winning to the repeal cause, and would give the government an excuse for suppressing the repeal movement.[67] The funeral of a riot victim in 1843, which was attended by 2000 to 3000 people including some repeal wardens, is considered to be the only evidence of public support for repeal in Belfast.[68] The evidence of over 2000 people attending weekly meetings of the Repeal Association has not previously been considered in analysing the success of the repeal movement in Belfast. In fact, Belfast was one of only two towns that held weekly repeal meetings.[69] This evidence shows that although there were no spectacular displays of support for repeal in Belfast in the form of 'monster meetings', there was a firm, consistent base of support and the campaign in the form of penny a month rent touched more people than has previously been realised.

Although some middle-class Catholics were members of the Belfast Repeal Association, they did not generally play an active part in the running of the organisation. Charles McAllister, wholesale druggist, oil, colour, dye stuff, spice merchant and manufacturing chemist was one of the few active middle-class members of the association. He often chaired meetings and attended the meetings regularly. Joseph Magill, a commission agent at the White Linen Hall, subscribed generously to the 'repeal reading room' and donated a collection of books.[70] Two solicitors, Bernard Lennon and John Maginnis, were active in helping those repealers charged with rioting after encounters with Orangemen. The most 'respectable' members of the Belfast Repeal Association can be ascertained by looking at the delegation sent to consult with O'Connell in Dublin. The delegation included Charles McAllister, Bernard Lennon, and William Mahon, proprietor of the 'Irish woollen warehouse'. The head repeal warden, Thomas McEvoy, a publican, had been nominated to go but modestly declined as he maintained that someone with a more fitting social standing should be sent.[71] Other middle-class Catholics such as John McDonnell, tobacco manufacturer, James Moore, rope and twine manufacturer, Henry Murney, tea and wine merchant and tobacco manufacturer, Henry Barry, shipowner, John Cramsie, wine and general merchant, Dr Alexander Harkin, surgeon, Bernard McHugh, draper, Bernard Hughes, bakery proprietor, and Charles McDonnell, tobacco and snuff manufacturer, limited their activities to selling the tickets to the St Patrick's Day dinner and using their influence on important occasions such as the meeting to denounce Young Ireland where most of them appeared on the platform.[72] Some of these men also helped organise the O'Connell tribute along with the parish clergy. Charles McAllister, Charles McDonnell, and James Skene, owner of the 'Stag Inn Coach' company, were the only Belfast members of the '82 Club, a gentlemen's club established by O'Connell and the Young Ireland leaders in honour of the Irish Volunteers of 1782 who declared the legislative independence of Ireland. Members of the club had to purchase specially made green 'Volunteer' uniforms with matching white gloves, all manufactured in Ireland. These were worn to club social events and Charles McAllister often wore his to the Belfast Repeal meetings. When he appeared at a Belfast meeting in uniform for the first time, he was given a huge ovation and was carried to the platform. Despite the support given to the repeal cause, these middle-class members, particularly those in the '82 Club (with the exception of McAllister), were occasionally denounced by the head repeal warden, Thomas McEvoy, for not attending the weekly meetings. 'They, being the natural leaders of the people, should attend their meetings and by their countenance cheer on those struggling patriots who were doing almost past their power as wardens and collectors in the repeal cause. I will always speak my mind freely on this point and if that body do not attend I am determined to represent their conduct to the Liberator and let him deal with them as he thinks proper. (cheers).'[73]

The most active members of the Belfast Repeal Association were the tradesmen, workers and the lower middle class in the Catholic community, some of whom lived in the Pound district. The *Vindicator* described the repeal wardens as 'all of them hard working men, yet forgetting the labours of the day' regularly collected the 'rent' and attended the weekly meetings.[74] The head repeal warden, Thomas McEvoy, was a publican, as were three others; two prominent repeal wardens were booksellers/publishers; two wardens, including the secretary Bernard O'Dempsey were painters/glaziers; two other wardens were clothes dealers from Chapel Lane; one warden was a hardware dealer from Marquis Street; one was a builder from the High Street area; one was a pawnbroker, one was a ship master; two were grocers, one from the Falls Road and the other from Pound Street; one was a brick manufacturer from Cullingtree Road in the Pound; two were flax dressers, one from Barrack Street in the Pound; and two were labourers, one from an entry off Durham Street. The other repeal wardens lived in houses which were too poor to be included in the Belfast street directories.[75]

The crowds of over 2000 attending the weekly meetings of the Belfast Repeal Association were said to be generally from the working class. In July 1844, the *Vindicator* described a crowded meeting thus; 'though the meeting consisted exclusively of the working classes, there was no want of propriety to give respectability to the proceedings nor of talent to give interest to them'.[76] Despite the desire to portray meetings as being as respectable as possible, the *Vindicator* regularly described repeal meetings as being 'composed principally of the honest and intelligent working classes'.[77] As the Pound was one of the main Catholic working-class areas and was home to four of the Repeal wardens, it can be assumed that many of those attending the meetings came from that district.

Up to a quarter of those attending the weekly meetings were women. In November 1843, special rows of raised seats opposite the platform were established for the ladies 'giving the fair occupants an opportunity of witnessing the entire proceedings without any of that annoyance to which they were previously subject'. At special meetings, such as the one held after O'Connell was released from jail in 1844, 'there were so many of the fair sex that the quarter set apart for them was filled completely by themselves' and 'so glad were their looks that you would suppose every woman a bride'. Apart from such observations, there are no descriptions of these women repealers. None of them ever spoke, except once or twice to propose a member or to hand in their own subscriptions. Some are named as being wives of prominent repealers such as Mrs Charles McAllister and Mrs James Skene but the rest are anonymous.[78]

At the weekly meetings, the benefits of repeal and the national repeal campaign strategy were discussed. Charles McAllister, Thomas McEvoy, another prominent local repealer or a guest speaker would give a speech on topics such as the depressed state of Irish manufacturing under the union, the benefits of repeal including promotion of Irish industry, agrarian reform, lower taxes etc. or the difficulties facing the government at Westminster, such as the Anti-Corn Law movement, the Chartists or trouble abroad, which could force them to grant repeal. By attending these meetings, Catholic workers became aware of politics on a wider and more sophisticated scale whereas in the past sectarian skirmishes or election rioting were their only understanding of politics. Attendance at these meetings or even talking to those who did attend was a particularly important method of politicisation for those Catholics who were illiterate and could not learn about politics by reading the newspapers. They had a clearer idea of the envisaged benefits of repeal and were willing to alter their behaviour in order to achieve the objective of the organisation as a whole. As it was not in the interest of the repeal cause, Catholic workers were persuaded to abandon controversial public rallies in Belfast and to stay inside on the Twelfth of July and ignore, if possible, the provocation of Orangemen. The Belfast Repeal Association brought working-class Catholics into the arena of national politics for the first time.

The founding of the Belfast Repeal Association also led to the increased involvement of Catholics, both electors and non-electors, in the electoral politics of the town. The repeal leaders' first attempt to mobilise electoral support for repeal was in February 1843 when the 'Belfast O'Connell Club' was established. Its main aim was the 'furtherance of every effort for Irish nationality as well as a vigilant attention to local interests'. It was decided that the club was to have a newsroom which would enable members to become politically educated, a business department which would monitor the rights of Irishmen and a club room for social intercourse. At the foundation meeting, the 43 people present, 40 of whom were electors, enrolled as members. The chairman declared that if they worked in the manner which this evening promised 'they would, before long, be able to return a Repeal member for Belfast'.[79] Unfortunately for the repealers, this prediction proved to be unrealistic. No repeal candidate was ever fielded for Belfast and the Belfast O'Connell Club appears to have folded soon after its foundation meeting. There is no further mention of it in the *Vindicator*. Although the dream of a Belfast repeal MP was never abandoned and continued to be mentioned occasionally in repeal meetings, it was obviously decided that repealers lacked sufficient electoral strength in Belfast and future electoral campaigns centred on increasing the support of Liberal candidates in their battle with local Tories.

In December 1843, the Belfast repeal leaders called a meeting of the Catholic electors of Belfast to form the 'Belfast Independent Registry Association'. This association was less ambitious than the aborted O'Connell Club and simply aimed to increase the number of registered Catholic voters who would lend their support to other liberal associations such as the 'Reform Club' in returning Liberal representatives for Belfast. Catholics were declared to be 'the more numerous section of the Liberal constituency' with 500 to 600 on the electoral role and if they were effectively registered and united, it would be the duty of the Whigs to consult their interests and wishes. Bernard Lennon donated his legal services to the association free of charge and Thomas McEvoy, the head repeal warden, agreed to act as agent at the registry sessions. At the foundation meeting there were 138 Catholic electors and 'many non-electors' present. It is interesting to note the participation of non-electors in an electoral association which suggests that electoral politics involved more people than those with the franchise as K.T. Hoppen has argued in *Elections, politics and society in Ireland*.[80] Hoppen maintains that those with the vote, such as shop keepers, publicans and anyone connected with the public, were often influenced to vote a certain way by those without the vote who formed a substantial part of their customer base. In the case of the Belfast Independent Registry Association, politically active Catholics without the vote were concerned about similar issues as those with the vote and so lent their support to the organisation. In turn, this support for the organisation may have encouraged more apathetic qualified Catholics to become registered voters. At the foundation meeting, the importance of non-electors was recognised in the following statement; '... a very small sum, by way of subscription, from the electors and non-electors – for it equally concerns both (hear, hear) – will be amply sufficient for all our purposes'.[81] Thomas McEvoy and Bernard Lennon worked hard canvassing for voters and attending the registry sessions. They often reported on their registry work at the weekly repeal meetings which would have made an even wider audience aware of the importance of registry work. It was probably as a result of their work that there was a consistent Liberal majority in the number of new registrations at the registry sessions in the mid 1840s.[82] Despite the failure of the Belfast O'Connell Club, the repeal leaders succeeded, through the Belfast Independent Registry Association, in involving the maximum number of Catholic electors and some non-electors in the electoral politics of Belfast.

The Belfast Repeal Association also fostered the development of Irish nationalism among the Catholic working class in Belfast. This nationalism was the nationalism of O'Connell, not the pure, romantic, uncompromising nationalism of the Young Irelanders. The majority of the leadership and membership of the Belfast Repeal Association supported O'Connell's policy of co-operation with the Whig government in exchange for reform in Ireland after 1846. However, this does not mean that O'Connell and the Belfast repealers were not nationalists. Ideally, they wanted an Irish parliament but after the anti-climax of the Clontarf meeting[83] it was clear that they were not going to win repeal by 'moral force'. As O'Connell and his followers were not prepared to resort to violence and the nature of the parliamentary franchise meant that they did not have the opportunities that the home rule movement had to exert influence later in the century, they had little choice but to extract as many reforms as possible from the government. As the head repeal warden, Thomas McEvoy, declared when O'Connell temporarily supported the plan for a federal solution, 'We will accept all we can get by way of instalment' but would 'never be fully satisfied with anything less than the legislative independence of our country'.[84]

Although misrule from Westminster was often given as the reason for the necessity of repeal of the union, there was also an underlying theme of Ireland as a nation having a right to an Irish parliament. This speech from one of the repeal wardens, Owen Kerr, is typical of those put forward advocating repeal: 'As long as Ireland wants her National flag, as long as the energies of her people are crushed by British legislation, as long as her wealth is drained by foreign landlords, her manufactures neglected and her people starving, in fine as long as she wants her native parliament in College Green, repeal will never be extinct (immense applause).'[85] This speech emphasises British misrule but also Ireland wanting her national flag and native parliament.

Elements of cultural nationalism are discernible in the Belfast Repeal Association. Sections of the Belfast repeal leadership supported the temperance campaign which, they maintained, proved Ireland's fitness for nationhood. The *Vindicator* reported the movements of the temperance campaigner, Father Mathew, nearly as faithfully as it reported O'Connell's and the editor, Mr Buggy, declared at a St Patrick's dinner that 'the glorious temperance movement has not only proved Ireland's fitness for perfect freedom but her ability to achieve it'.[86] Here is the origin of the connection between temperance and some nationalist/republican leaders which continued into the twentieth century. In the *Vindicator,* which was read by working-class Catholics in the 'repeal reading room', the virtues of the Irish people were often contrasted with the supposed absence of morals in England where young children were forced into hard labour in factories, women were unchaste, and the evils of socialism and incest were rampant. The 'repeal reading room', a Young Ireland idea, is evidence of a degree of cultural nationalism as it was established especially to enable the working classes to learn about Irish history and politics. All the daily and weekly repeal newspapers, including the Young Ireland paper, the *Nation*, were available in the reading room as well as a 'choice of the best national works' and 'no charge of any kind whatever is made'.[87] The *Vindicator* itself claimed to be 'the preacher of nationality' and encouraged the teaching of Irish history and geography in schools instead of Greek, Roman and English history. Since 1839 when Charles Gavan Duffy founded the *Vindicator*, poems appeared which proved to be 'an effective means of inculcating nationality among the population'. Articles by Young Irelanders such as Duffy appeared in the *Vindicator* emphasising the necessity of 'national education' involving national books, histories, music, painting, sculpture, costume, historical plays, historical novels and historical ballads. 'These are the seeds of permanent nationality and we must sow them deep in the people's hearts.'[88] The *Vindicator* also praised the revival of native music in Drogheda and advocated the establishment of a native music association in every parish as 'the cultivation of our native music would tend much to nationalise the people of Ireland and also to refine the manners and improve the habits of our humbler classes'.[89]

While the Belfast Repeal Association involved the Catholic working classes in politics proper for the first time and fostered the development of Irish nationalism, it also reinforced Catholic workers' sectarianism by mobilising them in support of specifically Catholic issues. The *Vindicator* itself saw a close connection between Catholicism and nationalism, as evidenced by their description of the absence of nationalism in Belfast before the founding of that newspaper in 1838. 'The Protestants had no nationalisation, they were merely Protestant and their politics were sectarian. On the other hand, there was a certain nationality among the Presbyterians. To be sure, it was anything but Irish – it smacked of Scotch feeling and strongly savoured of the plantation of Ulster. The Catholic party, strong only in the ancient patriotism of their creed, were without power, consolidation or organs ...'[90] The Belfast repeal leadership's outlook, as represented by the *Vindicator*, involved a strong commitment to defending Catholic interests. The *Vindicator* constantly carried reports of converts to Catholicism in England and elsewhere and it was reprimanded on one occasion by the national Repeal Association leadership for describing the Protestant church as an 'insignificant heresy'. In response, the *Vindicator* claimed that it had to tell the truth about the 'Church of blood and crime' due to its persistent attacks on the Roman Catholic Church.[91] Whilst ridiculing the paltry amounts of money collected by 'Trash' Gregg's Protestant Operative Society, the Vindicator noted that 'the day is not far distant when Catholicism will lift up its venerable head in high places. In Ireland, it has the giant's strength. In England, its daily increase is great; while state Protestantism is hated by the millions in both countries from its repulsive tyranny – and that other motley thing called dissenting Protestantism is nearly broken up – a thing without principle or vitality, exhibiting sad disfigurements and degraded below contempt by the frantic fanatics, who only take it up when they lose their reason'.[92] In early 1847, the *Vindicator* published a series of articles in response to the weekly lectures on the errors of Catholicism by the Revd Mr McIlwaine. The *Vindicator's* defence of its faith involved a criticism of Protestantism although it is difficult to see how they could have responded to McIlwaine in any other way.[93] Presumably, something of this commitment to the spread of Catholicism and the vigorous defence of its tenets must have filtered down to the rank and file.

Opposition to the Charitable Bequests Board, a specifically Catholic concern, dominated politics in early 1845 to such an extent that the *Vindicator* looked forward to the time when the issue would be settled and declared, 'Let us not forget the Repeal of the Union!'.[94] Although, the archbishop of

Armagh, along with two other bishops, had joined the Charitable Bequests Board, the Belfast repealers supported O'Connell's and Bishop MacHale of Tuam's opposition to the board on the grounds that it put church property under the control of the state. The Belfast repealers, such as Thomas McEvoy, were the main organisers and speakers at the public meeting held to denounce the board while the more 'respectable' Catholics did not attend. This is a clear case of the mobilisation of working-class Catholics in support of a specifically Catholic cause which, combined with the local repeal leadership's vigorous espousal of Catholicism, meant that nationalism was firmly identified with Catholicism in the minds of rank and file repealers and local Protestants. Protestants would have been particularly disturbed by this agitation as they saw Bishop MacHale, for whom, according to the Revd Dr Cooke, Catholic 'ascendancy was the lullaby of the cradle before reason dawned', as the driving force behind it.[95] While the repeal movement imbued the Catholic working class with a sense of Irish nationalism which transcended their simpler sectarian outlook, it did not eradicate sectarianism. Rather, the identification of Catholicism and nationalism reinforced and legitimised it.

It has been argued that sectarianism was not a strong enough base upon which to build political movements like repeal and that sectarianism may actually have hindered the development of such movements. This misconception is due to looking at the extent of the repeal movement in Ulster as a whole. It has been argued that as the Ribbon society was strong in Ulster and the repeal movement was generally weak, sectarianism must have hindered the development of political movements such as repeal.[96] Further research would have to be done to ascertain accurately the reasons for the weakness of the repeal movement in Ulster as a whole. However, one can surmise that outside Catholic strongholds such as Monaghan and Donegal and towns with a sizeable Catholic population such as Belfast, Derry and Dungannon, the opposition of local Orangemen and magistrates would have been an important factor. In such areas, it may have been logical for Catholics to band together in secret societies to defend their interests but not to agitate openly on political issues.

The fact that Ribbonism co-existed with the Repeal Association in Belfast suggests that sectarianism did not hinder the development of political movements like repeal.[97] In September 1845, the *Vindicator* revealed that there were as many as 1000 Ribbon society members in Belfast, including some repeal wardens and rank and file repealers. It was obviously feasible that a Catholic worker could support the repeal campaign and still feel that a secret society was necessary to protect their community from the Orangemen, particularly as the forces of law and order were not considered to be impartial. Once the Belfast repeal leaders discovered that Ribbonism had infiltrated the organisation, a purge was carried out. All those repealers suspected of being involved in Ribbonism were questioned by the repeal wardens. Some denied ever having any connection with Ribbonism while others admitted that they used to be members but had since distanced themselves from the society. All agreed to take an oath denouncing the society and by October 1845, McEvoy was able to report to the Repeal Association in Dublin that 'Ribbonism is extinct in Belfast'.[98] He may have eradicated Ribbonism from the ranks of the repeal wardens but it seems doubtful as to whether he could have eradicated it totally among the rank and file or forced the estimated 1000 members to leave the society.

Although the Belfast Repeal Association was committed in theory to winning over Protestants, particularly Presbyterians, it would not abandon Catholic causes to try to achieve this. The Belfast Repeal Association had two Presbyterian members who sometimes chaired meetings and a constant trickle of subscriptions from Protestants and Presbyterians came in from Belfast and areas of Antrim and Down. They appear to have supported repeal mainly because of the depressed state of the economy. When the Young Irelanders and O'Connell's Repeal Association in Dublin split ostensibly because the Young Irelanders would not support O'Connell's denunciation of physical force in all circumstances, the Belfast Repeal Association and the *Vindicator* whole-heartedly supported O'Connell with little thought for the effect this would have on the few Protestant supporters of repeal. Behind the physical force debate there were other fundamental differences between O'Connell and the Young Irelanders, many of whom were Protestants. The Young Irelanders were romantic nationalists who believed the cause of the nation to be of primary importance while religion should be essentially a private matter. O'Connell was a more practical politician who often appeared willing to exchange repeal for something that was more likely to be obtainable such as federalism or reform within the union. He also did not consider religion to be a private matter and supported bishops, such as MacHale of Tuam, in their opposition to mixed education and the Charitable Bequests Board.[99] At the time of the split, John Mitchell, one of the Young Irelanders, declared that 'he was one of the Saxon Irish of the North and they wanted that race in their ranks. They could not without them liberate themselves and it was their country (the Northerners) as well as theirs. If they drove them from them by needless tests, they would perpetuate their own degradation by establishing the old rule that Ireland must be governed by one faction and England would trample on their necks'.[100] The *Vindicator* did not heed Mitchell's advice and did not hesitate to identify Catholicism with the repeal movement. It declared, 'the war party [i.e. the Young Irelanders] would banish religion altogether from their deliberations – the peace party [i.e. O'Connell and the Repeal Association] would make it the basis of all their councils; the war party would have what is called infidel education – the peace party would have Christian education; the war party inculcate the right to dissent – the peace party urge the utility of unanimity; the war party would have recourse to arms even while the constitution was left to them, and by way of aggression – the peace party would not have recourse

to arms until they were driven from the constitution, and then by way of
defence; the war party would not prefer the Whigs to the Tories – the peace
party think there is some difference.'[101] The *Vindicator* and the Belfast repeal
leadership shared O'Connell's commitment to Catholic causes such as
denominational tertiary education and opposition to the Charitable Bequests
Board but they also had such reverential faith in O'Connell that it is hard to
imagine them disagreeing with any policy of his. It was probably 'their
unbounded confidence' in their 'beloved leader' as much as shared convictions
that led the Belfast leaders to denounce the secular nationalism of the Young
Irelanders.

Although the *Vindicator* predicted that Belfast would be the first to hold a
meeting to proclaim confidence in O'Connell, it was actually more than a
month after the split when the meeting finally took place. A number of
members of the Belfast Repeal Association were sympathetic to the Young
Ireland position and this caused the delay of the public meeting. The Belfast
repealers were also in the tricky situation of having invited William Smith
O'Brien, a prominent Young Irelander, to a dinner in Belfast just before the
split.[102] Although the conservative and whig press of Belfast accused them of
bringing the hospitality of Belfast into disrepute by not honouring the
invitation, the *Vindicator* maintained that O'Brien himself decided not to come
in the interests of repeal unity. When the public meeting was finally held, the
Young Ireland sympathisers had enough supporters there to ensure that the
disorder and noise was such that the meeting had to be abandoned. To prevent
the meeting denouncing the Young Irelanders after they had left, their
supporters turned off the gas so everyone had to grope their way home in the
darkness.[103]

When the meeting was reconvened a few days later, the pro-O'Connell
leadership ensured that tickets were mainly given to their supporters. The
meeting was said to have 'the approbation of the pious, respectable and zealous
prelates' and many of the middle-class Catholic repealers were on the platform
to lend their support to the denunciation of the Young Irelanders. One member
of the audience, 'a respectable townsman' asked for three cheers for William
Smith O'Brien. He was consequently thrown out of the meeting. 'By what
means he was ejected, *"moral"* or *"physical"*, we were unable to perceive,'
declared the *Northern Whig* reporter 'but we are quite prepared to say that his
departure was involuntary as he continued to protest that he was a "Repealer"
and "a friend of O'Connell".'[104] After the ejection of this individual, the
meeting unanimously proclaimed the Belfast repealers' 'unbounded confidence in the ability and integrity of our tried, trusted and beloved leader,
Daniel O'Connell, Esq., under whose guidance we rest assured the Irish
people, by moral means alone, can accomplish what they could not otherwise
effect – the Repeal of the detested union'.[105] In regard to potential Protestant
repealers, one of the speakers, Bernard Lennon, declared that Protestants

would only join a movement committed to peaceful means and besides, 'for his own part, he would be quite content if none should join in seeking it for as repeal would benefit the whole people of Ireland, they would reap their share of the advantages'. Despite the envisaged shared 'advantages', such sentiments reveal an accepted link between Catholicism and nationalism.[106]

The Belfast repealers who were expelled from the Repeal Association for 'Young Irelandism' were not openly advocating violence. They objected to the suppression of free speech within the association, the expulsion of the Young Ireland group and the banning of the *Nation* from the repeal reading room. In an explanatory letter to John O'Connell, one of those expelled, Edward Daly, declared that he was 'grateful for the services of some of the gentlemen called "Old Ireland", but if, to be so, I must be ungrateful for the services of those patriotic, talented, independent men, O'Brien, Barry, Duffy, etc., and rejoice at their loss, then I do not rejoice at my country's losing their valuable services'. He said he could not approve of the prescription of the *Nation* from the repeal reading rooms and could not subscribe to the doctrine that 'in an assembly of freemen, the right of free discussion is a crime'.[107] The head repeal warden, Thomas McEvoy, alienated some members, such as Dr Samuel McBurney, by declaring that although every man had a right 'to hold his own political and religious opinions, ... he did and ever would dispute the right of men to place their views in opposition to those of the great, tried and gifted man who had brought them from bondage to freedom ...'[108] The strongest criticism of O'Connellite policy came from John MacVeigh who denounced the entente with the Whig government. 'Some assert that the coalition with the Whigs is one of those bold master strokes of political expediency pardonable only in a great leader- that we should wait the result of this policy, suspend our agitation, or in other words, just keep the embers alive and quietly await the rich harvest which we will ultimately glean from finality Russell. A policy of this kind I protest against as weak and imbecile, as unbecoming a nation which has protested in the eyes of the whole world that she yearns for self-government, and has determined never to desist until she has attained her natural birth right, the right to be governed by her own Monarch, Lords and Commons. Such vacillation and time serving should be repudiated and despised.'[109]

Sixteen men, including one member, three repeal wardens and twelve associates were expelled from the Repeal Association. In addition to those mentioned above, were James Skene, a prominent Repealer, John Rea, a Protestant solicitor, and a Mr McLaughlin, a Protestant who formerly chaired Repeal meetings. These dissidents appear to be well educated, having among them a solicitor, a teacher, a surgeon and the owner of a coach company.[110] In September 1847, these Young Ireland supporters formed the Drennan Confederate Club. The Young Ireland leadership had decided to form Confederate Clubs throughout Ireland after their candidates were attacked by

O'Connellite repealers during the July 1847 election campaign. O'Brien emphasised that the clubs should be 'adult schools of nationality', a forum for lectures, discussion and meetings. Discussion of sectarian topics was banned and there was to be no expulsion without a hearing.[111]

The Drennan Confederate Club failed to win over a significant number of the rank and file members of the Repeal Association. Indeed, when the Young Ireland leaders, Smith O'Brien, Meagher and McGee visited Belfast to promote Confederate principles, a Repeal Association crowd ensured that the famous speakers could not be heard. Although some prominent Old Irelanders tried to obtain a hearing for the speakers, it appears that other members of the Repeal Association encouraged their rank and file to disrupt the meeting. The audience on the platform and in the reserved seats was considered by the Belfast Protestant press to be 'generally respectable' and may have included some middle-class Protestants who were not repealers while 'the body of the room was filled chiefly with parties belonging to the working classes'. These workers were committed Old Irelanders whose chants ensured that no speaker could be heard. They burned gun powder so the hall filled with smoke and their leader, a butcher, proposed a resolution of confidence in John O'Connell. When Meagher rose to oppose the resolution, 'about forty or fifty individuals from the body of the room rushed upon the platform, seemingly determined on the destruction of Mr Meagher and the other members of the deputation. They had armed themselves with a number of slender poles ... and belaboured all around them, right and left, till they had cleared the room of about one half of the audience. They then ascended the platform, a portion of which, during the melee, came down, hurting several individuals ... and proceeded to deal furious blows at the heads of Mr Meagher, Mr McGee and others. Mr Meagher resolutely refused to leave the position in which he had placed himself, and had it not been for the phalanx of Young Irelanders which surrounded him, and shielded him from many of the blows aimed at him, there is little doubt that, from the violence of the mob, he would have been taken from the hall severely injured.' After the police had removed the violent portion of the audience, some of the Young Irelanders were able to speak although there were still constant noisy and riotous interruptions. Mr Meagher declared that he had come to Belfast, 'not alone to advocate the principle of self government, but to assert a still greater principle – namely freedom of opinion. That is a principle, gentlemen, without which, ... Repeal would be not a blessing but a despotism.' He maintained that the Ulster patriots of 1782 'have taught me the principle which you impeach as treason. Blame them, they have taught me the creed which you designate as heresy ... I demand the Repeal of the Act of Union, and that this act may be repealed, I invoke the spirit of the North. Not for vote by ballot, not for an extension of the franchise, not for corporate reform amendment acts, not for eleven comprehensive measures, do I demand Repeal. These are not the grounds upon which an Irish citizen should claim, for his country, the restitution of her legislative power.' Meagher was not just addressing the O'Connollite supporters of repeal but those middle-class Protestants who were opposed to it. He asked, 'Is what we advocate tainted with sectarianism? Is it distempered with Whiggery? Does it predict the fall of Protestantism? I know full well that in the north Repeal has been identified with Popery, whilst the Union has been identified with Protestantism. The principles of 1688 and a legislative disconnection with England has [*sic*] been judged incompatible. Your fathers [in the Volunteers] did not say so.' He went on to outline the economic advantages of repeal and dismissed the danger of a Catholic ascendancy. He alleged that Protestantism was not safe under the Union as the English were increasingly relying on pro-Union Catholics for support. He emphasised that, unlike the Repeal Association, sectarian issues were not discussed in the Irish Confederation. They disapproved of the prominent role of priests in politics and rejected the motto, 'the priests and the people' in favour of 'the citizens of Ireland.' John Mitchel then explained the principles of the Confederation; the right of Ireland to a domestic legislature, the exclusion of religious issues from debate and absolute independence from all English parties. William Smith O'Brien concluded the meeting by proposing the resolution passed by the Volunteers at Dungannon in 1782 that, 'the claim of any body of men, other than the King, Lords, and Commons of Ireland to make laws to bind the kingdom is unconstitutional, illegal and a grievance'.[112]

The proposed second meeting which the Young Ireland leaders were to address was prohibited by the magistrates. Smith O'Brien led a deputation to Hercules Street where the most violent of the Repeal Association supporters resided in order to address them. The immense crowd following Smith O'Brien and the Hercules Street crowd were kept apart by the police and the Young Irelanders soon decided to return to their hotel.[113] When the second meeting was eventually held, it was prematurely adjourned due to the heckling of the Repeal Association supporters, one of whom declared that the Young Irelanders were 'resolved to take away the life and soul of the immortal Liberator'.[114]

The Young Ireland leaders did not consider their trip to Belfast as a failure. Smith O'Brien declared at the dinner held in Belfast in honour of the speakers that, 'to superficial observers it might appear that the mission of the deputation to the north was a failure. To him it did not appear to be so; for during his stay in Belfast, he had made the acquaintance of a number of gentlemen: men whose standing in society and high character, whose industry and efforts, made them an honour to the country to which they belonged.' In speaking of the riotous disruption at the meetings, he maintained that he was convinced that none of the respectable portion of the population, either Old Irelanders or Orangemen, countenanced the course that had been pursued [and for] the poor, deluded people, who had acted so improperly that day, he had no other feeling than that of pity …' The local Confederate leader, John Rea, praised the 'gallant conduct of the ladies, who had, despite every danger, attended their meetings …'[115]

The *Nation* regarded the visit as a success. 'The Orangemen offered no resistance. The respectable middle classes of Belfast came willingly to listen to the deputation; the only active enemies of Repeal were the emissaries of Conciliation Hall.'[116] Although their repeal principles were opposed by the Protestant press and the bulk of the Protestant middle class, the Young Irelanders determination to uphold freedom of speech was widely admired as shown by the *Whig's* description of the meetings which were actually reprinted in the *Nation*.[117] The Protestant *Warder* declared that the Young Irelanders' determination to stand their ground in a smoke-filled Belfast Music Hall while assailed with stones, bludgeons and gunpowder squibs, 'showed no lack of resolution and pluck' while 'the intolerance and rascality' of their opponents was fully exposed.[118]

The Confederate leaders' non-sectarian vision of repeal probably encouraged the formation of the short lived Belfast Protestant Repeal Association in July 1848. Its objective was declared to be a domestic legislature to be achieved by means of arguments and facts. Members had to be Protestants and repealers. Whilst they promoted co-operation with other bodies with the same objectives, they were independent, 'being determined to guard the just rights and privileges of the Protestants of the North. We go for Queen, Lords and Commons of Ireland and are necessarily opposed to anarchy and social disorder. It matters not to us whether a man be a Whig or a Tory, a Radical or Conservative; for while we shall prevent the intrusion of irrelevant matters into our meetings, we seek to unite all parties in a common league for the common welfare and shall interfere with no man's sentiments.' They would 'wield no weapons' to advance the cause. 'To raise and regenerate Ireland is our grand object; but Ulster, our birth place and our home, has a special claim on our sympathies. Fondly attached to it, we shall protect its interests as the apple of our eye. Finally, though we have emancipated our souls from rooted prejudices against the Catholic portion of our countrymen – though we embrace them as brethren – and shall invariably recognise their claims to equal rights with us, we shall stand by Protestantism, if need be, until death.'[119] The association was predominantly middle class. Its leader was a medical doctor, J.W. Beck, and one of its most prominent members was the poet Samuel Ferguson.[120] However, its uncompromising Protestantism could possibly have attracted a wider membership had the Confederate movement not collapsed after the 1848 rising.[121]

The fact that working-class Protestants did not attack the Young Irelanders as they did O'Connell suggests that they did not regard them as representatives of their Catholic rivals. The mixed nature of the Young Ireland leadership and local membership and their opposition to the Repeal Association meant that they did not fit into the sectarian pattern of working-class Belfast politics. Indeed, a few Protestant workers joined the Young Ireland movement. These workers were presumably attracted by the expected economic benefits of repeal (the reason most poor Protestant converts gave for conversion to Repeal was economic). The Young Irelanders' also praised what they perceived to be the qualities of the Orangemen. The *Nation* described them as 'brave, blind men whose courage and power would be invaluable in an Irish militia battling against religious tyranny'.[122] Their opposition to the O'Connollite Repeal Association also meant that support for the Young Irelanders was less likely to be seen as 'turning'. Although the number of working-class Protestants who joined the Young Ireland movement was not large, a 'John Mitchel Confederate Club' was established in Sandy Row in 1848 and 29 Belfast Orangemen were expelled from the Order for espousing Repeal principles.[123] Although most working-class Protestants were not won over to repeal, they did not regard the Young Irelanders with hostility as they allowed the John Mitchel Confederate Club to meet and did not attack Smith O'Brien or any of his colleagues when they visited Belfast. At the Twelfth celebrations in 1848, the Revd Dr Drew and the other Belfast ministers present felt it necessary to warn of the dangers of repeal and declare it impossible for a Protestant to support it. Even after the 1848 rising, there was some sympathy within the Orange Order for the Confederate leaders as Orangemen united with all classes throughout Ireland 'in demanding the reprieve of the Young Irelanders'.[124]

The hostility of the majority of Catholic workers and the neutrality of the majority of Protestant workers ensured that the Young Irelanders only made a minor inroad into the sectarian politics of the Belfast working class. On the eve of the 1848 rising, the two clubs in Belfast had only three hundred members although the *Nation* rather optimistically declared that two more clubs would soon be established. 'The people are arming. Another fortnight and Belfast will have from one to two thousand enrolled.'[125]

In early 1847, the Repeal Association in Belfast began to wind down, suffering under the effects of the famine and recession. McEvoy wrote to the Repeal Association in Dublin to inform them that 'the poor here are suffering under the most frightful privations from the want of sufficient and nutritious food which their ghastly and emaciated appearance but too visibly portrays. This alarming state of distress has deferred us from making our usual exertions in collecting subscriptions from the people.' The previous December, the Repeal Association in Dublin had stopped all funding for reading rooms and other local expenses as the national rent fell below £60 as the famine worsened. The Belfast repealers established a committee to deal with this new situation but the consequences of the end of national funding are not described in the *Vindicator*. It is only reported that the Belfast repealers began to hold monthly, rather than weekly, meetings. Despite the catastrophe of the famine and the bleak outlook for repeal, the Belfast repeal leadership did not lose faith in O'Connell or give up all hope, at least not publicly. The *Vindicator* even declared that one thousand people would not be dying every day in Cork if it had not 'pleased Almighty God to afflict O'Connell with his present illness. His powerful mind would have discovered an expedient fitted to meet a crisis … and his eloquence would have aroused the government and the country to a sense of their duty.'[126]

While the foundation of the Repeal Association politicised and nationalised the Catholics of the Pound, their sectarian outlook was not eradicated. The development of nationalism actually gave sectarianism an ideological legitimacy. Catholic repealers regarded themselves as comprising the ranks of those campaigning for Ireland's freedom whereas the Protestants were allied to the 'Saxon' enemy. The espousal of Catholic causes by the Repeal Association reinforced the connection between Catholicism and nationalism. The Young Irelanders' non-sectarian vision of Repeal only attracted small numbers of Catholic and Protestant workers and so made only a minor and temporary inroad into the sectarian nature of working class politics. Catholic and Protestant in Belfast were no longer separated solely by religion. Their shared support of Liberal candidates, which was due to the impossibility of a repeal candidate being successful, could not hide the fact that most Catholics and Protestants were also firmly divided by the politics of nationalism.

1843 RIOTS

The excitement surrounding the repeal campaign was the cause of the most extensive riots in the first half of the nineteenth century. While working-class Catholics were mobilised in support of repeal, working-class Protestants were mobilised in support of the union. The Protestant Operative Association organised an anti-repeal petition which attracted over 17,000 signatures. The association also held an anti-repeal demonstration attended by 3,000 people in June, 1843. On their way home from the meeting, the Protestant workers smashed the windows of Catholic houses in Sandy Row, yelling 'no repeal' and 'to hell with the pope'.[127]

Despite an appeal from Belfast's influential Protestants, such as the Revd Dr Cooke, not to cause trouble on the Twelfth which could provoke the government and so please the Repeal Association,[128] working-class Protestants were determined to demonstrate to Belfast Catholics that 1843 would not be the 'repeal year'. Unlike previous riots which were of much shorter duration, the Twelfth riots in 1843 continued intermittently for nearly two weeks. The Protestant *Belfast Newsletter* and the Catholic *Vindicator* agreed that the trouble began on the evening of the twelfth when an Orange crowd from Brown Street attacked Catholic houses in Peter's Hill and Boundary Street.[129] The police sent for the cavalry but the rioters dispersed before they arrived. The following evening, violence erupted in Sandy Row. According to the

Vindicator, an Orange crowd descended upon O'Hanlon's public house opposite the Ulster railway and smashed all the windows. An effigy of O'Connell was then carried through Sandy Row and burnt 'amid the usual howlings of that miserable faction'.[130]

On Friday and Saturday, the violence escalated. The *Vindicator* and the *Belfast Newsletter* emphasise the atrocities of the Protestants and Catholics respectively. The *Belfast Newsletter* reported that 'large numbers of people belonging to Sandy Row assembled on Friday evening opposite Christ Church to prevent a large body of Catholics marching from the Pound to wreck the church and Secession meeting house now being erected as such a threat was made the previous evening'. The two crowds threw stones at each other for a considerable time until the police eventually succeeded in separating them after themselves receiving many blows. Later that night, the two crowds burned effigies of William of Orange and Daniel O'Connell and ill feeling increased to such an extent that the police and magistrates were required to remain overnight to prevent further outbreaks. 'To such an extent did the excitement prevail that very few of the inhabitants of Sandy Row and the adjoining streets retired to rest during the entire night.'[131]

The *Vindicator* did not comment on the alleged threat to burn the churches and maintained that the Sandy Row mob 'committed a series of the most unprovoked aggressions exclusively against Catholics'. On Saturday night, 18 Catholic houses in Cullingtree Road had their doors, windows and furniture smashed. In one of these houses, a shoemaker called Cosgrave was in his bed dying of consumption. His wife asked the wreckers to stop or it would kill him. They replied, 'Damn the Papist – he is going to hell and we'll only send him there faster!' According to the *Vindicator*, the Catholics assembled in self-defence but were convinced to disperse by the magistrates in exchange for protection from the police and the military. However, after the police had gone, the Protestants returned and attacked the Catholics in their beds.[132] According to the *Belfast Newsletter*, the situation was reversed. After the two crowds had been fighting for a long time in a field next to Mulholland's mill, the magistrates and 'several other gentlemen' used their influence to convince the parties to go home. However, having seen the Sandy Row crowd retire, the Pound crowd returned and 'smashed the windows of almost every house in Cullingtree Road and Stanley Street occupied by Protestant families'.[133] The fighting occurred throughout the Sandy Row–Pound area as the crowds moved about and new riotous combinations emerged. The police evidence at the trial of the rioters was that houses belonging to both sides were damaged in Cullingtree Road, Durham Street, Stanley Place, Stanley Street and Albert Place.[134]

Although this major riot was eventually brought under control by the police, sporadic outbreaks of violence continued to occur for the next week or so. The *Vindicator* reported that on 18 and 19 July, 'Orange anti-repealers' attacked

Catholic houses in York Street. The 'drunken miscreants' then burned effigies of O'Connell and Father Mathew, the founder of the temperance movement in Ireland.[135] On the following Sunday, the funeral procession for the shoemaker, Cosgrove, who died during the riots, was attacked by a mob in Sandy Row. The *Vindicator* maintained that the funeral was not meant to be provocative and refuted claims made by the *Northern Whig* that the man had died on Tuesday and the funeral was deliberately postponed until Sunday. According to the *Vindicator,* the man died on the Friday and his funeral was not organised as a Repeal demonstration. Repeal wardens were present to try to ensure that no trouble occurred. The *Vindicator* reported that as the procession returned up Sandy Row, they were taunted by insults such as 'To hell with the Pope', 'Are you coming from Purgatory?', 'Is it a warm place?'. 'The women, to do them justice, were the most vociferous; one of them standing on a ditch and waving an Orange handkerchief as the signal for battle.' According to the *Vindicator*, the procession at first ignored the insults, dodged the stones and hurried home but near the Ulster Railway they were attacked again and 'a few of the younger portion of the Catholics' retaliated and 'gave them a desperate beating'. When the magistrate and the police arrived the Catholics told them they were attacked by the Sandy Row crowd but 'a number of the constabulary without more ado rushed upon the funeral party laying about them pell mell with the utmost fury!' Fighting broke out and the police were severely beaten. The cavalry was sent for but before they arrived both crowds had dispersed.[136]

The following evening, the *Vindicator* reported that the Orangemen of Sandy Row had burnt an effigy of O'Connell, yelling damnation to the Pope and repealers. They wrecked houses in Tea Lane belonging to Catholics. Three of these houses were 'utterly wrecked'. The Orangemen also 'brutally assailed some young girls, and for about an hour quite unmolested!'. In York Street a 12-year-old boy was assaulted by two Orangemen because he refused to yell 'To hell with the Pope'. An orphan girl was attacked on her way to work in Grimshaw's mill in Sandy Row for the same reason. This sort of violence was perpetrated by both sides. A Protestant girl from Sandy Row was attacked on her way home from the Revd Mr Johnston's Sunday school in Berry Street. Four Catholic girls, some of whom she worked with in a mill, threw stones at her at the college, kicked her, assisted by an old man and 'lumps of boys'. In a separate incident, two Protestant girls were severely beaten on their way home from church and one of their bibles was destroyed.[137]

The handling of the 1843 riots showed that, despite improvements, the administration of justice was still not impartial. Although the resident magistrates appointed by Dublin Castle were generally regarded as unbiased in their manner of dealing with disturbances, some of the local magistrates and the town police, an almost entirely Protestant force, were regarded as favouring the Orange crowd. Indeed, one policeman released a rioter he had taken into custody after discovering that he was an Orangeman and replaced him with a

Catholic. The policeman was later dismissed for his actions. Although equal numbers of Catholics and Protestants were tried and found guilty of rioting during the initial disturbances in 1843, an all-Protestant jury (which the *Vindicator* claims was rigged) dismissed all the charges against the Protestants involved in the subsequent funeral riot and returned guilty verdicts against all the Catholics.[138] The biased nature of the judicial system probably continued to encourage the Orangemen to commit acts of violence whilst at the same time it increased Catholic alienation from the state.

The segregation of the two communities probably increased as a result of the 1843 riots. The evidence submitted in court suggests segregation was already quite pronounced. The Belfast magistrate, Verner, described Sandy Row as containing 'a large majority of Protestants but also a number of Catholics. The Protestants there are considered very ardent ones.' Albert Place he considered to be Protestant while Durham Street he suggested was mixed. He described Cullingtree Road as mainly Catholic and Barrack Street as 'nearly all Catholic'.[139] Although there is no specific mention in the press of people actually moving out of hostile districts, the house wrecking during the riots and the subsequent intimidation suggests that some people must have sought safer abodes in their 'own' areas. The people living in houses that were completely wrecked such as the three Catholic families in Tea Lane would have been unlikely to rent a house in the same area. The protracted violence and intimidation in the two areas in 1843 sharpened and increased the divide between Protestants and Catholics.

Scholars such as Sybil Baker maintain that the Catholics were the most enthusiastic participants, if not the initiators, of the 1843 riots. This, it is argued, reflects their confidence derived from their increasing numbers. This Catholic aggression is regarded as a major cause of increased sectarianism in Belfast.[140] However, both the Protestant *Belfast Newsletter* and the Catholic *Vindicator* agreed that the initial violence was perpetrated by the Orangemen and the resident magistrate declared it was impossible to tell who was the main aggressor.[141] The riots were not caused by an increasingly confident and aggressive Catholic population. Catholics mistakenly felt secure in the belief that repeal would be granted. Moreover, the Belfast repeal leaders worked hard to try to prevent outbreaks of violence of which their leader O'Connell disapproved. This is not to suggest that Catholics were not involved in violent acts such as stone throwing and house wrecking. They obviously were but they had less reason to initiate the rioting. It was the Protestant workers who felt insecure and, as in 1829, in the face of opposition from their leaders, insisted on a show of strength. The false assertion that it was the increasingly aggressive Catholics of the Pound who caused the 1843 riots obscures the degree of anti-repeal feeling in Sandy Row and the origins of working-class unionism.

THE REVIVAL OF THE ORANGE ORDER

The official re-establishment of the Orange Order and the lapsing of the party processions act in 1845 allowed influential ministers such as Drew and McIlwaine to attend Orange processions and to address the crowds. This undoubtedly increased the legitimacy and influence of the Orange Order in districts such as Sandy Row. From 1846 onwards, the support of evangelical ministers for Orange processions and the advent of railway excursions combined to increase the riotous potential of the Twelfth in Belfast. Railway excursions heightened tensions on the Twelfth because larger numbers of Orangemen and their supporters participated in the celebrations, the railway station and town centre became Orange territory for the day and their return to the station in the evening was awaited by crowds of supporters and often opponents indignant at the display of Orange domination. Between 1846 and 1849, trouble followed these Orange excursions on the Twelfth with the exception of 1847 when, significantly, there was no railway excursion but a traditional march into the countryside.

In 1846, a large parade of Orangemen marched through the town to take the train to Lisburn having heard a sermon by the Revd Mr McIlwaine the previous evening. Upon returning to Belfast, they paraded along Bridge Street and Donegall Street where they were attacked by a Catholic crowd. According to the *Belfast Newsletter*, 'the intolerant spirit of Romanism prevailed to mar the harmony of the day'. Bridge Street was 'completely filled with men, women and children following the music and attracted by the display' when 'groups of three to four infiltrated the parade and attacked individuals including women'. The head of the procession continued to Donegall Street where they were met with stones and brick bats. They retreated to Bridge Street which was full with the rest of the procession so 'all who could fled into North Street and every other avenue where they could be safe from the principle danger. The screams of the women and children were heartrending as they made for every open doorway to give shelter and loudly appealed for admittance to those that were shut. The hall of our [i.e. *Belfast Newsletter*] office was speedily filled with poor creatures in a miserable state of fright.' The riot was eventually quelled 'but not before serious injury was inflicted on many of the Orangemen and the attacking party while being driven back by the police, assaulted the magistrates in a most brutal manner'. The *Newsletter*, however, reprimanded the authorities for not having deployed the military earlier in the day as 'the Repealers and Ribbonmen made no secret' of their intentions. 'They paraded the streets with green boughs, headed by a fife and drum, collected in several places in great numbers and manifested every symptom of intended opposition.'[142]

On 14 and 15 July, there was rioting in the evening in the North Queen Street/Pinkerton's Row area. The fighting was between local Orangemen and

Catholics known as 'mud larks' who had been brought to Belfast to be labourers on various public works projects such as the Belfast-Ballymena railway, the Cavehill railway and the Waterworks.[143] These Catholic labourers were probably among those from the south of Ireland given public employment in Belfast as a form of famine relief. Their speech, customs and the fact that they lived and worked together and had a sense of group camaraderie probably set them apart from the rest of the population and may have been a source of tension. This type of violence between navvies and other groups of men was not unique to Belfast. The often violent rivalry between Irish navvies and groups of English or Scottish workmen was notorious throughout Britain in the early to mid nineteenth century.[144] Another riot between a group of navvies and Orangemen took place in Ballymacarrett on the Twelfth of July 1849. One navvy died from wounds received during the riot and 'much excitement' prevailed during the funeral and inquest.[145]

According to the *Northern Whig*, in 1848 the procession was particularly large in order to disprove the propaganda of the recently formed Protestant Repeal Association claiming that the Orangemen had been won over to repeal. The procession marched through the main streets of town, watched by huge crowds of onlookers, and then took the train to Carrickfergus. They then marched to a nearby meadow where they were joined by the Larne district lodges. The gathering was estimated at between 4,000 and 6,000, 'more than half of which at least was composed of females'. All but a few of the crowd were 'what are called the working or labouring classes'.[146] The difficulty of gauging the size and nature of processions from newspaper reports is shown by the *Northern Whig* describing this parade as consisting of thirty lodges of 15-30 members 'calculating in this many little boys' and emphasising the working class and female composition of the gathering at Carrickfergus (seeming to downplay the importance of the event) and the *Belfast Newsletter* which declared that 'the members of the lodges were, without exception, men of evident respectability, judging from the decorum of their conduct and the neatness of their dress alone'.[147]

The gathering was addressed by a Carrickfergus minister and three other Church of Ireland ministers from Belfast. The Revd Mr Nickson of Carrickfergus recalled the injustices of James II, including forcing 'the loyal Dublin bakers to sell their bread at such terms that it was impossible to keep up their wives and children ...' The vicar of Belfast, the Revd Mr Miller, declared their watchword to be 'No Popery' and 'No Surrender' (cheers). He maintained that he was not a bigot as his prayers 'morning and evening were for his Catholic fellow countrymen that they might be regenerated by the spirit of God and set at liberty by the gospel of Jesus Christ ... At the same time', he admonished 'the principles of Popery, because it had infected with disease the hearts of so many of his fellow countrymen (loud cheers) and until they disengaged themselves from Popery they could not be ranked in fellowship with Protestants (cries of "never")'.[148] He concluded by answering those critics who objected to the clergy identifying themselves with politics. 'Why did they not come forward themselves and address the Orangemen? (hear, hear) Why were they sinking into the silence and insignificance of men who seemed willing to crouch before a pusillanimous government? (cheers) ... As long as they absented themselves from such platforms ... he would stand fast and steadfast beside the people. (loud cheering)'[149]

The Revd Dr Drew, minister of Christ Church, gave a speech after a cheer for 'Sandy Row' and another for 'the Sandy Row hero'. He declared the meeting to be of great importance. 'If there were no more Protestantism than even this', he 'would not despair of Ireland.' However, there were other meetings being held that day and 'by such means they would make links that would form a chain of inseparable connection between this country and England.' Drew declared, in his neighbourhood 'there were enemies abroad. A public announcement had been sent out stating that they, the Orangemen, did not know what they were, that day, about (cries of "we do"). It represented them as clergymen and squires and others assembling for no earthly purpose.' He then asked the meeting if they had 'any reason to be satisfied with such a monarch as King James II? (cries of "no") King James was a Papist, and had supported the Papacy; but the proudest day the nation saw was when he abdicated his throne and fled his kingdom (cheers).' Drew then went on to outline James's crimes such as dismissing Protestant judges and officers and taking 90,000 guineas which belonged to his brother and 'at that monarch's death, he would hardly allow a decent funeral (shame, shame)'.[150]

The Revd W. McIlwaine, minister of St George's, Belfast, finished off the speeches. 'There was a time', he declared, 'when the Irish wolfdog (Protestantism) was muzzled and the Italian hound fawned upon but the Italian hound had now turned on his mistress and he would soon be kicked out ... Was there a Protestant Repealer among them?' he asked (cries of "no, no"). 'If there was let him take the train and go away to the asylum. Suppose Queen Victoria was as bad as the Papists represented her, I would rather have her at any time than the Pope (cheers).' He finished by declaring that they, the clergy, had 'risked their character by coming forward that day to join them' and he hoped 'the meeting on separating would conduct itself in as peaceable and orderly a manner as possible. If their enemies threw stones at them, let them lift the stones and put them in their pockets, scorning to return the blows (cheers)'.[151]

In Belfast, the Orangemen were greeted at York Street by 'an immense assemblage composed mainly of girls'. They paraded to the Linen Hall with the Belfast band in the front and then the fifes and drums at the head of each lodge. The police and night constables were stationed along the streets and there was no trouble. Later that evening, however, there was trouble in various parts of the town. Opposite the college, a drunken man staggered against someone with a flag which sparked a fight. In Sandy Row, 'a little girl brandished a green branch whereupon the clothes were torn off the upper part of her body by a number of strong Orangewomen and nearly all the hair pulled from her head. She was saved only by the intervention of some of the men.' In Pound Street and Brown Street, there was stone throwing, windows were broken and a constable was knocked down. In Durham Street, 'a row occurred and stone throwing was kept up for some time in which Constable Farrell received a severe blow on the head. Shots were also fired.' Reinforcements were sent for and order was restored.[152]

In 1849, the Orangemen again assembled in town and marched to the station in York Street where they took the train to Antrim. Forty lodges marched in the parade, 'all the members wore the usual insignia and badges and in front of each lodge was a neat flag. The men were all dressed and orderly' and thousands lined the streets to watch the procession. A special train with 38 carriages conveyed the men, women and children to Antrim. Fifers and drummers played tunes such as 'The Protestant Boys', 'The Boyne Water' and 'Croppies Lie Down'. At Antrim, the Belfast crowd joined Orangemen from Ballymena and Antrim and the Belfast ministers, Miller, Drew and McIlwaine, addressed the crowd in a similar manner to the previous year. As in 1848, the ministers were the main speakers. There was only one nobleman present, Lord Dungannon. The deputy grand master for Co. Antrim denounced the bishop of Down and Connor for requesting members of the church to refrain from processions as it leads them to forget brotherly love.[153]

Upon returning to Belfast, the Orangemen's 'brotherly love' was to be tested. Many thousands of people gathered in York Street to meet the train. The Orangemen marched into town led by fifes and drums. The magistrate described the procession as 'very large and the number of people accompanying it immense. A high disposition to quarrel was evinced by both parties' and when the parade reached Donegall Place and Castle Place, stones were thrown at it from Hercules Street.[154] The Orangemen retaliated with stones and about ten shots were also fired at the Catholics. One girl in Hercules Street was hit in the cheek by a bullet. The constabulary 'immediately drove the Catholic party up Hercules Street and the Orangemen then proceeded through High Street and Bridge Street' and then dispersed to their lodge rooms. Subsequently, there were a few skirmishes in Brown Street and the Pound where a police detective was seriously injured in the face and head by stones. The *Northern Whig* declared 'owing to the arrangements made by the authorities and the active exertions of Graves, the stipendiary magistrate, and the police, who remained late on duty, the peace of Belfast was not further disturbed'.[155]

The riots of 1846, 1848 and 1849 were not on the same scale as those of 1843. This reflects the importance of the repeal question in inflaming animosity in 1843. In the late 1840s, the repeal movement was on the decline and the danger for Protestants had passed and there was no comparable political issue to inflame the passions. The riots of the late 1840s were a result of the lapsing of the party processions act, the support of influential ministers for Twelfth parades and the provocative nature of Orange railway excursions which were a challenge to the Catholics of the Pound and Hercules Street which they could not decline.

The renewal of the party processions act in 1850 raised the possibility of Protestant clashes with the police on the Twelfth of July. In 1850, on the eve of the twelfth, policemen were attacked in Sandy Row after attempting to prevent a procession. They arrested a lad of 17 and confiscated his drum. A crowd followed the police to the barracks, stoning them. After a series of warnings, the police, who were heavily outnumbered, fired shots into the crowd. Two people were seriously injured.[156]

The *Northern Whig* declared that further trouble on the twelfth was averted by the ban on processions and the decision of two Belfast ministers not to go ahead with special Twelfth sermons. The Revd Dr Cooke and Revd Mr Miller, the vicar of Belfast, had announced on Orange placards that they were to give special sermons on the Twelfth which was a Friday. The magistrates managed to convince the ministers not to proceed as it would violate the spirit, if not the letter, of the party processions act.[157] Although these ministers were persuaded to desist in 1850, ministers such as Drew subsequently held special Twelfth sermons. The continuous support of influential ministers for Twelfth celebrations made it more difficult for the party processions act to prevent the celebration of the Twelfth and its associated violence.

ELECTION RIOTS, 1832-1847

Between 1832 and 1847 there was another form of riot, election riots, which must be considered separately from other outbreaks of violence. Election riots were different because they were not completely spontaneous and were, to an extent, orchestrated from above.

The vast majority of people in Sandy Row and the Pound did not have the vote during this period. In Sandy Row/Durham Street approximately thirty men, mainly grocers, dealers and publicans, had the vote. The votes of these men reflected the political outlook of the district and their own role as community leaders, in particular, their role as Orange Order masters. Every vote in 1832, 1835 and 1837, except the vote of an artist, went to the Conservatives. In Barrack Street, the only street in the Pound proper to have any voters, the situation was not as straightforward. The sixty-odd votes in the 1830s were split between the Conservatives and the Liberals with a majority in favour of the Liberals.[158] This reflected the mixed nature of the street at this time as the Conservative voters were unlikely to have been Catholic. Although the vast majority of the Pound and Sandy Row inhabitants could not vote in elections, they had what one observer called 'a warm interchange of opinion on a basis of basalt'.[159]

During every contested election between 1832 and 1847, with the exception of the 1835 by-election, there were riots or violence of some kind. The poor Protestant and Catholic participants did not usually spontaneously riot at election time. Candidates recruited mobs by treating them at public houses.[160] The mobs were then used to intimidate voters and drown out opponents' speeches. It is unlikely that the members of the mobs understood the finer points of their candidates' policy, especially as the clamour was usually such that speeches could not be heard. However, election rioters obviously knew that Conservative candidates were sympathetic to the Orange Order and Liberal candidates were hostile towards the order and sympathetic to Catholic claims. Election intimidation often escalated into sectarian rioting and house wrecking which demonstrates the sectarian foundation and motivation of the crowds.

K.T. Hoppen has highlighted how common it was for candidates to hire mobs for election intimidation throughout Ireland.[161] In fact, election violence was also quite common in Britain; being recorded frequently during the many contested elections in the late seventeenth century and early eighteenth century and again during the first half of the nineteenth century. Voters were 'treated' and mobs hired to intimidate the opposition's supporters. Elections in Belfast are another example of this practice but the strong sectarian divisions in the town often led to serious consequences. The first contested election in 1832 provides ample evidence of candidates using mobs in their campaigns. The *Belfast Newsletter* described the election procedure in the Court House; the candidates were proposed and seconded and then each gave a speech. However, the conservative candidate could not be heard due to 'a chorus of sounds kept up by a crowd of fellows of the very lowest description, chiefly butcher boys and other equally respectable characters … They had been trained for this and their leaders directed them with signals.'[162] The *Northern Whig* maintained that Liberal voters had to 'bear up under the assaults of a band of ruffians, whom the other side have around them and whose savage conduct is tolerated and countenanced in the most barefaced manner. In fact, persons assuming to be respectable go so far as to place themselves at the head of this turbulent mob and lead them on. Peaceable individuals have been attacked and even the electors beaten on their way to the poll.' The mob also began 'to display Orange colours, as being in keeping with the principles of their favourite candidates.' The Conservative mob were 'maddened … by intoxication, (those candidates having kept open houses in Sandy Row and thus excited the evil passions of their low Orange partisans).'[163]

The celebration of the conservatives' victory in 1832 led to serious rioting and four deaths. A 'motley multitude' gathered outside the candidates' committee rooms where they were harangued by Mr Boyce, 'a noted Orangeman'. He declared that the conservatives' win was a victory for

Protestants and that they would continue to maintain their ascendancy. The candidates were then chaired around town led by a band playing party tunes while the mob brought up the rear. The procession entered Hercules Street where a brawl between orange and green crowds had taken place earlier in the day. A collision again ensued and the procession fled after a short struggle. Emerson Tennent, MP, had to escape through the post office and then clamber over walls and back yards until he reached the safety of Donegall Street. Before retreating, the Orange mob wrecked houses at the end of the street. After the Orange mob had fled, the police arrived and fired into the Hercules Street crowd without the authority of a magistrate. Four people were killed, none of whom were involved in the riot. The jury verdict at the inquest was that the deaths were a result of the shots of unknown policemen and 'at the time considerable rioting prevailed in the streets.'[164] Chairing of candidates was not again attempted in Belfast.

The events surrounding the election violence of 1835 provide some evidence of the organisation of mobs from above. During the week in which the election was held, the Conservative mob smashed the windows of every Catholic and some Liberal Protestant houses on their way home to Ballymaccarret. In retaliation, Orange houses in Brown's Square were attacked. On Saturday night, the Donegall Street school and the Revd Macartney's house were attacked as were Orangemen's houses in the streets off Smithfield. The Orangemen fired at their attackers, wounding eight. The over-enthusiasm of their mobs was probably not appreciated by the candidates. However, the candidates felt responsible for the actions of their mobs which suggests a degree of organisation from above. The Liberal candidate, McCance, declared that he would pay for all the damage caused by 'his friends' and the Conservative, Emerson Tennent, less magnanimously, promised to compensate his friends for any damage they had suffered.[165]

In 1837, 1841 and 1847, election violence was generally confined to the Court House, the scene of the election. The mobs excelled in their task of drowning out their opponents' speeches. The Liberal mob yelled 'Porkhead' to 'the noble aspirant to parliamentary honours', Lord Chichester, to the delight of the *Northern Whig* in 1847 while the Tory mob yelled 'No Tennent, No Whigs!'[166] The rival mobs often exchanged blows and stones. In 1837, the *Belfast Newsletter* reported that 'a considerable number of individuals on both sides appeared to have provided themselves with bludgeons of no trifling magnitude and for a while a sort of battle royal was maintained in the course of which several heads were broken ... The boards used in the construction of the booths had been literally split up and employed as weapons of offence and had the tumult not been quelled [by the police], it is more than probable that serious mischief would have been the consequence.'[167] In 1841, the violence spilled outside the Court House and onto the streets. The mobs stoned each other in the Queen Street area and when the Dragoons were called out, they were stoned by the Tory mob. A magistrate was injured trying to defend the home of Charles McAllister, a prominent Catholic Liberal and Repealer, from the Tory mob.[168]

Although election mobs were recruited and, to some extent, directed from above, the electoral contests excited sectarian passions which often could not be contained. The members of these mobs related to the electoral contests at an orange/green level and thus electoral politics proved to be another source of tension between working-class Catholics and Protestants.

ECONOMIC RIOTS

The Outrage papers for the period describe two economically motivated riots in Belfast in the period 1835-1850; a minor bread riot[169] and a more serious potato riot. In August 1838, a time of unemployment and high food prices, 'a mob of the lowest rabble' attempted to stop the export of potatoes from Belfast to Scotland.[170] These people whose occupations, religion and residence unfortunately remain a mystery attempted to prevent the sale of potatoes to exporters at Smithfield market and raided ships at the quay for potatoes. The *Northern Whig* declared that for some time 'a good deal of annoyance' had been exhibited to farmers bringing their potatoes to the quays. 'By way of rousing the feelings of the people still more on the subject, a bell has frequently been rung about the quays, at late hours, cautioning all persons from attempting to ship potatoes; and the same mode of excitement was resorted to in Smithfield yesterday morning. The parties engaged in the ringing affair even went so far as to assume the use of the sovereign's name as authority for their conduct.' At the quay where potatoes were being loaded for export 'a large mob [later described as consisting of up to 1000 people] assembled and violently proceeded to prevent the business being carried on. They rolled three casks of potatoes into the dock and taking forcible possession of the horses and loaded carts, drove them into Montgomery's market, amidst loud shouts, yells and cheering.'[171] The agent of the shipping company and some of his workmen succeeded in securing eight of the rioters but the police 'only prevented further outrage with much difficulty' and a party of cavalry and infantry had to be called in to protect the property of the shipping company and the lives of those loading the potatoes.[172] This riot caused much concern among the town's authorities and the press, particularly as it took place at a time when food riots were occurring elsewhere in Ulster. The resident magistrate published a warning notice reminding the public that the offence of obstructing food shipments from one part of the United Kingdom to another was punishable by death. Fortunately for the rioters, by the time they were tried the situation in the country generally had calmed down and the authorities considered it prudent to only charge them with a misdemeanour offence to which they pleaded guilty and were sentenced to one week's jail.[173]

This riot had much in common with food riots in Britain in the eighteenth and early nineteenth centuries which historians such as Thompson have described as originating in the breaking of a 'moral economy' or code under which the working classes operated. Rather than acting in a violent and desperate manner in response to hunger, these rioters acted when a custom was breached which resulted in disadvantage of some kind, such as bakers selling loaves below the regular weight or dealers selling grain to outsiders at a price the local poor could not afford. The rioters' manner of acting, far from being one of uncontrollable violence, was governed by an unwritten moral code. For example, food being sold at what was considered too high a price was sold by the crowd for a 'fair' price rather than just being confiscated.[174]

The potato rioters in Belfast obviously believed that the export of potatoes in a time of high prices was contrary to their 'moral economy'. Their use of the sovereign's name to legitimise their actions is a classical feature of moral economy rioting which derived from the practise in pre-*laissez faire* times of magistrates intervening in the market and forcing dealers, in times of distress and high food prices, to sell to local buyers first. Potato riots elsewhere in Ulster also fit the moral economy pattern. In 1837 people in Co. Londonderry prevented cartloads of potatoes being transported into Co. Antrim. The numbers of rioters was such that the military escort accompanying the potato convoy could not force it through the blockade. According to the *Belfast Newsletter*, 'the people then took possession of the potatoes, *repaid the carters the price they had given for them* and sent them home as they came'.[175] At the Ballymena market in 1842, a crowd of hundreds of poor townspeople prevented farmers from carting away potatoes which they had bought for seed. The crowd dragged the horses away from the farmers' carts, emptied the potatoes unto the streets and in some instances stoned the farmers involved. 'To crown it all', declared the *Northern Whig*, 'it is stated by many respectable inhabitants that numbers were forced back to the market place and obliged to sell their potatoes (which they had bought for 22d per bushed) for a shilling or in fact whatever price these legislators chose to name'.[176] In both cases, the crowds did not simply steal the potatoes but reimbursed the carters and farmers at what they considered to be a fair price, behaviour which, interestingly, seems to have provoked more outrage in the press than if the potatoes had just been confiscated.

The infrequent nature of economic riots in Belfast probably partly reflects the deep sectarian divisions among the working class. However, throughout the United Kingdom, the number of economic riots declined significantly in the nineteenth century due to the rise of laissez faire economic theory which discouraged those in authority from playing a paternalistic role during such disturbances. Grievances were increasingly channelled through trade unions instead of expressing them through food riots.[177] Therefore, the small number of economic riots in Belfast also fits the pattern for the rest of the United Kingdom.

A MORAL ECONOMY OF SECTARIAN RIOTING?

Belfast riots differed from most of the riots in England in that they were nearly always motivated by sectarian considerations rather than breaches of perceived customs regarding employment and food, rising expectations or political demands for enfranchisement. Food riots, machine wrecking, sabotage of factories in support of Chartist aims could all be conducted with minimal violence. These disturbances all had clear aims, such as to sell bread at a fair price, to destroy 'unfair' machines or to ensure that the general strike for Chartist aims was maintained. Only minimal violence was used to carry out these actions.[178] However, in Belfast the aim of rioters was simply to attack the other community or its institutions even if it was to make a political point such as 'no repeal'. As the object of Belfast rioters was to attack the other community, not to achieve a definable outcome such as the sale of cheap bread, one would expect an absence of the sort of 'rules' governing the use of violence which is apparent in English riots. However, Belfast riots in the early to mid nineteenth century were also remarkable for the low number of fatalities. This suggests that rioters in Belfast may also have followed an unwritten code of conduct.

During large scale riots such as in 1835 and 1843, the authorities were so overtaxed that a mob in one area could attack houses for up to an hour with no interference whatsoever. Despite the absence of any fear of immediate apprehension or retribution, no murders were committed by either side.[179] Although the Orangemen and the Ribbonmen had guns during this period, they were rarely used. When the two crowds directly confronted each other on the streets or in fields stones were the weapons used. Guns were fired in the air during Orange celebrations and defiant shots in reply were reported in the Pound but they were rarely used in battle. The only time guns were used in riots during this period was in 1813, 1829, 1830 and 1833 when Orangemen fired at crowds who had besieged them in their lodges or houses and in 1849 when Orangemen fired on a crowd in Hercules Street who were attacking their procession through the town centre.[180] This last incident was an ominous sign of the direction riots were to take in the later nineteenth century. Although witnesses such as policemen declared that all the rioters knew how to kill a man with a stone, such fatalities were rare. Magistrates described how even during the riots of 1857 the crowds deliberately kept a safe distance between each other and on one occasion were actually pleased that the military arrived to separate them when the situation was becoming too serious.[181] The available evidence suggests that the rioters did exercise some restraint and that the rioting had something of a ritualistic quality about it.

This is not to suggest that there was no bitterness between the two communities or that they did not take seriously their conflicting political beliefs. To balance the picture of a ritualistic confrontation, there is plenty of evidence of brutal sectarian attacks, such as the sectarian murders of 1832 and the violent intimidation in the wake of the 1843 riots. Catholic orphans who would not yell 'To Hell with the Pope' on their way to work in 1843 were beaten as were Protestant girls returning from Sunday school near the Pound. However, this type of cruel intimidation was not accepted by the communities in general. In 1848, a little girl carrying a green bough was attacked by some 'strong Orangewomen' in Sandy Row who stripped her of the top half of her clothes and began to pull the hair from her head. She was, however, saved 'by the intervention of some of the men'. This report of the moral standards of these men must be balanced by a report in the *Vindicator* describing the molestation of some young girls by Orangemen.[182] Although rioting did have a ritualistic quality and not all forms and degrees of violence were considered acceptable, there was a degree of bitterness and hatred between the two communities which manifested itself in these brutal sectarian attacks. However, the confrontation did not take the form of outright warfare until the future of Ireland hung in the balance in 1886 and even more precariously in 1920-21.

The ritualistic elements of Belfast rioting may have come from the tradition of agrarian confrontation between Orange and Green factions. These sectarian groupings had their origins in the faction fights of the eighteenth century which were completely apolitical and not necessarily sectarian. These factions were often based around familial ties but some had no apparent loyalty focus. The Peep O' Day faction, whose members eventually formed the Orange Order, was initially mixed in religion as were their rivals, the Defenders. Fights between factions occurred throughout much of Ireland, mainly at fairs and festivals such as patterns. Elaborate rules and customs surrounded these battles and something of this may have been transferred to confrontations in Belfast.[183]

Charles Townsend has suggested that Orange parades were firstly a celebration of Protestant identity and only coincidentally a provocation to Catholics.[184] Although Orange parades were a celebration of Protestant identity, the identity and the celebrations were inextricably bound up with opposition to the other community. There would have been no reason to celebrate a community's Protestant identity if they did not feel themselves to be somehow in conflict or under threat from the Catholic population of Ireland. However, there is evidence to support Townsend's related assertion that sectarian rioting helped to preserve in Belfast the sense of a rural community. Local loyalties, even today, are strong. A mural in East Belfast denouncing the Anglo-Irish Agreement epitomises the combination of the concern for high politics and local loyalty. It declares, 'Ulster Says No, Yukon

Street Says No'! Rivalry between different areas of the same religious complexion is also apparent. At football matches, Protestant Glentoran fans from East Belfast ridicule Protestant Linfield fans from the Shankill with taunting songs such as 'You'll never work again' and 'You have nothing to eat in your Shankill Road slums'. The Glentoran fans throw money at the Linfield fans as an indication of their alleged greater poverty and the police and dogs have to keep the two sides apart. In setting the boundaries of what are often quite small districts, promoting inquisitiveness and mutual defence, sectarian rioting did preserve a sense of rural community in working class parts of Belfast. The local loyalty and friendship among residents fostered by sectarian confrontation undoubtedly did ease the transition from rural to urban life. However, this was an incidental advantage of sectarian confrontation not the main reason why sectarianism was transported and maintained in Belfast.

It has been suggested that a climate favourable to rioting existed in Belfast because politics and religion were the only respectable recreational activities in the impoverished working-class culture of Belfast in the nineteenth century.[185] Undoubtedly, rousing sermons and political gatherings were cheap, respectable forms of entertainment and did tend to heighten sectarianism and promote rioting in Belfast. However, there were other forms of entertainment available such as church outings, walks in the nearby countryside, dances, penny theatre, drinking in the pub and street games such as marbles (although not all of these would be considered respectable). It was probably not so much the lack of alternative forms of entertainment that caused sectarian rioting but its huge appeal that made any other amusement appear dull by comparison. This is an assertion, however, which cannot be readily proved. It is based on my observations of more recent disturbances on the Falls Road and Garvaghy Road. Whilst observing the nationalist residents of the Garvaghy Road who were assembled in order to block the intended Orange parade through their area in July 1995, I spoke to a number of the participants who told me they did not like the Orange parades 'but to tell the truth', they said, 'we're just here for the crack'. The anticipation and excitement of the day was obviously more appealing than any of the varied amusements available today. The same applies to the riots on the Falls Road in July 1995 after the release of Private Lee Clegg having served two years of a sentence for the murder of a Catholic joyrider. Although the young men setting fire to hijacked trucks and cars were right outside an indoor swimming pool and only a short bus ride away from the beach, they obviously preferred the excitement of police pursuits and setting vehicles alight. Undoubtedly, they were angry at Clegg's release but one did not have the impression that they were acting due to uncontrollable fury. The whole process was remarkably orderly. Hijacked cars were driven in, the driver would jump out and youths would come forward with petrol and expertly set the vehicle ablaze. Residents of all ages calmly watched and others returning home from work in their cars were diverted down a side street. The numerous spectators, women, small children, old people and small groups of young men, found the spectacle of burning vehicles and retreating police cars more amusing than the television. If the Pound and Sandy Row inhabitants of the nineteenth century were like their modern contemporaries, they would have been attracted to the excitement of political confrontation even if there were other amusements to be had.

To some extent, Belfast rioters, like Thompson's food rioters, enjoyed a degree of legitimacy in their own communities. Even though the law was often against them, the Orangemen believed they had a right to march and to act violently in response to political challenges like repeal. They were encouraged in this belief by the sympathy shown towards Orangeism by some of the town's magistrates and the police. Catholic rioters believed the magistrates and police to be biased towards the Orange faction (despite them occasionally clashing with that faction themselves) and therefore were unlikely to give legitimacy to the law. They believed they had a right, regardless of the law, to challenge Orange parades, attack public houses used for lodges and respond in kind to house wrecking. Unfortunately, the occupations of rioters are not usually given in newspaper reports so it is difficult to ascertain whether the rioters were representative of the working-class districts in which they lived, as English rioters were,[186] or whether they were from the lowest class such as labourers or the unemployed. As two different newspaper reports could describe the same Orangemen in a parade as being 'of the very lowest class' and 'in general, respectable', it is difficult to ascertain their true nature.[187] The evidence for riots in the second half of the nineteenth century suggests that rioters were fairly representative of their communities.[188] If the rioters were representative of their areas, it is more likely that they enjoyed a measure of legitimacy within their communities. Although many residents may have deplored violence and remained silent out of fear, there was sufficient tacit acceptance of the rioters' belief systems for areas to become Orange and Green battle zones. By the early 1840s, rioters on both sides knew that if they were arrested, legal help would be supplied without charge, an indication of some middle-class support and an additional source of legitimacy and affirmation.

CONCLUSION

In the 1830s and 1840s, the sectarianism imported into Belfast developed into a lasting political division. The widespread support for Irish nationalism among Catholic workers was matched by an equally strong opposition to it on the part of Protestant workers. The serious riots of 1843 which occurred against a background of agitation for and against repeal are evidence of this political division. The origin and development of sectarianism in Belfast and the existence of this political division have not been correctly analysed by some historians.

Budge and O'Leary maintain that the Orange Order was responsible 'for the growth and possibly the origin of' sectarianism in Belfast.[189] This claim ignores the fact that the Orange Order did not exist in a vacuum and that it thrived in Belfast at least partly as a counter to the Ribbon society. Moreover, institutions such as the Orange Order were a reflection of existing attitudes rather than a cause. The Orange Order did possibly play a role in institutionalising sectarian beliefs, conferring legitimacy on them and spreading sectarian feeling by encouraging others to join. However, in the early nineteenth century, the Orange Order in Belfast was not a very strong, well organised institution helping to spread anti-Catholic feeling. In the early nineteenth century, Orangemen had no lodges and instead met in public houses. They often acted against the orders of the district leadership, as in 1825 and 1829 when they marched on the Twelfth. The lodges in working-class areas appear to have acted with a fair degree of autonomy which suggests that they were a reflection of local sectarian attitudes. In his evidence to the Commission on the State of Ireland, Rev. Dr Cooke emphasised the fact that sectarian factions had long existed in parts of Ulster under different names before the foundation of the Orange Order and the Ribbon society. 'The names of Orangemen and Ribbonmen which have become notorious in Ireland have merely been the coming out of the leaven that had infected the lump before.'[190] When the Orange Order was banned between 1836 and 1845, communal hostility actually increased with the riots which accompanied O'Connell's visit in 1841 and the twelfth riots of 1843. The institution of the Orange Order was not the cause of sectarian strife but a reflection of it; only assisting its expansion from 1846 onwards by conferring clerical, and subsequently elite, legitimacy on the sectarian outlook of the Protestant working class.

Peter Gibbon in his *Origins of Ulster unionism* maintains that the identity of Sandy Row Protestants was 'local' rather than 'ethnic'. The 'ethnic' hostility which was necessary for the development of unionism only arose, according to Gibbon, after 1860 when the new industries, such as ship building, created a class of skilled Protestant workers who knew that their future depended on the British link. Gibbon argues that the 'mill worker' population of Sandy Row were 'Orange' because, being unskilled, they were dependent on their employers for employment and housing. These 'Orange patrons' are said to have recruited through the Orange Order.[191] This analysis is doubly flawed. The most important occupational group in Sandy Row in the early nineteenth century were weavers, not mill workers. As the economic condition and independence of the weavers was declining, it could still be argued that they were becoming increasingly dependent on the Scottish company agents for whom they wove and the new employers of wareroom weavers. However, far from the 'nepotistic' relations described by Gibbon, there is evidence of antagonism between weavers and employers. Moreover, the majority of the main textile employers in Sandy Row voted liberal in the 1830s. Indeed, the biggest manufacturer in the Sandy Row area, John Murphy, was a Liberal-voting Quaker and his partner, Robert Grimshaw, was a prominent liberal who attempted to prevent sectarian violence in the workplace.[192] In the early nineteenth century, the Sandy Row Orangemen were led and influenced by men from their own class, publicans and grocers, not textile employers.

Gibbon maintains that the early to mid nineteenth century riots reflected local rivalry, not an appreciation of a wider Protestant/Catholic battle. He emphasises that the riots occurred in 'shatter zones' and that women played a prominent part.[193] Women were prominent in riots throughout the nineteenth century and their participation does not reflect a lack of understanding of wider Protestant and Catholic interests. Gibbon also maintains that in the latter part of the nineteenth century rioting ceases to be solely in 'shatter zones' and occurs throughout the town as Protestant and Catholic institutions were attacked and defended.[194] However, in the early nineteenth century, Catholic institutions outside the 'shatter zones', such as the diocesan seminary, Dr Denvir's house, the Donegall Street school, the Royal Hotel when O'Connell was staying there and the soiree for O'Connell held in the Music Hall, were attacked by Protestant crowds. Catholic crowds attacked the foundation meetings of the Belfast Protestant Operatives' Society. If targets outside the 'shatter zones' indicate a sense of 'ethnic' identity on the part of the rioters, as Gibbon maintains, then this sense of identity was present in the early 1840s and even earlier.

The Sandy Row Protestants and the Pound Catholics displayed a sense of ethnic identity based on nominal religious adherence from the 1820s and 1830s. The repeal campaign of the 1840s then transformed this sectarian conflict into a political one. The foundations of unionism and nationalism among the working class were laid well before the 1860s and the development of heavy industry. The Pound Catholics' membership of the Repeal Association and the Sandy Row Protestants' violent opposition to repeal prove the foundations of unionism and nationalism already existed in the early 1840s.

4

The Pound, 1850-86

In the second half of the nineteenth century, the Pound went from being a district held together mainly by a sense of ethnic solidarity, based on nominal religious adherence, to a community with its own schools, church and religious associations. The district became more Catholic (in the religious rather than the ethnic sense) which increased its distinctiveness from Protestant Belfast. This strengthened its identification with the rest of Catholic Ireland and reaffirmed the appeal of Catholic nationalism. The significant support for Fenianism and subsequently the home rule movement reaffirmed the support for nationalism demonstrated in the 1840s during the repeal agitation. The working-class Catholics of the Pound (and a section of the Catholic middle class) had decided by the 1870s, if not as early as the 1840s, that their future lay in joining the rest of Ireland in the quest for some form of self government. A.C. Hepburn's argument that the Catholics of Belfast had an ethnic or religious identity similar to Irish Catholics in British cities and that nationalism had to be imported into the north from the south in the 1890s is not supported by the evidence. Although the 1880s was the period when the unionist/ nationalist division became fortified and fixed in electoral terms, the origins of the division can be traced back to the early decades of the nineteenth century and this chapter concludes with a critical analysis of historians such as Comerford and Walker who maintain that this division was not inevitable until the 1870s or 1880s.

RELIGIOUS INSTITUTIONS AND SOCIAL ORGANISATION

Between 1850 and 1886, the presence of the church in the lives of the Pound inhabitants increased dramatically. Until 1866, the Pound inhabitants did not have their own church and had to try to find room at St Mary's, St Patrick's or St Malachy's. In 1841, Bishop Denvir declared that 'On Sundays you will find the chapel yards, nay the streets for a considerable space, covered with a kneeling throng who have no roof over their heads during divine worship.'[1] Although he did oversee the establishment of St Malachy's in 1844, Bishop Denvir appears to have lacked the organisational talent and the will to tackle the problems of the ever increasing Catholic population. In 1856, Archbishop Dixon of Armagh informed Rome that there were only four priests in Belfast serving a Catholic population of 40,000. Therefore, it was 'physically impossible' for even half of them to be confessed. Indeed, it was 'scarcely credible that one third frequented the sacraments'. Each week one priest attended the dying who had not been to confession for 20 or 40 years.[2] These descriptions of Belfast as a whole suggest that institutionalised religion played a minor role in the lives of the people of the Pound despite the fact that Catholicism was the defining characteristic of the district. Although the fact that priests were always called to death beds shows that Catholics had not become disillusioned with their faith, the lack of church accommodation and priests and the exertions of Protestant missionaries offering some spiritual outlet and school places for children may have resulted in some conversions. Patrick Dorrian claimed that between 1840 and 1865, more than 1000 people per year were 'lost to the church'.[3] It is impossible to know if any Pound Catholics converted to Protestantism. Despite the Catholic church's institutional weakness in the district, the well established sense of ethnic identity based on Catholicism would presumably have prevented significant numbers of Pound Catholics from 'turning'.

The rate of attendance at church and confession increased after Bishop Dorrian took over the diocese in 1865. The new bishop was a strong supporter of Ultramontanism and had the organisational talent required to establish new Catholic institutions in Belfast. In May 1865, he launched a general mission in Belfast. Twenty-four priests, including some drafted in from outside the town heard confession for ten hours every day. By the end of May over 20,000 people had confessed, some for the first time.[4] These missions became a regular feature of religious life for Belfast Catholics. Special missions were arranged to coincide with papal events and in other years ordinary missions were held by the religious orders such as the Dominicans whom Dorrian had invited to Belfast. Church accommodation increased dramatically with the completion of St Peter's cathedral in 1866. Prior to the establishment of this cathedral, in 1863, mass attendance had been estimated by Archbishop Dixon at about one third of the population despite five masses being held in each of the three churches.[5] St Peter's cathedral situated in the Pound could accommodate 3000 people and adequately fulfilled the needs of the district. The church attendance rate in the Pound presumably increased substantially as a result of Dorrian's missionary drives and the completion of their own cathedral.

Bishop Denvir had feared the reaction from Belfast's Protestants that the introduction of religious orders might provoke and so did not avail himself of the help such orders could offer in instructing the Catholic population.[6] The Sisters of Mercy were the only order invited to Belfast by Denvir. They ran a girls schools in Calendar Street in the town centre. Dorrian considered the spiritual and educational needs of the Catholic community as outweighing any apprehensions of a Protestant backlash against the religious orders. By the end of his episcopate, there were two male religious orders and five orders of nuns.[7] The Christian Brothers operated a primary and intermediate school in the

Pound district and the Irish Dominican sisters ran a school for poor girls further down the Falls Road.[8] The introduction of religious orders increased the distinctiveness of the Catholic religion at a time when the upsurge of evangelicalism within Protestantism was already emphasising its differences with Catholicism. Protestants had always regarded religious orders with suspicion and their introduction to Belfast heightened the differences between the two communities and reinforced sectarian attitudes.

Bishop Dorrian encouraged the introduction of more Italianate devotions associated with Ultramontanism. Earlier in the century in Belfast there had been some innovations in Catholic ritual but under Dorrian these reforms were extended and embraced a broader section of the population. These Italian forms of piety placed more emphasis on the adoration of the Eucharist, devotion to the suffering Christ, devotion to the sacred heart, the Virgin Mary and 'popular saints such as St Joseph and St Anthony'. Processions and pilgrimages were encouraged as was more participation in the sacraments.[9]

The account of the opening of St Peter's cathedral gives a good description of the new richness in Catholic ritual. Cardinal Cullen presided at high mass which was accompanied by Haydn's Number Three Grand Imperial sung with full orchestral accompaniment. Crowds lined the streets to greet Cullen's carriage. Special trains brought Catholics from Cookstown, Magherafelt, Castledawson and other Ulster towns. Tickets for the high mass were 10s. for the nave and 5s. for the aisles. Pound residents, however, were more likely to have attended the evening pontifical vespers; the tickets for which cost 2s. 6d. in the nave and 1s. in the aisles. Cardinal Cullen again presided and the vespers were sung by the Revd Dr Butler which was followed by a sermon by the bishop of Dromore, Dr Leahy. 'Several hundreds' had to be turned away for lack of room. In all, there were twelve bishops and two cardinals present.[10] The proceedings must have been awe inspiring for Belfast Catholics, particularly the working class for whom such elaborate rituals must have seemed a world away from their dreary environment. As Ambrose Macaulay maintains, such a confident and powerful display by the Catholic church in Belfast marked 'a symbolic change in attitudes and expectations of Catholics'.[11]

The provision of Catholic education in the Pound, as in the rest of Belfast, improved dramatically in the second half of the nineteenth century. Until the 1850s, there were no Catholic run schools in the district and in 1863 Bishop Dixon of Armagh estimated that of 12,000 Catholic children of school age in Belfast, only 2370 were enrolled at Catholic-managed schools.[12] The 26th report of the National Education Commissioners shows that in 1859, there were only two Catholic managed schools in the Pound; one in Cullingtree Road with male and female departments and a boys' school in Alexander Street West. Both were run by Catholic lay people connected with the St Vincent de Paul Society. The Cullingtree Road school had 96 boys and 56 girls on the roll during the year with an average daily combined attendance of 65. The

Alexander Street West school had 344 boys on the roll and an average attendance of 84. There were other Catholic managed schools not far from the
district in Chapel Lane and Millfield (with a combined average attendance of
262) and the Donegall Street school situated somewhat further away (with an
average attendance of 204)[13] but these schools were far from meeting the needs
of the population of the Pound. Some children attended the non-denominational Model School on the Falls Road, some attended Protestant-managed
schools and many more probably did not attend school at all. Some of these
children attended the Sunday schools run by the St Vincent de Paul Society
which offered the poor basic education as well as religious instruction.

The situation had improved somewhat by 1868 when the Royal Commission
of Inquiry into Primary Education conducted a census of Belfast schools. The
census records a new Catholic boys school in Milford Street in the Pound with
an attendance of 106 pupils (all Catholics) on the day of the census. The
Christian Brothers school in Barrack Street in the Pound established the
previous year was attended by 362 pupils (all Catholics) and a new national
school under Catholic management just outside the district in Conway Street
was attended by 188 Catholic pupils. The older schools in Brook Street
(Cullingtree Road) and Alexander Street West had a combined attendance of
421. The total number of children attending schools within the Pound proper
amounted to 889 compared to 149 ten years previously. There were also 104
Catholic children attending the non-denominational Model School on the Falls
Road (despite its denunciation by the clergy), 61 Catholics, predominantly
girls, attending the national school attached to Chartres Mill and, most
worryingly for the clergy, there were still 66 Catholics attending the Protestant
charity school in Barrack Street, 'the Ragged school' which had no guarantees
to protect the children's faith apart from what the mistresses saw fit.[14]

The Christian Brothers school was an important institution in the Pound. It
provided free or cheap relatively high quality education to the inhabitants. The
Brothers had a reputation for instilling the 'three Rs' into working-class boys
and keeping order with stern measures. An area inspector from the national
board declared that he had never seen 'such a soldier like precision of discipline
as is attained in the schools of the Christian Brothers in Belfast'.[15] The
Brothers also offered the opportunity to enrol in intermediate education and
thereby qualify for a white collar job or the priesthood. Seventy children out of
a total of 800 were intermediate pupils in 1882.[16] Few boys from the Pound
could have been spared from earning a wage to continue with their education
but it gave a chance to the lucky few. The Christian Brothers schools were also
known for their nationalist ethos epitomised by their motto 'For Faith and
Fatherland'. Future nationalist leaders such as Joseph Devlin were educated at
the Brothers' schools and the nationalist teachings of the Brothers may have
played some part in their political development.[17]

By the 1880s, many of the schools in the Pound had been rebuilt and

extended to include infant and evening classes and new schools such as St
Peter's with male, female and evening departments had been established.[18] In
1892, schooling became compulsory for children under 12, thereby increasing
the demand for school places. The Catholic community of Belfast appears to
have met this challenge. In 1902, the administrator of St Peter's could claim
that there were enough school places for any Catholic child who sought one.[19]

In the second half of the nineteenth century, an increasing number of
confraternities were established in Belfast. This was not an entirely new
development. A Rosarian society was established in connection with St Mary's
church as early as 1774. Bishop Denvir encouraged the establishment of a
Christian Doctrine Society in 1834 which sought to instruct the working
classes in Catholic religion. In the mid nineteenth century, volunteers would
visit the poor known to be Catholics and encourage them to send their children
to Sunday school.[20] Denvir also oversaw the foundation of the St Vincent de
Paul Society which provided charity and education to the Catholic poor. Under
Bishop Dorrian, these societies mushroomed and branches were established in
all the Catholic churches of the town. In 1865, before St Peter's was actually
completed, a branch of the St Vincent de Paul Society was established in the
parish. Its leader was William Downey, a linen lapper from Alexander Street
West in the Pound. The society held its meetings in the Alexander Street West
school house.[21]

By the 1870s, numerous other confraternities had been established in
connection with St Peter's parish. The Total Abstinence Society was established
in 1877 and the membership for the greater Belfast area was 1500 by the
following year.[22] In the early 1880s, the curate of St Peter's, the Revd McGreevy,
established a total abstinence society for women which had a membership of
1700 in 1885.[23] The St Peter's branch of the Holy Family confraternity had 1300
male and female members in 1878 and by 1885 the membership had reached
1600.[24] As well as providing either fellowship based on temperance or a more
specifically spiritual function, both societies offered social events such as annual
outings to the country with games, athletics and refreshments. These outings
took the form of grand processions with banners and music. As the parades were
often attacked by Protestant crowds,[25] they also provided additional experience
of ethnic conflict and confirmed their members' commitment to their religion
and community and their opposition to the Protestant society around them. The
Holy Family confraternity also put on concerts and 'dramatic entertainments'
which were attended by the bishop and the Catholic elite of the town.[26]

The Catholic Young Men's Association established a branch in Belfast in
1872 but there is no evidence of its degree of popularity in the Pound. The
association had a reading room and its members marched to church with
banners. The first president of the association was John Duddy, the president
of the Belfast Home Rule Association, suggesting that this confraternity may
have had the nationalist ethos it often had elsewhere in Ireland.[27]

The Irish National Foresters Benefit Society was another organisation in Catholic Belfast which had a nationalist ethos. Members had to be 'Irish by birth and descent' and, although there was no religious test, the vast majority of its members were Catholic.[28] Like other friendly societies, it offered its members benefits in times of sickness, funeral payments and payments to families in the event of the death of the member. The society also offered conviviality and fellowship and organised social events such as St Patrick's day dinners.[29] The composition of the membership in Belfast cannot be established but such organisations usually attracted the upper levels of the working class and the lower middle class. The independence from state welfare such as access to paid private doctors gave the members a valued sense of respectability.[30] The membership of Nationalist heroes such as Michael Davitt, William O'Brien and Joseph Biggar gave ordinary members a sense of pride in the organisation.[31]

There were also church based societies for children such as the St Peter's Temperance Association for youth established in February 1883. By 1885, the membership of the boys' stood at 2500 and the girls' at 2400. The associations were open to boys and girls aged between nine and eighteen who were willing to take a total abstinence pledge until they were thirty years old. Annual retreats were organised for the members with services every evening for a week. The service opened 'with the recitation of the rosary, followed by an exhortation adapted to the intellectual capacity of the youthful auditory and closing with benediction of the most holy sacrament. Numerous priests were occupied during the week in hearing the confessions of the members and yesterday a grand general communion took place at the ten o'clock mass.' According to the *Belfast Morning News*, 'aided by these two associations, the Revd P. Convery has the gratifying knowledge that the vast majority of the youth in his parish attend regularly to their religious duties. The benefits derived from such associations not only to the individuals themselves, but to the community at large in the foundation of sober, steady habits and in the rearing up of creditable citizens are ... obvious.'[32]

A lay organisation centred on the parish was the St Peter's Mutual Improvement Club which met every Sunday in Brook Street in the Pound from early 1885. One of the members would give a lecture on a topic such as 'the communal system in Russia' or 'progress' which would then be 'criticised' (discussed) by the other members. The only member who can be identified is P. Magee, a reeling master from Pound Street.[33]

The Catholic Institute, established in 1859, was an important lay organisation which reflected the increasing confidence of the Catholic community in Belfast and the desire for self improvement typical in industrial towns of the Victorian era. The Institute aimed to provide for the educational and recreational needs of its members at rates so low that the poorest could avail themselves of its services. Classes in chemistry, mechanics and art and design were offered, lectures on literature and Irish history were given and there was a library and reading room which non-members could also use for a small fee. The Institute, situated in Hercules Place, was also used for St Patrick's Day dinners as well as being made available to visiting clergy as alternative accommodation to staying in Protestant run hotels.[34] Although the main shareholders and leaders of the Institute were merchants and doctors, two residents of the Pound, Patrick McShane and John Hackett, were among the twenty men whose names appeared on the memorandum of association. McShane was an illiterate provision dealer who bought £3 worth of shares. He was the only signatory of the memorandum to sign it with 'his mark'. Hackett's occupation cannot be established as he lived in Scotch Street which was comprised of houses too poor to be listed in the Belfast street directory. It can be assumed that he was from the labouring or artisan class. He bought only one share for one pound. Of the 526 people who bought shares in the Institute, 44 lived in the Pound. Of those that can be identified there were 10 grocers, dealers or publicans, 1 slater, 1 tobacco spinner, 1 tobacconist, 3 flax dressers, 1 linen lapper, 1 clerk, 1 plasterer, 1 baker, 1 carpenter, 1 labourer, 1 bricklayer, 1 national school teacher and 1 salesman. There were also, however, eight men who lived with a householder who was a labourer or lived in a house too poor to be included in the street directory.[35] Although shopkeepers and artisans were most prominent among the Pound members, the fact that flax dressers and those from poorer streets were also members sets this institute apart from similar educational and self-help organisations in British industrial cities. Studies of institutions such as the co-operative movement and mechanics institutes in Britain reveal that they were predominantly used and operated by the 'respectable' artisan class who had practically no contact with labourers or people living in very poor streets. These respectable artisans had more social contact with the lower middle classes and ran their organisations independently resisting any interference from the middle and upper classes, accepting them only as honorary patrons.[36] By contrast the Catholic Institute in Belfast was representative of all classes of Catholics in Belfast from wealthy merchants and doctors to grocers, publicans, white collar workers, artisans and labourers. While the Institute was a product of the self help ethos of the Victorian era, the divided nature of Belfast society and the strong sense of Catholic identity allowed the lower classes as well as the artisans to participate.

The leaders of the Institute were disappointed not to have received more support from the Catholic middle class and clergy. However, the list of shareholders shows they were well supported by the lower middle class, artisans and labourers. Bishop Dorrian was hostile towards this Catholic lay initiative. He was suspicious of some of the institute's leading members, particularly Andrew McKenna whose newspapers, the *Ulster Observer* and the *Northern Star* sometimes 'strayed over the edge of constitutionalism',[37] and feared that the institute could be infiltrated by Fenianism. It is quite possible that it could have been a breeding ground for Fenianism despite the intentions of its leaders as the Fenians often recruited activists from other organisations. However, Dorrian's main objection to the organisation appears to have been the lack of episcopal control over an organisation dedicated to improve Catholic morals and education. The philosophy of Ultramontanism encouraged bishops to assume the right to control any organisation purporting to be Catholic. Dorrian declared to Rome, 'I have to make a stand to purge [the Institute] from the Presbyterian leaven.'[38] Accordingly, when the leaders of the Institute decided to sell the property for a profit and obtain other premises elsewhere, Dorrian took the opportunity to force the committee to dissolve the Institute unless they agreed to his approving all lectures and reading material and having a right of veto over the committee members. If they ignored his request, any members of the Institute would be ex-communicated. This caused a sensation in the British press as well as the local press. The *Northern Whig* declared 'Hell or My Dictatorship'. Understandably, the leaders of the Institute were not comfortable with such anti-Catholic allies as the *Belfast Newsletter* and this strengthened Dorrian's hand.[39] The Institute dissolved itself and the flax dressers and labourers of the Pound, together with other Catholic artisans and workers of Belfast, lost an opportunity for self improvement, education and recreation. Dorrian declared to Rome that 'the sore here wanted to be opened that our people might be cured of their Presbyterianism'[40] and, indeed, when the St Mary's Hall was opened for recreation, lectures and training in music, science etc. in 1876 it was firmly under clerical control.[41]

In the early to mid nineteenth century the Pound was a Catholic ghetto held together mainly by a sense of ethnic solidarity. There was no church in the district, no Catholic managed schools and no institutions except the secret Ribbon society and the Repeal Association. By the 1880s, the inhabitants had become more religious in that they were regularly attending church, confession and participating in Dorrian's missions. A range of confraternities brought significant numbers of the inhabitants together for spiritual and recreational purposes under the umbrella of the church. As the controversy over the Catholic Institute demonstrates, the church was determined to control any lay organisation purporting to be Catholic. Whilst the increased presence of the church undoubtedly enriched some people's lives and strengthened a sense of community in the Pound, it also stifled lay initiative in the case of the Catholic Institute and increased the fears of the Protestant population regarding Ultramontanism. As the Pound became more Catholic (in the religious rather than the ethnic sense), its distinctiveness from Protestant Belfast was reinforced. Its identification with the rest of Catholic Ireland was reaffirmed and the appeal of Catholic nationalism became even greater.

FENIANISM

The Fenian society was an underground movement, founded by survivors of the 1848 rising for the purpose of overthrowing, by force, British rule in Ireland. At its height in 1865, it had 50,000 members, including many soldiers serving in the British army.[42] Many historians of Belfast, such as Budge and O'Leary, Wright, and Maguire,[43] have overlooked Fenianism in the town mainly because it was a secret organisation and only limited information appeared in the press, whereas others, such as Brian Walker and A.C. Hepburn, have overlooked it because they started from the premise that nationalism was not a force in the north until much later in the century. The eminent historian of Fenianism, R.V. Comerford, has sought to downplay the republican (and even nationalist) nature of Fenianism and emphasise its role in providing recreation and social fulfilment to artisans in Irish towns. In this section, I will argue that Fenianism was strong among the Catholic lower classes of Belfast and that this demonstrates a continuing commitment to nationalism among that class, not just a need for recreation.

Fenianism had significant support among the Catholic working classes of Belfast, including those of the Pound. At its height in 1865, it probably numbered well over one thousand members. Co. Antrim had one of the highest rates of people arrested under the Habeas Corpus Suspension Act which was introduced in 1866 to combat the Fenian conspiracy. Antrim's arrest rate of 33 (most of them in Belfast) per 10,000 of the population was comparable to other Fenian strongholds such as county Cork with 35 and Limerick with 31. Only Dublin with 112 significantly exceeded the arrest rate in Antrim.[44] In 1866, the Belfast Resident Magistrate, Orme, declared to Dublin Castle, 'It is well known that there was an extensive organisation here [in 1865] and that drilling and other military preparations were carried on.'[45] The head 'centre' of Belfast, Frank Roney, maintained in his autobiography that he had no problems recruiting the first thousand members in Belfast in the early 1860s and that by 1865, after the coup of recruiting William Harbison, a sergeant, and several soldiers of the local garrison and gaining access to their weapons, Belfast was never in a more perfect condition for revolution.[46] The Pound was one of the Fenian strongholds. One of the local 'captains' Francis Rea, a power loom tenter, lived in Pound Street, Charles Carroll, a tailor with a high Fenian rank, lived in Hamill Street and many rank and file Fenians also lived in Hamill Street, English Street, Irvine Street and Cinnamond Street. Police reports mention Fenian meetings being held in houses in Nail Street, Hamill Street and Derby Street in the Pound as well as in public houses close to the district in Carrick Hill and Chapel Lane. Ammunition was also manufactured and stored in the area.[47]

During 1865-66, the Catholic church and the local authorities dealt the movement severe blows. Bishop Dorrian's denunciation of the movement and his campaign to force those who attended confession during his mission in 1865 to leave the society resulted in the desertion of 'several hundreds' according to the resident magistrate.[48] Frank Roney admitted in his autobiography that the Church's campaign against Fenianism did some damage although a strong nucleus of men remained.[49] More damaging were the arrests in 1866 under the Habeas Corpus Suspension Act which not only destroyed the leadership of some cells but prompted many other Fenians to flee the town.[50]

In January 1867, the police raided the house of Charles Carroll in Hamill Street in the Pound and discovered a Fenian munitions factory. The police surrounded the house and broke down the front door. Michael Donaghy, a labourer from Hamill Street, rushed at the police with a pair of tongs and struck a constable on the head. The police forced their way into the house and found a pan of boiling lead on the fire and a bullet mould nearby along with a can full of about six dozen bullets. Over a hundred weight of lead was found in the house altogether. Those arrested included four labourers, a weaver, a hackler, a blacksmith and a chimney sweep, all residents of the Pound. Three shoemakers from Irvine Street in the Pound were arrested in the same week. The police searched the house of Michael Hanlon, a gardener from Skiegoneil with the rank of 'colonel' who had been arrested in Carroll's house, and found great quantities of ammunition, pistols, swords and pikes concealed in a wall. All the men arrested in January 1867 were defended by the talented and somewhat eccentric John Rea who argued that the bullets were for bird shooting at Christmas time and that only Carroll was involved in their manufacture while the others were chance visitors. Rea succeeded in getting some of the men released and the charges against the others reduced from treason felony to possession of ammunition in a proclaimed district.[51]

Still more damaging to the Fenian movement in Belfast was the arrest of William Harbison in early 1867, just after he had attended a meeting of the Fenian leadership in London.[52] The movement lost their main military strategist and access to the weapons of the Belfast garrison. Harbison, his brother Philip and two other leading Fenians, including Francis Rea, the captain from the Pound, were arrested and charged with treason. Harbison died in prison of a heart attack and his funeral was attended by 12,000 people and watched by 'many thousands more'. The remaining defendants were defended by John Rea who succeeded in winning numerous delays of the trial. The local authorities, always apprehensive of Rea's talents, decided to release the defendants after the threat of Fenianism had passed on the condition that they go to America.[53] Roney was also arrested and sent to Mountjoy prison where a priest informed him that an informer was going to give evidence against him and that he could face trial for treason. That night the prison governor visited his cell and revealed that he would favourably consider an application for release on the condition that he go to the US. The governor, a friend of Roney's father who was a fellow member of the St Vincent de Paul

Society, had the power to release him so long as he had not been charged. The next morning he was released before the charges could be formally brought against him.[54]

The weakened state of the society in Belfast and the fact of it being a garrison town meant that the local Fenians did not participate in the failed rising of March 1867. However, the organisation continued to exist. In January 1868, the resident magistrate reported that although 'the [Fenian] system is still going on here, I do not believe Fenianism is at present at the same force it was last year in this locality.' Police reports up until 1869 mention Fenian meetings being held three times a week particularly in the Pound and Chapel Lane 'but no great importance [was] attached to the proceedings.' Their activities appear to have been mainly confined to raising funds for released prisoners to go to America and for a memorial to William Harbison.[55]

Some Fenians were probably involved in the home rule processions of the 1870s which were often held without the approval of the leadership of the local Home Rule Association and on occasions seemed to countenance the use of force. The banners in these processions bearing life-size pictures of Robert Emmet and harps without crowns also suggest Fenian influence. By 1879, the Irish Republican Brotherhood (as the Fenians were now known) was quite strong in County Antrim where there were 153 adherents per 10,000 of the Catholic population.[56] Some of them presumably lived in Belfast where their influence (in the form of interjections in favour of the 'rifle' and exclamations in favour of an Irish Republic) was felt at Home Rule meetings.[57]

The Belfast Fenians whose occupations can be identified were a mixture of artisans, white collar workers, shopkeepers, semi-skilled workers and labourers. Of the leaders who can be identified, the Belfast 'head centre' Frank Roney was a moulder; William Harbison, the main military strategist, a sergeant in the Antrim militia; John Griffith, a 'centre', a clerk; Michael Hanlon, a suspected 'centre', was a gardener; Henry O'Hagan, a suspected 'centre', was a bricklayer; and Francis Rea, also a suspected 'centre', was a power loom tenter. In total, the occupations of the identifiable Fenians were; shoemakers 4, labourers 4, clerks 4, draper's assistants 3, blacksmiths 2, mechanics 2, pawnbrokers 2, weaver 1, hackler 1, chimney sweep 1, tailor 1, gardener 1, moulder 1, compositor (unemployed) 1, tenter 1, spirit grocer 1, publican 1, barber 1, bricklayer 1, soldier 1 (the magistrates suspected that more soldiers were involved).[58]

In a study of the composition of the Fenian society in Ireland as a whole (as measured by those arrested under the Habeas Corpus Suspension Act), Comerford has established that the Fenians were predominantly from the artisan/lower white collar class.[59] The composition of the Belfast Fenians, including not only those arrested under the suspension of Habeas Corpus act but also those charged with other Fenian related offences, does not quite fit the pattern for Ireland as a whole. Of the 34 identifiable Belfast Fenians, only 18 were artisans or white collar workers. It is also questionable how far occupations such as shoemaker and tailor could be classed as part of an artisan elite. Often men worked in these trades without having completed an apprenticeship and due to the over-supply of workers, the pay was not as high as that earned by skilled workers such as moulders whose numbers were regulated through the apprenticeship system. Perhaps only 13 of the 34 Belfast Fenians could be said to have belonged to an artisan/white collar elite.

Comerford argues that the composition of the Fenian society throughout Ireland indicates that the society was fulfilling the social and recreational needs of an artisan elite who would otherwise have had no outlet for their talents. He places the Fenian society in the context of Victorian self-improvement organisations such as the mechanics' institute and recreational organisations such as brass bands and association football. Comerford provides evidence of young Fenians with plenty of disposable income to contribute to the movement and to its social events such as drinking, sport and picnics as proof of its fulfilling a social role for the artisan elite. He also describes how Fenian groups would often drill openly and go to picnics and sporting events which seem contrary to the nature of a secret society.[60]

The composition of the Belfast Fenian movement does not fit Comerford's description of the society and the comparison with artisan organisations in Britain is misleading. All classes of people who lived in the Catholic ghettos of Belfast were represented in the Fenian society such as shopkeepers, clerks, shop assistants, skilled tradesmen as well as labourers, mill workers and chimney sweeps. The artisans and white collar workers may have been over-represented considering their numbers in the town as a whole but the society still had too many members who were unskilled workers to be equated with British artisan organisations. Self-help organisations in Britain such as mechanics' institutes and co-op stores were composed of men who had hardly any contact with labourers and those living in very poor streets.[61] The Fenians in Belfast were meeting in squalid streets of the Pound such as Nail Street and Hamill Street as well as better off locations such as Derby Street.[62] The nature and composition of respectable working men's organisations in Britain and the Fenian society in Belfast are not comparable.

Comerford's examples of men drilling in broad daylight past police stations are admittedly contrary to the nature of a secret society. However, this could indicate a foolish desire to display bravado towards the enemy rather than proving that drilling was a form of entertainment or an opportunity for young men to discover 'personal identity and achievement in group display'.[63] The Belfast Fenian leader, Frank Roney, confirms this when he lamented, 'It was impossible to suppress the foolish burst of patriotism displayed by these indiscreet, light-hearted members' which let the government know that something was afoot.[64] Comerford also reads too much into the use of cricket and racing to cover Fenian meetings, suggesting that the meetings themselves were primarily of entertainment value. Sporting events were a cover not just for Fenian meetings but IRB and IRA meetings in the late nineteenth and early twentieth centuries.[65] (Were these later rebels also only looking for something to do on the week-end?)

In the case of Belfast, drilling and military preparations appear to have been taken seriously by the local Fenians. Roney claimed that drilling occurred every night and 'was done so systematically and carefully as to attract no attention from those outside the organisation'. Arms were steadily being imported into Belfast and Roney and another leader, Nolan, could enter the military barracks in Queen Street at any time of the night. 'The armoury of the Antrim Militia was practically in our keeping, and with the aid of the Irish soldiers stationed at Belfast, Carrickfergus and other adjacent points most of whom were members of our organisation, the arms and supplies stored there were at our disposal. Belfast was never in such a condition for successful rebellion as it was at that period and up to 1865.' Roney and other leaders spent many hours being trained in military matters by Harbison and when Roney attempted to sneak up on a drilling party to test their security he was nearly killed when he was spotted.[66] Other members of the organisation spent many hours melting lead over fire in order to make bullets.[67] The military preparation appears to have amounted to more than the recreational activity allowed for by Comerford.

Comerford maintains that working men's organisations were not numerous in Ireland because there was little elite or church support which resulted in 'Fenianism filling the vacuum'.[68] However, in Britain working men usually formed such organisations themselves, accepting middle- or upper-class men only in honorary roles and resenting any interference on their part.[69] The reason why there were fewer working men's organisations, such as co-ops or indeed a strong labour movement in Ireland, was because workers were preoccupied with the national question. The organisations which did exist in Ireland, such as confraternities, are dismissed by Comerford as not being lively enough for the bright young men, who unlike their British counterparts, were apparently only satisfied with military preparations as entertainment. Comerford, seeming to contradict his own argument, draws attention to the fact that those associations which did exist, such as the Catholic Young Men's Society, often became nationalist despite the intentions of their founders.[70] This seems to indicate the strength of nationalism rather than an absence of social organisations, which Comerford maintains is the *raison d' être* of Fenianism.

Comerford asserts that 'Fenianism found a following not because there were tens of thousands of Irishmen eager to take up the gun but because there were tens of thousands of young Irishmen in search of self realisation through appropriate social outlets.'[71] Every organisation offers a sense of belonging. In this, the Fenian society was no different from the Orange Order, the present republican movement or a football club. It is not a unique quality or what is most important about Fenianism. The Fenian society should not be seen as primarily a source of entertainment and social fulfilment for an artisan elite. Unlike brass bands, football clubs and the Catholic Institute, the Fenian society was a revolutionary movement and its members faced the possibility of imprisonment, exile, transportation and even death as John Newsinger has pointed out in his criticism of Comerford.[72] The three Belfast Fenians whose photos survive were all married with four children and their families suffered greatly during their imprisonment. Imprisonment affected the health of others and in William Harbison's case caused an early death.[73] The emotional appeal of nationalism and their experience of living in a society divided on sectarian lines was what made these men take the risks which led to their imprisonment and their families' suffering. There were associations in Belfast which they could have joined, such as confraternities and, until 1865, the Catholic Institute, if they were only interested in self improvement or entertainment.

The predominance of artisans and the involvement of town and rural labourers in the Fenian movement as a whole can be explained by reasons other than the need for a social and political outlet. Town dwellers were more progressive and less under the control of the church which was opposed to secret societies. Agricultural labourers were the social class in the countryside whose customs were most resilient in the face of clerical condemnation.[74] Peasants, who were more conservative and subject to clerical influence, understood the national question in terms of the land question which the Fenians did not take up as a major theme, thereby ensuring the dominance of urban and non-landed groups.

Fenianism in Belfast should be seen in the Irish context of the merged tradition of Ribbonism, constitutional Nationalism and Republicanism rather than in the British context of Victorian artisan organisations. The merging of Ribbonism into the Fenian movement in Belfast is indicated by its absence from police and magistrates reports after 1864 once Fenianism took hold. The leader of the Belfast Fenians, Frank Roney, claims in his autobiography that the Fenians took part in the 1864 riots, fulfilling the role of defenders against the Orangemen previously undertaken by the Ribbon society. There is no reason to suppose that Roney was lying about this as, being himself avowedly non-sectarian, he admits that it pained him to be fighting fellow Irishmen. It was 'not a pleasant undertaking ... especially when we had been preaching the doctrine of National unity and the destruction of sectarian prejudice'.[75] The Fenian society in Belfast also fulfilled the mutual aid society function which had previously been provided by the Ribbon society. Informers revealed that unemployed Fenians were entitled to unemployment benefit paid out at a barber's office of 10s. per week for single men and 12s. per week for married men.[76] Although some of the Fenian leadership in Belfast were hostile to the sectarian principles of Ribbonism,[77] Fenianism's duplication of Ribbon activities and its presence in Ribbon strongholds like the Pound suggest that it drew on membership of the Ribbon society. The membership of both organisations came predominantly from the same social class, i.e., the working class but not generally from the most destitute.[78] The link between Ribbonism and nationalism in Belfast persisted after the heyday of Fenianism. In 1873, a committee of some of the rank and file nationalists formed to organise a procession on the Fifteenth of August, in opposition to the bishop and the leadership of the Home Rule association, was reported by the police as possibly containing some Ribbonmen.[79]

Fenianism also drew on the traditions of Republicanism and to some extent constitutional nationalism in Belfast. The leaders of the movement in Belfast were Republicans who admired the United Irishmen and the Young Irelanders.[80] Frank Roney's mother, who was a Presbyterian before she converted to Catholicism at the time of her marriage, knew Mary Joy McCracken, the sister of the executed United Irishman, Henry Joy McCracken, and told the young Frank stories of the heroism of the young woman watching her brother's execution and afterwards taking a lock of his hair. Roney stated that this story was recited to him 'time and time again' and 'I felt that if, when I became a man, I failed to avenge his death, I would be derelict in my duty to my God and my country.' As a boy, Roney went with his mother to visit the McCracken house which was kept in darkness, the drapes only being opened on St Patrick's day.[81] Frank Roney's great aunt, a Presbyterian who lived in Downpatrick, also told him tragic and heroic stories about the United Irishmen and the cruelty of the British. Her fiancee survived the battle of Ballynahinch only to be informed upon by a beggar woman. British troops took him back to her house and hanged him, without trial, in front of his loved ones.[82] Although his father was a dedicated Repealer and was for 'Queen, Lords and Commons of Ireland',[83] the influence of his mother's family ensured that Roney was a Republican. John Griffith, another leading Belfast Fenian, had been a Young Irelander in his youth. These men, together with other leading Fenians, climbed to the top of Cave Hill and, in imitation of Wolfe Tone and the United Irishmen, pledged themselves to fight for an Irish Republic. During a recruitment drive in Downpatrick, Roney and Nolan, visited the grave of the United Irish leader Thomas Russell. Although they were both Catholics, they knelt at the grave of 'this martyr of liberty and with devout fervour prayed that almighty God would receive the soul of this Protestant hero with mercy and forgiveness.'[84]

The ideological commitment to Republicanism may not have been as strong among the rank and file Belfast Fenians. However, the leadership may have succeeded in imparting something of this ideology to the rank and file who were influenced more by the Ribbon tradition. The Ribbon society, whilst being sectarian, also shared a commitment, if somewhat hazy and undefined, to Irish independence[85] so Fenianism would have been attractive to its members just as the earlier Repeal movement had been. According to Roney, only in Co. Monaghan was the commitment to the sectarian nature of their society so strong that a section of Ribbonmen refused to join with the Fenians.[86]

Whilst being predominantly part of the Republican and Ribbon tradition in Belfast, Fenianism should not be seen as a completely separate development from the tradition of constitutional nationalism. Some nationalists may have become Fenians in the 1860s as constitutional nationalism seemed to offer no way forward at that time. After the failure of the Fenian rising in 1867 and the new possibilities offered by the development of the Home Rule movement in the 1870s, some Fenians appeared to have become involved in constitutional politics. At the leadership level, the Home Ruler, Joseph Biggar had secretly given substantial funds to the Fenian society in the 1860s and John Griffith, another prominent home ruler, was probably a Fenian 'centre' in the 1860s. In Belfast, as in the rest of Ireland, Fenians appeared on home rule platforms after the 'new departure', the understanding reached between Parnell and the IRB leader, John Devoy, in 1879 which allowed individual Fenians to participate in the home rule movement in exchange for Parnell's abandoning the policy of federalism in favour of some form of independence under the crown. Often speeches at home rule meetings seemed designed to appeal to former Fenains or members of the IRB with violence never being denounced on moral grounds, only rejected for practical reasons.[87] The banners of the home rulers in their processions, such as life size pictures of Emmet and harps without crowns, suggest Fenian influence. The participation of a Presbyterian band from Newtownards in the home rule procession in Belfast in 1872 is interesting given Roney's revelation of Presbyterian converts to Fenianism in the area.[88]

The particular form which nationalism took in the 1860s in Belfast was dictated by circumstance. Constitutional nationalism appeared to be a dead end with the failure of the repeal movement and the Independent Irish party of the 1850s. Until franchise reform and the innovation of obstructionist tactics at Westminster created opportunities for nationalist goals to be pursued by peaceful methods, revolution appeared to be the only option for Irish nationalists. When a Fenian agent visited the Ulster Patriotic Association in Belfast, a nationalist debating society whose members spent their Sunday afternoons debating the best way to achieve nationalist goals, he could offer them membership in a nation-wide movement with an *actual plan* to achieve an independent Ireland.[89] Comerford's assertion that the Fenians were only 'locked into' an armed struggle strategy because of the influence of Irish America and their leader James Stephens' 'earlier machinations' and that if it were not for these factors 'Ireland would not have been a particularly trouble-some part of the UK in 1867'[90] ignores the commitment of these men to an independent Ireland and the fact that at that time revolution seemed the only hope of achieving it. The men debating in the Ulster Patriotic Association were looking for a way to achieve Irish independence and Fenianism offered them a strategy when constitutional nationalism appeared bankrupt. This is not to say that all Fenians would only have been satisfied with an Irish republic achieved through violence. As mentioned above, with the failure of the Fenian rising and the rise of the Home Rule Association in the 1870s, some Belfast Fenians appear to have become involved in constitutional politics.

Comerford concludes that, 'Certainly the Fenians of the mid nineteenth century were not answering the call of any inexorable national spirit, but rather they were, by and large, trying to find, through the invocation of nationalism, a more significant place for themselves in the world.'[91] Possibly Roney, Griffith and even the rank and file Belfast Fenians were searching for 'a more significant place for themselves in the world'. However, they were also part of a well established nationalist tradition. Roney grew up with stories of United Irishmen martyrs and Griffith was a Young Irelander. The rank and file men came from the Ribbon tradition of primitive republicanism and sectarian defence against loyalist Orangemen. The nationalism of the Fenians was more than the 'cloak' allowed by Comerford. It was the driving force behind the society.

Comerford also seeks to play down the extent to which the Fenian prisoners and the Manchester martyrs roused the nationalism of the rest of the Irish population. He asserts that the nationalism of 1867-8 was 'a proclamation of grievance – a loud assertion of identity and call for a new deal for Ireland,' a future in the UK where Ireland would be ruled in accordance with 'Irish ideas' as Gladstone expressed it.[92] It is misleading to interpret the enthusiasm for Gladstone's policies such as dis-establishment of the Church of Ireland as indicating the absence of the desire for Irish independence. There was no opportunity to achieve Irish independence in 1868-9 so people were happy to take whatever benefits Gladstone was offering in the meantime.

The suffering of Fenian prisoners and the execution of the Manchester martyrs did rouse the nationalist sentiments of Irish Catholics. In Belfast, William Harbison's funeral was watched by 30-40,000 people. Comerford is probably right that the attendance was high partly because the rising had taken place and failed and Catholics who disapproved of physical force now felt free to demand leniency towards the Fenian prisoners.[93] It is not being suggested that the example set by the Fenian prisoners turned the rest of the Catholic population into physical force Republicans; however, like Isaac Butt who formed the Home Government Association after being inspired by the patriotism of the Fenian prisoners he had defended, their patriotism was roused. In Belfast, police reports reveal there were plans to hold a 'funeral' procession in honour of the Manchester martyrs as had been held in the south of Ireland. Collections for the parade had been made and black crepe had been bought but the authorities, threatened by ultimatums from Sandy Row Protestants, issued a declaration against demonstrations of a 'treasonable character'.[94] The Catholics of Belfast, like their co-religionists elsewhere in

Ireland, were outraged at the execution of the 'martyrs' and only the mixed nature of the town and the decision of the magistrates prevented them from holding a 'funeral'. Meetings demanding the amnesty of the Fenian prisoners were held from January 1869, including a rally of between 8,000 and 10,000 to Hannahstown in October 1869. The campaign increasingly gained the support of the bishop, the clergy and middle-class Catholics.[95] The fact that pamphlets of speeches made by Fenian prisoners in the dock sold in their thousands throughout Ireland shows the widespread attraction of nationalism[96] and when the opportunity arose for achieving wider nationalist aims, as it did with the obstructionist home rule movement, people flocked to it deserting the Irish Liberals en masse.

HOME RULE

The Home Rule Association in Belfast was very strong among Catholics, particularly the working class. It was, without a doubt, a nationalist body and contained a broad range of nationalist opinions from home rulers to separatists. The Belfast Home Rule Association was one of the first branches established in Ireland and its establishment was a local initiative. It was an early and enthusiastic supporter of obstruction tactics at Westminster and after the understanding reached between Parnell and the IRB in 1879, succeeded in recruiting some Fenians to the movement. During the 1870s, a more advanced nationalist group known as 'real nationalists' (probably members of the IRB) existed alongside the Home Rule Association and succeeded in mobilising the Catholic working class for nationalist processions. The popularity of home rule and this more militant, advanced form of nationalism in the 1870s and 1880s shows the enduring appeal of nationalism in Belfast which is sometimes overlooked by those who see the nationalist 'invasion' of Ulster in 1883 as proving that nationalism had to be imported into Ulster from the rest of Ireland.

The fact of there being in Belfast a numerous and concentrated population of Catholics with a middle class to provide the organisation probably explains the early establishment of the Home Rule Association in Belfast in comparison with some other parts of Ulster. The fact that Belfast was a centre of Fenian activity also assisted its development as there were some Fenian activists in the town looking for a new way to advance the nationalist cause. The bishop of Down and Connor, Patrick Dorrian, was a firm believer in self-government for Ireland. He did not join the organisation himself as he wanted Protestants to support the organisation and he believed his involvement would not facilitate this. However, he allowed the priests of the diocese to take part in the movement and his blessing must have encouraged some Catholics to join. The newspaper edited by one of his priests, Fr. Michael Cahill, adopted a very favourable position towards home rule and Dorrian refused requests from

Cardinal Cullen to interfere in Ulster elections to support Liberals against home rulers.[97]

The aims of the Belfast Home Rule Association in its early years were moderate and reflected those of the movement as a whole. Its leaders professed to favour not separation from Britain, but rather a strengthening of the union by granting Ireland a measure of self-government within a federal system. At the organisation's second meeting in June 1872, John Griffith, one of the leaders, declared, 'We are not wishing to separate, but to strengthen the bonds of empire; we want to create a true union instead of a false one (loud applause).'[98] The reasons for self-government given by John Duddy, the president, were that 'the heart was not more necessary to the circulation of the blood through the human system than was a native parliament to the national life and prosperity of Ireland'. Only an Irish parliament could 'develop resources, stimulate trade and commerce and stop the tide of emigration'.[99] The federal policy was adopted, both locally and at an all Ireland level, to try to appeal to a broad section of the population, including Protestants. Economic arguments were used rather than ideological justification for an Irish parliament as this was more likely to appeal to Protestants. Indeed, Duddy declared that he hoped to see the Orange hero, William Johnston, on a Home Rule platform.[100] John Griffith sought to reassure Protestants by quoting the words of Thomas Davis, 'Good men and true, we heed not creed, nor race, nor clan, we have a hand for you.'[101] Moreover, a limited amount of self government was the most the association had any hope of obtaining from the British. The moderate aims of the association contrast with the composition of some of the leadership and its supporters, many of whom had more advanced nationalist views.

Joseph Biggar, the founder of the association in Belfast, secretly gave considerable financial support to the Fenians in the 1860s and John Griffith was probably one of the head centres in Belfast who was arrested twice under the Habeas Corpus Suspension Act and was charged with treason in 1867.[102] By the early 1880s other ex-Fenians were appearing on home rule platforms such as Edward Gilmore who had been charged with treason in 1867 and Patrick Doran who had been held under the Habeas Corpus Suspension Act in 1866. They were still regarded as involved in Fenianism in 1868–9 and both were office holders of the William Harbison Memorial Fund.[103] Gilmore was first mentioned as appearing on a Home Rule platform in 1882 and Doran, somewhat later, in May 1885. In December 1885, Doran was an election agent in West Belfast for the Home Rule candidate Sexton and he also helped to establish a branch of the Irish National League in Hannahstown.[104]

By 1876, the Belfast home rule leadership was sounding less moderate in aims and methods and demanded a more active and effective policy on the part of the Irish parliamentary party at Westminster. Rather than nationalism having to be imported into Ulster as A.C. Hepburn has claimed, in the mid to

late 1870s Belfast was at the forefront in the campaign to accelerate agitation
and support obstruction. In January 1876, the Belfast leaders organised a huge
home rule rally to which the MP for Louth, Mr Sullivan, had been invited as
the guest speaker. The MP did not turn up and did not organise a replacement
leading the *Belfast Morning News* to criticise the movement in the south.
Perhaps a southern member of parliament's speech would not have been any
better but 'what was needed was the presence of such men to rejuvenate the
movement.'[105] The meeting was held to give support to members of parliament
during the next parliamentary session as 'if the constituencies are lukewarm so
will be the members' performance'. The Belfast leaders had evidently given up
any dreams of winning over Orangemen like William Johnston to Home Rule
and instead mocked the Orangemen's threatened resistance to it. Duddy
declared that William Johnston had made similar threats regarding church dis-
establishment, i.e., that if it was implemented '300,000 Orangemen would
know the reason why.' The Church had been disestablished and he 'supposed
Mr Johnston and his friends knew the reason why (laughter)'.[106]

At a rally for 'Irish National Independence' in Belfast on 15 August 1876,
Duddy demanded the expulsion of those Whig members of parliament who
had been elected by falsely pronouncing themselves home rulers. He declared
that the home rule party must press on England 'without squeamishness'
whenever she faces trouble. 'The time has come when the Home Rulers should
change their tactics and begin to advance.' They 'should show themselves
resolute and determined men, change their strategy at once, assume the
offensive, strike some bold and decisive blow at the power of England which
would bring her to a sense of her duty.'[107]

The Belfast home rulers were early and enthusiastic supporters of the policy
of obstructing proceedings at Westminster. In September 1877, Parnell and
Biggar spoke at a huge home rule meeting which passed resolutions in favour
of obstruction. John Duddy, the local leader, introduced the resolutions
declaring that England 'has robbed and plundered us for centuries; she refuses
to give us equal rights with her own English subjects; she mocks at our
demands; she insults our representatives; and instead of offering to us, who are
the injured parties, conciliation, she gives us coercion. Instead of saying to us,
"if you will only forgive and forget the injuries that we have inflicted upon you,
we will admit you to equal laws; we will allow you to manage your own affairs",
they say "we are the best judges, and we will give you as much liberty as we
think good for you and if you don't like that we will make you like it."'[108]
Parnell emphasised the effectiveness of the policy in winning amendments to
the South Africa bill and amused the audience with accounts of their
obstruction antics. He scoffed at the idea that the Irish people would save the
British government from obstruction by voting them out of power. 'The
London *Times* is already down on its knees before the Irish people, entreating
the Irish people to save them from Mr Biggar (loud laughter and cheers).' In

an appeal to any Fenians in the audience, Parnell declared, 'If, after having made a good and resolute fight for Ireland's rights with the whole strength of the Irish members, or with the sound part of the Irish members, we see it is impossible to gain any good for Ireland by parliamentary action, then let us behave with common honesty. Let us go back to the Irish people and tell them that we have exhausted every constitutional means to obtain redress for Ireland, and it is useless (cheers). Let us tell them that we are no longer responsible there and our stay there any longer is a sham and a mockery. Let us tell them that we are no longer responsible, and no longer their representatives (hear, hear) ... Let us show that these constitutional measures have failed; and not in us, but in England will be the result (cheers).'[109]

The meeting of over 3000 people appeared unanimously and enthusiastically in favour of obstruction. The policy suited the more advanced nationalist views of the Belfast home rulers. Even the local priest Fr. Michael Cahill, who chaired the meeting, described the English as 'the common enemy', to the consternation of the moderate nationalist *Belfast Morning News* who thought it unfair for men such as Gladstone to be described as such. Duddy rejected any suggestion that a policy of moderation could win over the Orangemen. 'A few years ago the Home Rule League told us that if we were moderate and conciliatory here in the north, we would soon have the Orangemen in our ranks fighting for Home Rule. How has this prediction of theirs been verified? Are the Orangemen less bigoted, less sanguinary, or more tolerant than they were a hundred years ago? (no, no) Let Derry, Lurgan and Belfast answer these questions.'[110]

The policy of obstruction may have won over more Fenians to the Home Rule Association in Belfast, as elsewhere in Ireland, and the new departure[111] may have facilitated further Fenian recruitment after the summer of 1879, however some Fenians still remained opposed to constitutional means. The speeches of the Revds Isaac Nelson and Michael Cahill at a Home Rule meeting in October 1879 were interrupted with calls for an 'Irish Republic' and declarations in favour of the use of 'the rifle'. It is interesting that Cahill responded by denouncing violence not from a purely moral standpoint but from a practical one. 'There are two means of getting back our legislature – either [by violence] or a constitutional system, and if we can accomplish our end by a constitutional system we are bound to follow it in preference ... ('no' and cheers).'[112]

Parnell obviously considered the local Fenians to be either an important element in Belfast and/or potentially valuable activists for the Home Rule cause as his speech was partly an attempt to win them over. He started with the strategy he was frequently to use of not defining what degree of self government he would accept when the time came. 'Whether we are to have a restoration of the Irish parliament of 1782 or whether we are to have a plan of federalism such as that which was formulated by the great Isaac Butt, or whether in the course of years and in the march of events the Irish nation shall achieve for itself complete separation from England – (cheers) – is a matter which must be left to the course of events for solution. I myself believe that England and Ireland might live together in amity connected only by the link of the crown ... In other words, I think the Repealer, the Federalist, and the Separatist should work as far as they can in common upon a common platform, and where their views diverge then they can agree to differ (cheers).'[113] This may have placated the Fenians in the audience as Parnell and Biggar, the other principal speaker, were not interrupted as the local clerical Home Rulers had been. It is difficult to know if this 'new departure' inspired declaration immediately led to more Fenians actually joining the Home Rule Association as the only members listed by name in the newspaper reports were those who appeared on platforms and they tended to be middle class. There were, however, no more reports of Fenian interruptions at meetings and in 1882, the prominent Fenian, Edward Gilmore, appeared on a home rule platform and in 1885 Patrick Doran, another prominent post-1867 Fenian, was listed as a home rule election agent.[114]

By 1884, the Belfast Home Rule Association had grown considerably. The town had been divided into parish branches which met weekly. The St Peter's branch, which included the Pound, was called the 'Charles Stewart Parnell Branch'. One of its committee members was Alexander McGlone, a painter from Quadrant Street.[115] The office holders of all the parish branches appear to have been from lower socio-economic groups than the leaders and prominent members of the Belfast branch as hardly any of them can be found in the street directory, even if they had an unusual name. The proceedings of the parish branch meetings were rarely reported in the press but presumably their main function was to recruit members in the parish.

The movement suffered a setback in late 1884 when the local leadership fell out with Parnell and the organising committee in Dublin which was attempting to control the local branches. The Belfast leaders had organised an Ulster convention of home rulers in July 1884 which was scuttled by Parnell who disapproved of two of the resolutions to be adopted. One resolution denouncing landlordism favoured the nationalisation of land instead of peasant proprietorship. The other resolution called on the organising committee to accelerate the organisation of the Irish National League in every town and village which Parnell interpreted as a criticism of the work of the organising committee. There was also no customary declaration of confidence in the Irish parliamentary party. The correspondence between Parnell and the Belfast leaders also shows a degree of misunderstanding between north and south. Parnell accuses the Belfast men of not understanding the need for caution in expanding the organisation due to the coercion legislation which applied in the south. The Belfast nationalists were insulted and declared that they had had more experience in facing violence as a result of their political beliefs. The convention was still-born as Parnell sent a circular to all Ulster branches denouncing it.[116]

The Belfast branch's advocacy of land nationalisation shows its independence and more progressive nature than the movement as a whole. It may indicate its distance from rural Ireland and perhaps a sympathy with agricultural labourers who had left the countryside to come to Belfast and to whom peasant proprietorship offered nothing. The Belfast leaders' impatience with the organising committee's cautionary policy may have stemmed from their tendency to hold advanced nationalist views. This conflict with the national organisation confirms that far from nationalism having to be imported into Belfast, a nationalist ideology with more progressive social policies had developed in the town.

The Belfast Home Rule Association continued to function for a while longer despite being at odds with Parnell. Michael Davitt, a long-time advocate of land nationalisation, accepted an invitation to speak at one of their meetings in December 1884 and his declaration in favour of abolishing landlordism and resting the administration of the land 'in the hands of the nation' could be seen as supporting the local position.[117] However, a few weeks later the INL leaders organised a meeting in Belfast regarding the distribution of the new parliamentary seats without consulting the Belfast leaders. John Duddy, the Belfast president, appealed to people not to attend but the meeting was well attended and had the support of the bishop and the press.[118] Their position becoming ever more untenable, Duddy and the central council of the Belfast Home Rule Association resigned in January 1885 leaving Belfast, for a short time at least, without a home rule branch.[119]

Joseph Biggar went to Belfast to re-establish a branch of the INL in January 1885. The administrator of St Peter's, Fr. Patrick Convery, was elected the new president of the branch. Many of the men who had been prominent in the old organisation joined the new branch. However, despite a conciliatory appeal to the previous main office holders, Duddy and his associates refused to join.[120] By December, the membership of the new association had reached over 1,000 members. It is not clear if the rift with Duddy hampered recruitment among the rank and file. Duddy was still highly regarded by some at the time of his death in 1890 as evidenced by the existence of a beautiful high cross memorial to him near the entrance to Milltown cemetery. In any case, the post-Duddy leadership were not entirely satisfied with the membership figure of 1,167. Although it was considered to be something of an achievement to have increased the numbers from 31 to 1,167

Membership was boosted in June 1886 by the admission of 300 'ladies'. There was some doubt as to the legality of admitting women and the approval of the organising committee in Dublin had to be sought but they welcomed the idea. The women were thanked for their work in collecting 27,000 signatures for a home rule petition and Father Convery declared that, 'an acquisition of such energy as they had displayed in furtherance of the national movement should be a stimulus for men to come forward to the meetings and join the League'.[121]

The new INL organisation in Belfast faced an electoral challenge for the first time in 1885 when the extension of the franchise and the creation of four constituencies in Belfast made it possible to put forward a home rule candidate. The home rule members were mobilised to register as many voters as possible and transport was provided to bring the aged to the polling station.[122] Several residents of the Pound were involved in the formal nomination of the home rule candidate for West Belfast.[123] The candidate, Thomas Sexton, a barrister who resided in Dublin, had been unanimously chosen by a Belfast convention of home rulers. Although Sexton tried to emphasise his commitment to labour causes, such as compensation for accidents suffered at work, in an attempt to win some Protestant votes, the campaigning centred on the attempt to register all qualified Catholics, defend their claims against any challenges at the revision sessions and ensure they actually voted on the day. At one election meeting, Father Convery compared Sexton with Sarsfield who defeated William of Orange at Limerick, not something one would do if one seriously wanted to win over Protestant voters.[124] The constituency of West Belfast was roughly divided between the Catholics of the Smithfield, Pound and Falls Road and the Protestants of the greater Shankill[125] and the election was a competition as to who could get more of their co-religionists to register and vote. The conservative candidate, Haslett, won by 37 votes. The Belfast home rulers, however, were not completely downcast as the home rule victory in Ireland, including parts of Ulster, was overwhelming. In particular, they were delighted with the victory of T.M. Healy in South Derry and bonfires burned for him in Catholic districts.[126] Despite the fact that Gladstone's home rule bill did not pass through the House of Commons, the Belfast home rulers remained optimistic about the prospect of self government. Father Convery declared that, 'the principle of Ireland's right to govern herself had been brought to the front and Mr Gladstone would be regarded as the friend and benefactor of the Irish race (cheers) ... and it was as sure as the sun shone that the Irish people would have their parliament in College Green before two years (cheers).'[127] The spirits of the association were also lifted by the victory of the home ruler Sexton over the conservative Haslett in west Belfast in 1886.

The Belfast Home Rule Association was almost entirely Catholic. Although the Belfast leaders tried to emphasise the moderate aims of the association and the high percentage of Protestants on the organisation's central authority, very few local Protestants joined the association. The exceptions among the prominent members were the founder of the association, Joseph Biggar, the Revd Isaac Nelson, a Presbyterian minister, and John Ferguson, a Protestant of unknown profession, who sometimes addressed meetings. The total number of Protestants in the association in 1875 was only 24.[128] The association supported specifically Catholic causes such as the denunciation of Judge Keogh, the judge who had declared priests had exercised undue influence in the Galway election of 1872, and chastised the local boards for the under-representation of Catholics.[129]

The Home Rule Association had a working class membership and middle class leadership. The leadership was composed of a large number of spirit merchants and spirit grocers, other small and medium sized businessmen, some professionals and a sprinkling of white collar and skilled workers. Of the local men who appeared on platforms at meetings or were listed as office holders, eight were spirit merchants, including the president John Duddy and the treasurer William Carville, thirteen were publicans or spirit grocers, twelve were other merchants or proprietors of large businesses, sixteen were drapers, builders, booksellers, grocers, pawnbrokers or dealers, five were professionals such as lawyers, doctors and architects, seven were white collar workers and seven were skilled workers. Numerous priests always appeared on the platform at Home Rule meetings and Revd Michael Cahill, the editor of the Belfast nationalist paper, the *Ulster Examiner*, was particularly prominent, often chairing meetings. When the association was reorganised as a branch of the INL in 1885, the administrator of St Peter's in the Pound, Revd Patrick Convery, became its president.[130]

Although all sources describe the bulk of the home rule members or those attending the meetings as from the working class, the leadership composition shows that a representative section of the Catholic middle class was committed to home rule. The prominence of the drink trade in the Home Rule Association reflects the prominence of that trade amongst the Catholic middle class.[131] Other merchants, retailers and professionals were all represented. It is difficult to know what proportion of the Catholic middle class were supporters of home rule. It was probably not a majority and those in the upper middle class were accused of remaining aloof,[132] but a respectable number of the Catholic middle class certainly supported the movement. The thousands of workers who filled the body of the hall at Home Rule meetings are, unfortunately, largely anonymous. All that can be established is that they were artisans or workers and that they came from all the Catholic districts of Belfast.

The home rule movement received considerable support from the inhabitants of the Pound. Fourteen of the forty-nine identifiable lay activists came from the Pound (and many others came from further down the Falls Road or the Smithfield area bordering the Pound), including one clerk, one engineer, one hairdresser, one painter, six spirit grocers, two pawnbrokers, one owner of a building business and a plumber (or a spirit grocer: there are two entries for this name, both in the Pound).[133] Father Andrew McAuley, the administrator of St Peter's from 1873 to 1882, was a supporter of home rule and he often appeared on platforms at meetings along with his curates and priests.[134] Father Patrick Convery, the administrator of St Peter's from 1882-95, became the president of the Belfast branch of the INL in 1885. The support of these administrators, particularly the very popular 'Father Pat' as Convery was known, must have encouraged many Pound residents to support the home rule movement by joining or at least attending its public meetings. The nationalist ethos pervading the parish under Convery is epitomised by the ceremony to celebrate the opening of the St Peter's tower and bells when the bells not only chimed out spiritual tunes but nationalist airs such as 'The Wearing of the Green' and 'Let Erin Remember'. Father James McGreevey, one of the parish curates, wrote a poem for the completion of the spires and bells.

> The bells of St Peter's, The bells of St Peter's!,
> Oh ring them out gaily – nor ever forget,
> That the voice of their chiming from yon lofty steeple,
> Shall echo the shouts of our liberty yet!

The poem was enthusiastically received by the people of the Pound and 'for many years appeared inevitably on their concert programmes'.[135]

Even in the very early years of the movement in Belfast when its professed aims were so moderate, the association was linked with a mass of supporters whose aims and methods were more extreme. This mass of supporters included some who were not necessarily members of the Home Rule Association[136] but who used the home rule slogan, attended special home rule meetings and held processions in favour of home rule to which leaders such as Biggar were invited. One police report describes them as 'not exactly the Home Rule party but the lowest section of the Catholic party.'[137] These 'real nationalists' as they came to be known had more advanced nationalist views, supported the idea of the use of force and believed they should challenge the territorial dominance of the Orangemen. On one occasion the police describe some members of a parade organising committee as 'suspected Ribbonmen'.[138] These characteristics suggest that some of them were ex-Fenians or members of the IRB. These men sometimes organised processions with the home rule leaders and at other times held processions in opposition to both the Home Rule Association and/or the Catholic Church. They also held their own social functions such as St Patrick's day evenings. Clifford Lloyd, a resident magistrate, described this body of Catholics in 1879 as comprising 'the lowest and poorest of the population with but little to lose and often much to gain by serious disorder'. Their insignia was 'as a rule of a seditious description which while being offensive to every loyal subject must be doubly so to a self-styled ultra-loyal population of Protestants and Orangemen remarkable for their intolerance and who in their turn display banners recalling to mind Catholic defeat and oppression'. Lloyd maintained that the home rule parades were 'not supported or countenanced by the presence of any of the upper classes of the same religious denomination'[139] although in the past, in 1872 and 1876, some home rule leaders did attend.

In 1872, a home rule parade was organised in conjunction with the Home Rule Association and Joseph Biggar spoke to those who marched to Hannahstown. The banners of those making up the procession were somewhat at odds with the moderate aims of the association. Separation rather than strengthening the union through federalism appeared to be the message. Banners with pictures of Emmet and Tone and harps without crowns and inscriptions such as 'Amnesty to the Political Prisoners' and 'Who Fears to Speak of 98' along with the less controversial representations of St Patrick and the Volunteers of 1782 prompted the Chief Secretary's Office to note on the police report of the parade that the sentiments expressed appeared to amount to more than 'home rule'.[140] The massive rioting which resulted from an Orange attack on the returning procession led the Catholic bishop and the home rule leadership to denounce most attempts at parades in the future. However, they were not always successful in enforcing their will against those calling themselves 'real nationalists'.

A committee made up of these men organised a parade to celebrate O'Connell's birthday on 6 August 1877 in opposition to the bishop and the home rule leadership. A letter from the bishop denouncing the intended procession was read out from the altars on the previous Sunday. He pleaded that 'we want peace and industry, especially in times when trade is dull.' Celebrating O'Connell's birthday was 'a thing you never did before'. O'Connell's 'motto was peace. There are many things which, like you, I have to complain of but the way to victory is peace, conciliation and abstention from empty displays ...'[141] The main nationalist papers, the *Ulster Examiner* and the *Belfast Morning News*, also condemned the parade. The *Examiner's* editorial urged people not to attend as it was got up purely as a counter demonstration against the Twelfth of July. 'You have assembled in your thousands whenever the nation has called upon you ... [but] there has been too much sunburstry, green flags and oratory.' Instead people were urged to devote half a day's pay to the families of political prisoners.[142] Despite these pleas and the threat of some employers to not allow any workers who took the day off back to work for three weeks,[143] about 2,000 people took part in the procession. Arches were also erected in the main Catholic districts. The resident magistrate's report maintained that the parade was 'disapproved of by all of the respectable portion of the community' and it was 'composed of the lowest class and followed by a number of shoeless boys and girls'.[144] Although it had been rumoured that Joseph Biggar would address the meeting at Hannahstown, he did not attend and no arrangements were made for any speechmaking so the parade returned to Belfast early in the evening.[145] This celebration of a new occasion did provoke a concerted Orange attack on the procession which led to several days of rioting.[146]

A police report from 1873 reveals the extent of preparation behind these unofficial nationalist parades. Before the advice of the clergy and the Home

Rule Association not to parade was heeded, preparations were made by 'the lower classes of Catholics' for a nationalist procession to celebrate the Fifteenth of August. Three flags were being prepared at a drapers in North Street and hundreds of sashes had been ordered from the same place. One flag was said to have a representation of St Patrick with a harp without the crown and a round tower and the inscription 'God Save Ireland'. The other two flags had been taken away without any inscription and were being prepared at a public house in Mill Street. A Mrs Moore of Hercules Street, 'well known as a warm supporter of party displays', had ordered 500 sashes for sale or distribution 'all with the words "God Save Ireland" and the harp without the crown'.[147]

In March 1879, another more spectacular nationalist parade took place in the face of clerical and home rule opposition which the *Belfast Morning News* described as being a 'Fenian parade'. The organisers of the parade, Neal Boyle and Thomas Connolly, cannot be positively identified but it appears that Connolly was a butcher from Durham St in the Pound. Their names are not found among those arrested under the Habeas Corpus Suspension Act in 1866-7 but they could have escaped arrest or have been new members of the IRB. There was a fair degree of hostility between these 'real nationalists' and the home rule leadership with both groups distributing placards and denouncing each other. The parade organisers' placards declared:

> Irishmen – A cowardly epistle has been posted through the town signed by order of committee. In it the cowards ask you to believe that there is a deception about to be imposed upon you on St Patrick's day by saying we 'knavishly address you as Nationalists'. Now, we are willing to contest the title with them, and show that we are really the true Nationalists of Belfast, and are not going to be led at the feet of a few (well, we will not mention any trades)[148] traitors who have never done anything but oppose the liberty of the people, though some of them are well paid for advocating it. Irishmen, we do not wish to denounce this parcel of traitors as well as we could, but if they carry on much further we will announce something to the so-called Nationalists that they will not be pleased at. Now, Irishmen, you are again called on, as we are assured by the support you have given already you are willing, to assemble in your thousands in Smithfield, at nine o'clock sharp, and show these mock patriots that there is no further call for them. – By order of the Real National Committee, 28 Marquis Street. – God Save Ireland.[149]

The 'real nationalists' seem to have had considerable support and were well organised, suggesting the presence of the IRB in the real nationalist committee. The magistrate's report described the procession as consisting of 'about 5,000 people of the lowest order and was the usual character of such displays'.[150] According to the *Belfast Morning News*, also a hostile source, 1,500 people took part in the procession and five times that many accompanied it to

Hannahstown in very bad weather. Most Catholic districts of the town were represented including the Pound, New Market, Smithfield, New Lodge Road and Ballymacarrett. Eight bands took part in the display including the National Brass Band, Emmet Flute Band, Grattan Flute Band, Erin's Hope Flute Band, Wolfe Tone Flute Band, Falls Road National Flute Band, Young Ireland Flute Band and the Young Blood Flute Band. The only main Catholic bands absent were the church bands. 'Each contingent had a band and a banner and before the order to march was given twelve stands of colours and a number of bannerettes were displayed.' In Barrack Street, Divis Street and Milford Street in the Pound, as well as in other streets in Smithfield and the Falls area, green arches were erected. The processionists 'wore sashes of green and gold and rosettes of the same material'. On the banners 'which were handsome and costly, were representations of St Patrick, O'Connell, the Manchester Martyrs, Erin with the harp and round tower, etc. and such inscriptions as "Hereditary Bondsmen, know ye not, Who would be free, themselves must strike the blow", "Ireland for the Irish", "God Save Ireland", "Emmet", "Grattan", "Sarsfield", and in one or two instances "Home Rule". The streets were crowded along the route of the procession ... [and] the processionists were cheered from the windows of the houses in Mill Street, Divis Street and the Falls Road and green ribbons and handkerchiefs were waved to them as they passed.' The bands played tunes such as 'The Wearing of the Green', 'God Save Ireland', 'The White Cockade' and 'The Marseillaise Hymn'.[151]

The speeches at Hannahstown demonstrate, as was pointed out by the *Belfast Morning News*, that the procession did not consist of 'Home Rulers proper' but of 'Real Nationalists' or 'Fenians'. The chairman, Neal Boyle, declared that 'they were not content with the present dilatory method which was being pursued by many of those who professed such a strong attachment for Ireland. There was another system which could be practised with far more success, and which he thought would be much more likely to succeed if they were only unanimous in their views of carrying it out. The "no drop of blood" policy of O'Connell did very well in its time, but it had long since been rendered useless in consequence of a miserable repetition and misconstruction of the meaning which was sought to be conveyed by that talented Irishman. (cheers) They had had too much experience of a miserable, truculent spirit in Irish politics to be caught again by a similar chimera, and what they wanted now was something which they could adopt with satisfaction to themselves and that would prove a gentle reminder to their legislators that it would be in their interest that they should concede something on behalf of Ireland (cheers).' Home rule itself was not necessarily rejected, rather the purely constitutional method of attempting to achieve it. The other speaker, Thomas Connolly, declared, 'If they settled upon Home Rule, they would have it or else they would know the reason why it was refused. There was a growing spirit in the country which would brook no defeat ...'[152]

The parade was re-routed by the magistrates from Smithfield directly down the Falls Road to avoid a clash with the Protestants of Brown Square. The processionists were not willing to change their route and serious clashes with the police took place. One of the leaders, addressing the magistrates, declared, 'it was a disgrace that the Orangemen were at liberty to march through any part of town they chose, while the Catholics were restricted to certain districts'. The processionists became excited, the bands struck up again and the parade attempted to force its way through the police lines. Despite cavalry charges and baton rounds, some of the processionists, covered by their stone-throwing friends, managed to push through the first line of police. Shots were fired at the police and the riot act was read. The police fired at the crowd who retreated, still throwing stones in retaliation.[153] Later at Hannahstown, Neal Boyle, one of the procession leaders, declared, 'There could be no denying that there is one law for the Catholics and another law for the Protestants after what they had witnessed that morning. They had been treated as though they had no liberties to enjoy. They had been treated as though they had only been conquered yesterday. But the day would come, and he hoped soon, when they would assert their rights, and prove to England and to the world that Irishmen were not the dolts they took them for, but that they were endowed with gifts which fitted them to occupy positions in the world other than the mere serfs of a dominant and tyrant power (cheers).'[154] The fact that these 'real nationalists' considered it to be part of their duty to challenge the territorial domination of the Orangemen shows the link between these men and the Fenians, and the Ribbonmen before them.

The Fifteenth of August 1880 appears to be the last occasion when this group of nationalists organised a parade in opposition to the home rule leadership. Individuals and bands still attended home rule parades outside Belfast and bands continued to parade the streets on weekends but no organised demonstration was again attempted during this period. The new departure and the absorption of more Fenians into constitutional politics may explain the increasing compliance of the 'real nationalists'.

The vast majority of the Belfast home rulers were clearly motivated by the desire for Irish independence, whether they were home rulers or separatists. Invariably, speakers at home rule meetings emphasised Ireland's right as a nation to its own parliament. They saw themselves as part of a long line of movements and individual heroes opposed to British rule. They were not primarily motivated by 'a search for material benefits' as historians such as Comerford have suggested.[155] On the contrary, rather than specific grievances motivating the Belfast home rulers, the government's remedying of grievances such as the 1869 dis-establishment of the Church of Ireland and the 1870 Land Act were cited as early as 1873 as arguments *in favour* of Home Rule as some of the causes of divisions between Irish Catholics and Protestants and landlords and tenants had been ameliorated or removed.[156] Grievances such as emigration were mentioned as additional justification for an Irish parliament. It is natural that the home rulers would attempt to portray an independent Ireland as more prosperous but in reality Belfast's prosperity probably depended on the union. This shows the secondary importance of economic arguments. They were moulded to suit positions determined by political and religious reasons.

In 1877, Parnell addressed a pro-obstruction home rule meeting in Belfast. The account of this meeting in the moderate Catholic paper, the *Belfast Morning News*, shows clearly that the Belfast home rulers were motivated by the desire for independence, not reform. The *Morning News* editorial declared that 'It might appear to the ordinary reader that the fact of many columns of a newspaper being filled with printed matter is in itself evidence that some fearful grievance has roused the energy of patriots. But there could be no greater mistake committed.' The speeches were only 'empty rhetoric', i.e., nationalist rhetoric, but the 3000 people in attendance seemed eager to listen to it. Regarding Parnell's suggestion of abandoning constitutional politics if all constitutional methods fail, the *Morning News* declared that he should know 'how young men are easily moved by patriotic calls. We don't want any more young men in the dock.'[157]

Nationalism, not grievances surrounding land or the university question, inspired the Belfast home rulers. The Revd Dr McCashin of St Malachy's College, Belfast, made this clear at the home rule meeting called to celebrate the release of Parnell and the other Land League leaders in May 1882 when he declared, 'Why did Mr Parnell throw off his coat? Was it for the land question? No. He said in Cork that he threw off his coat in order to get a government for Ireland, and that that coat would never be put on until he had achieved his purpose ... Lop off as they liked all the branches of the tree of injustice, in the land question and every other question, there would never be peace in Ireland while England ruled the Irish people. Let the government give them what they might, either willingly or unwillingly, until they ruled themselves they would never have peace and contentment – they would never rest until that end had been attained.' Even if the English were willing to rule them justly, 'they knew not the necessities; they did not know that there was something in the human breast, something implanted by God himself, and that the Irish would never feel that they were free until they had the power vested in them of legislating for themselves.'[158]

The speeches of the home rulers, even those clerical leaders who were so opposed to processions, reveal a strong commitment to nationalist ideology. On St Patrick's day 1874, the Revd Michael Cahill, editor of the *Ulster Examiner* and frequent chairman of home rule meetings, replied to the toast 'Our native land' proposed by Bishop Dorrian at the dinner held by the moderate Catholic Association (the advanced nationalists held their own soiree).

It was not the land alone that they were enamoured with, it was the love of liberty which existed in the land – in the glorious history of their forefathers. That was the reason why they should love their native land, and confer on her the tribute of every faculty of which they were possessed (applause). When they looked back into other ages, and saw the glorious achievements of their ancestors, or, when casting their eye on the historic page of their country's history, they found that every page was dotted over with diamonds, and those diamonds were the noble actions of those who proceeded them – on that account they were compelled to be enamoured of their native land (applause). When they remembered the glorious struggles of their ancestors when they met in fierce conflicts the invading foe, and when, under the glorious Brian, they conquered at Clontarf – that was a reason why they should be proud of their native land. When they remembered the many struggles their forefathers had at the time of the English invasion, in which their ancestors so nobly comported themselves, that was another reason why they should be proud of their native land. When they remembered the great O'Donnell, and the glorious achievements of Red Hugh of Ulster – (applause) – And again coming to more recent days, when they remembered the glorious struggle made at Ballynahinch, and when they remembered the bloody conflicts which took place at Wexford, they had still further reason to be proud of their native land. When they remembered the great conflict that raged round the walls of Limerick, when they remembered the stand that was there made, and how the haughty conqueror at the Boyne was compelled to give up his influence before the immortal Sarsfield, they had still further reason to be proud to call this their native land ... Much as they owed to the achievements of their ancestors in resisting, as they were consciously bound to resist, every inroad made upon their liberty, there was still a higher claim on behalf of their native land, and that was the opposition which their ancestors had given to those who endeavoured to filch from men that faith which was implanted in the soil (applause). The whole country seemed now uprising, as if to assert new independence, and he believed there was not a man or woman in the room who would not make every exertion in his or her power to endeavour to further that cause. It had been cast in their teeth that the independence for which they were struggling was a separation from the sister kingdom. Now he declared positively that that was not their intention ... Their only object was to have that which was unjustly taken from them – a parliament of their own in College Green (loud applause). And why did they ask for that? Because of their attachment to their native land (applause).[159]

This speech epitomises the nationalism of the vast majority of the Belfast home rulers. It shows the inextricably linked nature of Catholicism and nationalism, the viewing of Irish history as a long series of resistance to Protestantism and English rule and the home rule movement's place in this 'glorious' struggle. The only reason given for an Irish parliament is 'attachment to our native land'. There is not even any mention of current grievances such as land or education in this speech at a time when Comerford asserts that, 'In the early 1870s, as for long before and long after, popular Irish nationalism was a matter of self assertiveness of the Catholic community and of a search for material benefits, rather than a question of yearning for constitutional forms.'[160]

The politicisation of the population of the Pound and other working-class Catholic districts was reinforced during this period, not only by the activities of the Home Rule Association, such as meetings, but by nationalist parades. These parades, when permitted by the police, took routes which went past nationalist sites such as the place of execution of Henry Joy McCracken and his grave site. As the procession passed St George's Church in August 1876, 'the processionists raised their hats in respect to the memory of McCracken and on passing [the place of his execution] the "Dead March in Saul" was played …'[161] This was a new phenomenon in Catholic parades indicating the increased politicisation of the Catholic working class resulting from Fenian influence and home rule agitation. Even after organised nationalist processions were abandoned in the early 1880s, the informal parading of individual nationalist bands and their supporters served to maintain the nationalist spirit of ghettos like the Pound. These bands paraded nearly every weekend during the summer months from 1877. They were named after nationalist heroes such as Wolfe Tone, Robert Emmet and Henry Grattan and had special uniforms in national colours (The green uniforms of the Emmet band were said to particularly enrage the Sandy Row crowd). When they paraded, they were usually accompanied by a crowd of (sometimes rowdy) supporters and many others came out of their houses to watch them pass.[162] The bands also held special dances to which their members, their supporters and their girlfriends were invited.[163] The nationalist bands succeeded in subtly indoctrinating the population into nationalist ideology, completing the work done by the Fenians/IRB and home rule movement amongst the more politically active.

By ignoring Fenianism and the early home rule movement in Belfast, A.C. Hepburn has come to the erroneous conclusion that 'Until the last decade of the nineteenth century, … the minority in Belfast was defined fairly narrowly by its Catholic religion, was under clerical leadership in social and political as well as spiritual life, and had more in common with Irish migrant groups in British and overseas cities than with the rest of Ireland … *In particular the popular political nationalism of the late nineteenth century was developed entirely in the south and subsequently imported into the north*.'[164] These claims are clearly refuted by the evidence that Belfast was one of the Fenian strongholds in Ireland, it established its own Home Rule Association in 1872 and helped to establish others in counties Down and Antrim, it was an early and enthusiastic supporter of the policy of obstruction, it contained a group of influential advanced nationalists who mobilised the population for great nationalist processions and supported a popular culture of nationalist bands whose constant parades filled ghettos like the Pound with music and imagery celebrating Ireland's struggle for independence. The religious composition of Belfast did make it different from other parts of Ireland but it did not make it any less nationalist. In fact, the hostility between Catholics and Protestants was one of the driving forces behind the nationalism of working-class Catholics.

Hepburn also contends that there was a fundamental change in the nature of the leadership of Belfast Catholics in the 1890s from a clerical leadership which sought accommodation with local Protestants to a nationalist leadership whose origins were the Catholic ghettos of the town. Hepburn comes to this conclusion by looking at the conflict between the nationalist leader Joe Devlin and Bishop Henry who wanted to run Catholic candidates in municipal elections who would seek accommodation with Protestants on local issues. Devlin finally won this battle and Hepburn sees this as the triumph of nationalism over purely Catholic politics which meant the end of any hope of Belfast Catholics developing an Ulster identity rather than an Irish nationalist one. Hepburn then compares Devlin's triumph with the changes in leadership of blacks in American cities where an older elite had favoured integration with white society until a new elite from the ghetto (like Devlin) rejected this policy.[165] However, in Belfast there was no radical change in the leadership of Catholics in the late nineteenth century. The repeal movement in the 1840s and the home rule movement in the 1870s and 1880s both relied on leaders and organisers from Catholic ghettos. Although both had some mercantile and professional leaders from mixed parts of the city centre and the suburbs, they did not and could not provide the entire leadership for movements whose main strengths were in the ghettos. The spirit grocers and publicans from districts like the Pound were an essential part of the leadership of both organisations.

The victory of nationalism in the 1890s came at the expense, according to Hepburn, of incorporating Catholic concerns which meant the movement had no chance of attracting Protestants.[166] This process had occurred long before the 1890s in Belfast. The Repeal Association's campaign against the Queen's Colleges and the Charitable Bequests Act[167] and the Home Rule Association's adoption of the Catholic line on education demonstrate clearly that nationalism had already ensured its triumph among Catholics by winning the approval of the church. Bishop Henry's short lived domination of local politics (and it was only local politics) should not be seen as indicative of Catholic politics during the entire nineteenth century until the victory of Devlin. The accommodation whereby Nationalist leaders were allowed relative autonomy in the political sphere and in turn took up Catholic causes and sought priests as organisers existed during Bishop Dorrian's episcopate in Belfast.[168] It was not a new departure for Belfast which Devlin and Bishop Henry negotiated after Henry had accepted defeat.

There was no question of Belfast Catholics developing a regional Ulster identity in the 1890s. From the 1840s, the bulk of the Catholic working class and a section of the Catholic middle class believed their future lay in supporting an all Ireland Catholic/nationalist movement for some form of Irish independence. The popularity of the Fenian and home rule movements from the 1860s onwards reaffirms this. Bishop Henry was able for a short time to abrogate the accommodation between the church and constitutional nationalists at the local level by fully exploiting his position of power and influence over people who were very devout Catholics and susceptible to such influence. In the end, even this was not enough to limit the power of nationalism among Belfast Catholics so his brief success should not be seen as indicative of the state of Belfast politics for the entire nineteenth century as Hepburn tries to portray it.

To claim, as Brian Walker does, that Ulster politics could have developed into something other than a unionist/nationalist divide during 1868-86 is equally fanciful.[169] Walker maintains that Ulster politics could have developed differently, for example, into a division between all of Ulster and the rest of Ireland based on the industrial nature of the province and its custom of tenant right. The strength of the Orange Order among working-class Belfast Protestants and the existence of the Ribbon society, the Repeal movement and the Fenian society among Belfast working-class Catholics shows that the unionist/nationalist divide was already well established. There was no chance of Protestant and Catholic workers forming an alliance based on their shared membership of an industrial society. The religious divide in the countryside was also too deep to prevent anything other than unionism and nationalism from being the long term political allegiances. Wright stresses that the Catholic peasants of Ulster always rejected the plan, sometimes entertained by Protestant peasants, of securing the Ulster custom in the province without insisting on its implementation elsewhere in Ireland.[170] The religious link with Catholic peasants elsewhere in Ireland was always stronger than any shared economic interest with their Protestant neighbours. Peasants from both communities supported Liberal candidates on the land issue but with the transformation of the Land League into the National League, politics was again divided along religious lines. The sectarian realities became clear in electoral terms during Walker's period but they had long existed and ensured that politics would take a unionist/nationalist form.

It is a mistake to assume that nationalism can be neutralised or eliminated by redressing grievances. Grievances fuel nationalism but their elimination can rarely destroy it once it has already been mobilised as a force. Walker's claim that 'possibly a more sensitive and effective government reaction to the situation in Ireland in the early 1870s could have undermined home rule and nationalist demands'[171] is not tenable. The speeches of the Belfast home rulers emphasising that they would still demand legislative independence regardless of how well they were governed by Britain prove that reform could not have destroyed nationalism. Would the sensitive handling of the land question have made Father Cahill forget about the 'glorious' struggles of Brian Boru, Sarsfield and the United Irishmen and the wickedness of the English 'enemy' in trying to eradicate 'the faith implanted in the soil'? It is unrealistic to imagine that 'a Liberal/Conservative and eventually a Labour/Conservative split might have been the division in Ulster and Irish politics as happened in 19th century and early 20th century Scotland and Wales where nationalism failed to win wide support'.[172] The obvious differences between these other parts of the UK and Ulster and Ireland clearly show that there was little, if no possibility, of Ireland being a contented part of the UK. Wales and Scotland (apart from the Highlands) were Protestant. Although they were predominantly Dissenters, they did not have to fight for religious equality in the same way as Irish Catholics did in the nineteenth century and they shared a common Protestantism which was closely linked to British identity. They did not have a landlord class which was lacking in legitimacy and identified with a conquering enemy. As a result, they had not experienced strong nationalist movements in every generation since the 1840s. By underestimating the almost insurmountable problems inherent in the flawed nature of the union and the land system, by downplaying the nationalist and militaristic nature of Fenianism and interpreting repeal as a reform movement, these historians have come to the erroneous conclusion that Ulster politics could have developed into something other than a unionist/nationalist divide. Comerford's thesis has been accepted by historians such as Walker who can now disregard the nationalism of the Fenian organisation as simply a 'cloak' for their leisure activities, leaving them free to claim that the nationalist nature of Irish politics only developed during their period.[173]

This study of the Pound reveals the long term commitment to nationalism among working-class Catholics. The origin of nationalism among the Pound inhabitants derived in the first instance from their experience of rural Ulster. The sectarianism and primitive republicanism of the Ribbon society was transferred into the Pound where it thrived due to the rivalry with the neighbouring Orangemen of Sandy Row. The Pound inhabitants, including the Ribbonmen, were therefore predisposed towards nationalist politics and became involved in the more sophisticated nationalist politics of the Repeal Association when a local branch was established in 1842. Their Ribbon traditions and the sectarian division in Belfast predisposed them towards all Ireland nationalist movements such as repeal and, subsequently, Fenianism. Participation in the politics of repeal and, even more so, in the politics of

Fenianism, gave working class nationalism a wider ideological element as heroes of the past, many of them Protestant such as Grattan and Wolfe Tone, were incorporated into what had been a basically sectarian nationalism. However, despite the incorporation of these Protestant nationalist heroes, nationalism was firmly linked to Catholicism which perpetuated sectarianism rather than eradicating it. The increasingly Catholic nature of the Pound from the 1860s reinforced the attraction of Irish nationalism as the differences between Catholics and Protestants became even more pronounced in religious terms.

The Belfast branch of the Home Rule Association was one of the earliest branches established and one of the most enthusiastic in supporting the advanced Parnellite wing of the movement. The intermingling of the new Catholicism of the Pound and the nationalism of the Home Rule Association is epitomised by Father Patrick Convery, the administrator of St Peter's and active promoter of confraternities, also being the president of the Belfast Home Rule Association and the new bells of St Peter's ringing out nationalist tunes before the tower's opening ceremony. The strength of the nationalist tradition in the Pound, and in working-class Catholic Belfast in general, belies any attempt to argue that Ulster politics could have developed into something other than a unionist/nationalist divide. The Pound inhabitants would have agreed with the Revd Dr McCashin's assertion that even if the English were willing to rule them justly, 'they knew not the necessities; they did not know that there was something in the human breast, something implanted by God himself, and that the Irish would never feel that they were free until they had the power vested in them of legislating for themselves'.[174]

Sandy Row, 1850-86

This chapter focuses on two key events in the Sandy Row district during the mid to late nineteenth century – the Ulster revival of 1859 and the formation of the Belfast Protestant Working Men's Association in 1868. These events are important because they reinforced the Protestant and unionist nature of the district, ensuring that the inhabitants would be violent opponents of home rule in 1886. This chapter is shorter than the equivalent chapter on the Pound because there is less information on communal and political institutions in Sandy Row. It is not clear whether this reflects weaker development of community institutions or that they were not as visible. There is definitely not the same degree of press coverage of community organisations as there was for Catholic organisations in the Catholic press. There is also not nearly the same amount of material on political organisations in Sandy Row. Whereas the Catholics of the Pound were involved in the Fenian and home rule movements for which there is a substantial amount of documentation, the Protestants of Sandy Row were, relatively speaking, generally satisfied with the status quo and so did not receive the same amount of attention from the police and magistrates resulting in fewer records. The secretive nature of the Orange Order, the main political institution in the district, also means that information about the institution is sparse.

THE 1859 REVIVAL

The 1859 revival was important in the development of the Sandy Row district. It consolidated the gains made by the evangelical churches in the early to mid nineteenth century and, by making the conversion experience all important, increased the social division between Protestant and Catholic workers. Although contemporary sympathetic observers of the revival maintained that it made the Protestants of Sandy Row more peaceable towards their Catholic neighbours, the heightened divisions caused by the revival bringing religious issues to the forefront of everyday life and the controversy surrounding Catholic converts contributed to a long term worsening of relations.

Hempton and Hill define a revival as a situation where religious issues are at the forefront of a community.[1] People experience, through prayer meetings or sermons, a deep sense of their own sin during which time they suffer mental and even physical anguish before experiencing a sense of release and joy when they realise that God has forgiven them because of their faith in Jesus Christ. Revivals had occurred in Ulster in the past and in the United States and parts of Great Britain.[2] Although revivals often occurred at times of economic and social stress, this was not always the case and recent literature stresses the importance of the religious experience of those involved. What was a necessary prerequisite for all revivals was a belief and an expectation that a revival was desirable and imminent.[3]

However, in the case of Ulster, it is generally accepted that an underlying cause of the revival's success was the anti-Catholicism which prevailed in the region. The Ulster Protestants' perception of their increasing vulnerability due to the new confidence of the Catholic Church and its political gains meant that they were receptive to the revival in a way that Protestants in other countries such as Britain were not. As Myrtle Hill has argued, the revival offered 'reaffirmation, justification and divine approval to a society which had undergone half a century of social, political and religious upheaval'.[4]

The expectation that a revival was imminent existed in parts of Ulster in 1859 when news was received of the great revival in the United States. Prayer meetings in Kells, Co. Antrim, became active revival meetings and ministers and lay people who had experienced the revival there travelled to other parts of Ulster spreading the word. In Belfast, Presbyterian ministers such as Hanna and Morgan urged young men to follow the example of those who had instigated the revival in the US and Antrim.[5] A female convert from Kells addressed a meeting in Hanna's Berry Street church and during her address some of the congregation were affected and others in attendance were later smitten at work.[6] Hanna's daily revival meetings quickly became so popular that huge crowds were left outside unable to gain admission. Other Presbyterian churches as well as Methodist churches began to hold meetings and the crowds often seemed prepared to go to any meeting regardless of denomination.[7]

The revival occurred predominantly among working class people and Sandy Row was one of the main revival centres in Belfast. Revival meetings were held in the Presbyterian churches in Albert Street, actually the southern border of the Pound district, and in the College Square North church as well as in Christ Church and the Methodist church in Wesley Place. The Methodist church was particularly notable for a large number of cases of smitten people during June. Ministers of all denominations also held outdoor services in the evenings and at lunch time, sometimes as many as five ministers would be preaching at the same time in different locations in the Sandy Row district.[8] Large numbers of people smitten were reported during June and July throughout the district. The *Banner of Ulster* reported that 'in Stanley Street, Durham St and several other localities there have been spiritual manifestations almost without number'. All ages and sexes were said to have been affected. During the evenings, young women sat singing hymns in a field between Sandy Row and

Great Victoria Street and it was claimed that 'at about ten at night the voice of praise greeted the ear from nearly every alternate house in Sandy Row'.[9] On one occasion, Hugh Hanna 'addressed an assembly of 25 boys in the neighbourhood of Stanley Street casually collected in a kitchen'. During prayer, 19 were smitten and 15 turned out to be 'cases of strong conviction'. The *Banner of Ulster* maintained that 'this circumstance has created great astonishment in the neighbourhood, and thus more seriously impressed the people'.[10] When a number of people were smitten in such a dramatic manner, it did cause great excitement among the rest of the population. When six cases were reported in Mary's Place, the crowds surrounding the houses were so large that the reporter could not get near to the houses in order to establish what exactly had occurred.[11] The atmosphere in the district during June and July must have been one of tremendous religious excitement with saturation preaching at all hours of the day both indoors and out, women collapsing at work, ministers praying in people's kitchens and huge crowds collecting to observe those who had been struck down.

Women in Sandy Row, as in other working-class areas, were particularly affected. The *Banner of Ulster* declared, 'one of the most extraordinary features of the awakening from its very commencement has been its almost electric spread among female workers'. Women would collapse and cry out in agony as they grappled with the realisation of their sins. Some even went into a trance for days and experienced what they claimed to be visions of heaven. Women were smitten during meetings, in the mills and in private homes, often while other affected women were being prayed over. After gaining relief, 'a general feature in their condition', according to the *Banner of Ulster*, was 'their ardent affection for those impressed, or whom they desire to be impressed, in the same manner. This feeling is frequently expressed in the most impulsive manner, both by words and gestures – those affected rushing into one another's arms with mutual ejaculations of endearment and mutual aspirations for divine mercy and guidance.'[12]

Why were these young women particularly susceptible to the revival? Janice Holmes has pointed out that explanations relating to the difficulties of adjusting to industrial life are inadequate. In Belfast, industrialisation was already well established and, despite the harsh conditions, many young women enjoyed the financial independence they attained through mill work.[13] Gibbon's claim that the hysteria was due to frustration associated with the inability to marry is not a full explanation.[14] This is not to discount that there may have been some sexual element in the responses of some women, particularly in their adulation of the Revd Hugh Hanna. The *Banner of Ulster* described how once the smitten women were 'in a calmer state of spiritual fervour, they [regardless of their own religious denomination] expressed an earnest desire to be visited by a particular minister (the Revd Hugh Hanna) who has since been most assiduous in his attendance to them, even proceeding to their houses for the purpose of prayer and advice'.[15] There may have been some underlying attraction for some of these women, who, after all, were just ordinary mill workers, in having a famous and charismatic man such as Hanna praying over them in bed and indeed this often led other women present to collapse and also require his attention.

However, this mania for Hugh Hanna is hardly an adequate explanation for the revival as a whole. Other aspects of the revival clearly held attractions for some women. In this period, for a short time, the most important division in society was between the saved and the unsaved. Women's lowly status and any previous improper behaviour could to some extent be cancelled out by joining the ranks of the saved. Indeed, if the woman had experienced visions or claimed to be able to read whilst in a trance or claimed to have experienced any other religious phenomenon, she instantly acquired celebrity status.[16] The churches were somewhat uncomfortable with these excesses but working class people were fascinated, and often convinced, by them. This shows, as Janice Holmes has pointed out, that working people retained a belief in the supernatural which separated them from their clergy and it also demonstrates that the revival had a momentum of its own and was by no means always under the control of the church. Subconsciously, some women took advantage of the temporary irrelevance of institutional religion to improve their standing in society.[17]

However, the women themselves described their participation in the revival as a strictly religious experience and, as Janice Holmes emphasises, this should not be lost sight of.[18] Women's visions give some clue as to what attracted them to this religious experience. Many women who experienced visions described how Jesus himself presented them with a beautiful dress or a coat in heaven. Many others saw departed relatives and some claimed to be able to read whilst in a trance although they were illiterate. This indicates a longing to see relatives gone forever, a desire for education and a longing for nice things such as clothes, as well as individual recognition (Jesus himself gave them the dress).[19] It shows what was missing in these women's lives and religion provided some comfort.

Sympathetic contemporary accounts maintain that the revival drastically changed the behaviour of the people in districts such as Sandy Row. According to the *Banner of Ulster*, which wholeheartedly supported the revival, church attendance increased dramatically, the public houses were empty, people no longer indulged in flippant amusements and there was a decline in the sale of cheap London publications 'dangerous to morals'. Young men who had previously beaten their wives had become 'kind, sober and industrious'. The Orangemen ceased to spend the fines collected from breaking the rules of the institution on drink and instead spent it on religious works which were then distributed to the poor free of charge.[20] Opponents of the revival, however, asserted that the claims of reduced drunkenness and crime were untrue.[21]

Hempton and Hill have pointed out that sympathetic accounts of revivals tend to exaggerate both the irreligious condition of the population prior to the revival and the effect the revival had on changing their long term behaviour. In reality, the rise of evangelical religion in the early to mid nineteenth century prepared the ground for the revival.[22] In Sandy Row, Christ Church had been instilling evangelicalism into the Church of Ireland population since the 1830s and the Town mission had been holding services in the district for decades. This is not to deny that for two months or so in 1859, more people came under the influence of evangelical Protestantism or that there was a change, albeit temporary in many cases, in some of the inhabitants' behaviour. Religion was indeed at the forefront of the community as evidenced by the descriptions of the district given above. However, the long term behavioural effects were probably not as impressive. Generally, revivals did not increase church attendance substantially in the long term and backsliding in relation to drinking and 'flippant amusements' was common.[23]

There were some visible gains for the churches as a result of the revival in Sandy Row. The College Square North Presbyterian church was overcrowded and 500 people sought to have a minister appointed to them and a church established. In 1859–60, they had a minister but no church and they were forced to borrow rooms for services. In 1861, a church was built for this congregation in Great Victoria Street. At the opening soiree, the Revd Dr Cooke described the church 'as truly a revival church'. They had started with only 50 families and now there were 200. Initially there were only 15 Sunday school pupils and now there were 200.[24] In 1860, a new Primitive Wesleyan church was established in Mill Lane, off Sandy Row. It drew large crowds to its opening services and is evidence of the success of Methodism in responding to the revival enthusiasm.[25] The Church of Ireland continued to rely solely on Christ Church and the Magdalene to serve the district although during the revival ministers also held open air services in locations such as the Boyne Bridge. However, in 1868, it was determined that a new church was required and the St Andrew's congregation was established and a new church built in Hope Street, complete with schools.[26] The increase in churches generally led to an increase in schools as well. In 1859, there were only three Presbyterian schools in or close to the Sandy Row district and the Christ Church schools were the only Church of Ireland schools. By 1868, there were eight schools in the district under Presbyterian, Church of Ireland or Methodist management educating pupils from all Protestant denominations.[27]

The ministers of the new Presbyterian and Church of Ireland churches in the Sandy Row district were both devout Orangemen, ensuring that the anti-Catholic tone Drew had given to Protestantism in the area was reinforced. When the Church of Ireland minister, Gaunt, was attempting to raise funds for the building of a church for his congregation, he declared that he may be a hindrance as he was regarded as 'some kind of Lucifer match to set the combustible materials of Sandy Row on fire (applause), that he was too much of an Orangeman (applause) though he did not show half the Orangeism that he intended, had opportunity presented (loud applause)'.[28] Montgomery, the new Presbyterian minister, was an Orangeman and a close associate of Hugh Hanna.

After being moved to Loughinisland in 1859, Drew continued to visit Sandy Row for important occasions ensuring that his influence in the district continued to be felt. At the foundation stone ceremony for the new Orange hall in 1868, Drew gave a speech which conferred clerical legitimacy on the sectarian attitude of the crowd. He declared, 'I used to preach a great deal against Popery and one Sunday night six fellows with big sticks came to Christ Church just to give me a sample of Popery.' He had been warned of the impending attack and escaped. The following week the Sunday school teachers offered to walk him home but he refused their offer. On the way home he heard 'tramp, tramp, tramp' like a company of soldiers behind him. 'I thought that all the cardinals of Rome with Bishop Dorrian at their head were coming to slaughter me, but what did I see when I turned around but 24 young women marching abreast after me (great laughter and applause). Girls, said I, what are you doing? Oh Sir, said they, we're guarding you (laughter and cheers). Where are such girls now who would follow their minister; and if the pope had showed himself that night they would, I am sure, have scratched his face (roars of laughter).'[29]

The membership of religious organisations, such as intellectual improvement societies, temperance societies, the YMCA etc., in the district cannot be established so it is difficult to assess their influence. However, it is interesting to note that the sorts of lectures given by these organisations often contained anti-Catholic themes. The president of the College Square North Young Men's Intellectual Improvement Association, the Revd Joshua Collins, gave lectures on topics such as 'the little horn' in which he argued that according to one view Mohammedism was 'the little horn' alluded to in the bible but the general opinion and his own was that 'the papacy realised all the prophetic conditions of the passage'.[30] A typical lecture given at the YMCA was about a persecuted Protestant minority in Europe, 'The Waldenses, and signs of the times.' This Protestant community in the Alps had been helped financially by Cromwell. Their watchword was 'death rather than the mass'. 'The rack, the scaffold, the stake, with every mode of torture devised by the inquisition could not shake the undaunted spirit of martyrdom which actuated its members; and hence the brave and liberty loving spirit of Britain stretched out a helping hand to the insulated and oppressed.' Current events showed that 'the doom of Popery draweth nigh'. Italy would then be free of 'Popery, tyranny, priest craft, Jesuits, monks, nuns, traditions, indulgences, masses, wafer gods, and holy water. (great applause)'.[31]

The Orange Order was, of course, the most explicitly anti-Catholic organisation in the district and during the second half of the nineteenth century, the number of lodges in Belfast and Sandy Row increased dramatically. In 1856, there were 42 lodges in Belfast but by 1875, there were 147; a substantial increase even allowing for the town's increasing population. In 1875, there were 20 lodges in the Sandy Row district and in 1868, a large Orange Hall was erected. The occupations of the masters who can be identified show the all encompassing nature of the institution. In 1875, there were two spirit grocers, two labourers, one clerk, one mill worker, one painter, and one porter.[32] The Orange Order was an important community institution. It provided fellowship to its members and the varied occupations of the masters show that it successfully integrated all classes of inhabitants in the district. Whilst the most recent literature maintains that craft exclusiveness, rather than the Orange Order, was the main reason for the Protestant domination of the trades in Belfast, it is accepted that the order could have played an important role in securing work for unskilled men.[33] Members of the order often possessed firearms and they played an important part in defending the district during rioting.[34] The order also performed a social function for the district as a whole. It organised 'soirees' for its members and friends where speeches dealing with current topics would be given. The crowds would then have tea and dance and sing until the early morning.[35] The Twelfth of July celebration was the activity which touched the entire population of the district. Listening to the bands practising, the collection of money for arches, the building of arches and watching the parade were activities which involved all the men, women and children of the district in some way. Accounts of the Twelfth throughout the nineteenth century mention that the Orangemen were accompanied on excursions by women and children and huge crowds lined the streets to watch them pass. The Twelfth was a community festival, but one inspired and maintained by religious and political conflict.

Although sources sympathetic to the revival claimed that it made Protestants less hostile to Catholics, the controversy and conflict surrounding Catholic converts led to a worsening of relations. The evidence cited for the alleged improvement in relations is the absence of parades and trouble on the Twelfth.[36] However, it should be noted that there was no trouble in other years, such as 1858, and the party processions act was in force which ensured there could be no legal parade. Even if the short term obsession with religious matters decreased the desire of the populace to celebrate the Twelfth, the importance of religion during this period naturally led to bitter division between Catholics and Protestants who differed on one of the fundamental tenets of the revival, that is that salvation comes only through faith in Jesus Christ and the conversion experience. Predictably, the Catholic church sought to prevent the revival converting its members and the Protestant churches believed it was their duty to attempt such conversions.

Emotive articles in the Protestant press about the alleged hostility of priests and Catholic neighbours towards converts reflect the tension surrounding the revival. The *Banner of Ulster* maintained that priests would often visit converts at the request of the family and try to convince them to remain in the Catholic Church. Protestant ministers who visited converts in the Pound were allegedly harassed and on occasions driven away by threats of violence. A girl from Brook Street in the Pound 'took ill with this glorious work' and she called for the Revd Hugh Hanna but instead her cousin brought her a priest. She supposedly told him to leave her sight at once but 'the bigotry of her parents would not allow her any other clergyman'. The *Banner* added reassuringly that there was reason to believe 'that she and her sister have found peace in Christ'.[37] One girl struck down at a Methodist open air service was allegedly told that water would be thrown on her if she continued to 'show that description of heresy'.[38] Catholic managers in the mills discouraged the revival in the workplace and in a few instances allegedly dismissed workers who were reading scripture.[39]

The *Banner's* reporting of a dramatic court case involving a Catholic convert reveals the degree of Protestant hostility towards the Catholic church for attempting to protect its members from the revival. A young convert from Catholicism was fought over by her family and the Revd Hugh Hanna and the case had finally to be decided in court. As the girl was eleven days under the age of consent, the court ruled that she return to her mother who put her in a Dublin penitentiary where, according to the *Banner of Ulster*, she was kept in a small room for 3 hours daily with her hands tied behind her back. She tried to escape but 'fell into the hands of the Romanists'. After she was released she returned to Belfast and Hanna's Berry Street church.[40] She became a servant in the house of a 'respectable Presbyterian'. Her mother, accompanied by a 'Romish mob of 100-150', composed of 'the lowest rabble' attacked the house and caught the owner by the beard and hurled him against his own shop.' The mother and two of the mob were sentenced to one month's jail.[41] Although these accounts are undoubtedly biased, it is clear that the revival did cause tension between Catholics and Protestants in working class areas.

Although the revival consolidated the gains made by evangelical churches among the working class, it did not lead to the submersion of the rough working-class culture which to some extent united poor Protestants and Catholics in areas like the Pound and Sandy Row. As the churches were so involved in organising 'respectable' leisure time activities such as soirees and picnics, much of respectable popular entertainment was segregated. However, mixed respectable entertainment possibilities also existed such as excursions to the country organised by employers and trips to Queen's Island and the Botanic Gardens where people could participate in organised sack races or visit the amusement arcades.[42] Sections of the Protestant and Catholic working class also continued to indulge in rough, unrespectable activities which united them in opposition to the values of their respective churches and respectable people in their own communities. Drinking in the pub and frequenting singing saloons and the penny theatre continued to be popular in the second half of the nineteenth century.[43]

Although it can be safely stated that the respectable working class culture did make inroads into the traditional rough culture from the 1830s onwards, it is not certain if it became the dominant culture. Complaints about 'bullet throwing' matches sent to the chief secretary's office in the early 1880s demonstrate that far from rough working class culture being in decline, new forms of rough entertainment were being introduced into the town, much to the distress of the middle class inhabitants. Bullet throwing involved two players throwing heavy leaden bullets resembling cannon balls along a road. These matches took place every Saturday evening near Snugville Street and special encounters were held on the Antrim Road just outside the town. On some occasions crowds of 'several thousands' were present and the prize money amounted to £30, a considerable sum. On such occasions, the excitement spread throughout the town and betting on the outcome was widespread, much to the dismay of the respectable press. These contests occasionally took on a sectarian flavour with the Falls Road supporting the challenger from Cork and the Protestants supporting a Shankill champion.[44] However, the rivalry appeared to be relatively good natured with no riots resulting from the competitions. Although church-based entertainment deepened the divisions between Protestants and Catholics, the working class taste for betting, games and bawdy theatre united some members of the two communities at some level in opposition to middle-class values.

Even though the revival probably did not permanently alter the behaviour of most of those swept up in it and others in Sandy Row remained untouched, it was a phenomenon which the community as a whole experienced in some sense. This experience was not shared by the Pound and other Catholic districts and it reinforced the division between the two communities. The revival was widely regarded as demonstrating God's blessing on the Protestants of Ulster, an opinion which could be absorbed even by those who were not personally smitten or even regular church attendees.

THE BELFAST PROTESTANT WORKING MEN'S ASSOCIATION

The widening of the franchise in 1867 and the campaign to repeal the party processions act resulted in divisions within the hitherto united Conservative politics of Sandy Row. In 1868 the Belfast Protestant Working Men's Association was founded to organise the return to parliament of a candidate who would advance the interests of Protestant working men, many of whom had been enfranchised by the 1867 reform act. The BPWMA invited William Johnston of Ballykilbeg to stand as the Protestant working men's candidate in the 1868 elections. He had taken a stand against the party processions act by organising a Twelfth of July parade in 1867 which resulted in him spending some weeks in jail. The local aristocracy and conservative leaders were regarded as having let down Johnston by declaring their intention as grand jurors to enforce the party processions act. A bitter electoral contest took place between Johnston and the two official conservative candidates, Charles Lanyon and John Mulholland. Johnston secretly did a deal with the Liberal candidate Thomas McClure who agreed to finance Johnston's campaign. Johnston and McClure beat the two official Conservative candidates in what some hoped would be a watershed in Belfast politics.

The official Conservatives' main concern was the prospect of the disestablishment of the Church of Ireland. In their campaign, they were supported by the Ulster Protestant Defence Association, an aristocratic led organisation, which had been established to protect the status of the Church of Ireland. The UPDA had an auxiliary organisation in Christ Church in Sandy Row which attempted to mobilise the population behind the official candidates. The UPDA made pleas to workers to shun the meetings of the Belfast Protestant Working Men's Association but this was largely unsuccessful. Although 200 parishioners and other Protestants joined the Christ Church auxiliary of the UPDA,[45] its success in curbing the enthusiasm for Johnston and the BPWMA in Sandy Row was negligible. Appeals from the conservative *Belfast Newsletter* to workers not to attend the BPWMA as it was a plot by ultramontanists and the *Northern Whig* to divide Protestants by denouncing Protestant leaders and the Co. Down aristocracy apparently had little effect as the BPWMA meetings were always crowded.[46]

The BPWMA had widespread support in Sandy Row. The treasurer, Richard Johnston, was a grocer from Durham Street and another leader, John Williams, was a publican from Sandy Row. When Williams spoke at meetings, three cheers for Sandy Row were given by the audience.[47] Johnston recorded in his diary the enthusiastic support he received in Sandy Row during the campaign. His canvassing on the Shankill and Sandy Row 'met a most enthusiastic reception in both places'. In the streets off Hutchinson Street in Sandy Row, he recorded, 'crowds of children caught my hands'. He spoke on a number of occasions in Sandy Row and huge crowds listened attentively.[48] Johnston usually emphasised his absolute commitment to the repeal of the party processions act and the attention he would give to the concerns of the working class. At one meeting of 4-5000 of his supporters in front of Linfield mill, he declared that he trusted that the electors will 'know how to discriminate between those who have stuck by them through thick and thin in days gone by, and those who, for the first time, have declared themselves in favour of the repeal of the Party Processions Act ... There are some gentlemen ... [who] are offended and greatly disgusted with the Orange democracy, while at the same time [they] would not hesitate to talk about the Orange aristocracy.' He declared that if he'd been sentenced to death, 'it would have been John

Mulholland as High Sheriff who would have executed me (laughter and cheers) so they are not satisfied with the two months in jail, but they must bring John Mulholland down here to be my political executioner in the city of Belfast (groans). [W]e are here today to sound the death knell to tyranny and hypocrisy and to seek protection for the artisan against tyranny and dictation of all sorts; and we'll keep an eye on those men, whether in foundries or factories, who seek to tyrannise over or deprive the artisans of Belfast of their freedom.' 'I thank you for this meeting tonight and for the enthusiasm you have manifested and I know you will all work for me, men, women and children of Sandy Row (cheers).'[49] His message was popular. The BPWMA claimed that 'there is not a voter in Sandy Row that is not going to vote for Johnston'.[50]

The denunciation of Church of Ireland ministers had little effect on the supporters of the BPWMA which suggests that it is simplistic to blame ministers for the sectarian attitudes of the Protestant working class in Belfast. They only listened to ministers when they liked what they heard. At a BPWMA meeting in the Music Hall, one speaker declared that it was said that the church is against us. 'That's a sure and certain sign of our success (hear, hear and laughter).' The speaker compared the clergy's doctrine of submissiveness with that preached in Derry before the apprentice boys shut the gates. 'That was the answer they gave to the clergy when they told them not to do what was right, and let us give a similar answer when we are asked not to vote for Mr Johnston, let us cry "no surrender" (loud applause and kentish fire).'[51] At a meeting in Northumberland Street, a clergyman, despite being an Orangeman, could not get a hearing for the Conservative candidate, Mulholland. He appealed to the audience, 'I appear here as a working man and an Orangeman.' A voice replied, 'come out and I'll give you a smoke'. The minister persisted, 'I am a Conservative and by the blessing of God I'll always continue one ...' A voice interrupted, '3 cheers for William Johnston of Ballykilbeg' and the cheers drowned out the minister.[52]

It has been said that, minus the anti-popery rhetoric, Johnston was more of a Liberal than a Conservative. He was in favour of 'a considerable measure of reform' and supported tenants' demands for tenant right, which set him apart from the Conservatives, as did his belief that 'the peculiar interests of labour should be watched over by those who have the confidence of the employed'.[53] However, the anti-popery policies were a very important part of his electoral appeal. One of the BPWMA's main criticisms of the Conservatives was that they were not uncompromising enough in their Protestantism as the following speech from the secretary, Robert Maxwell, makes clear. 'A short time ago an election took place in a certain ward in Belfast and the town council thought to push upon the Protestant electors of Smithfield a Catholic (groans). They wouldn't take him (loud applause). They then and there became independent and put in their own man in spite of the town council and their power (cheers).' Richard Johnston, the association's treasurer from Durham Street maintained that the association 'should have been set up long ago to form a brigade who would upset any Papist brigade in the House.' At the same meeting a resolution was passed to support 'the Protestant institutions of our country by every legitimate means and to stand by our brethren of all evangelical denominations in defence of our common Protestantism'.[54] The leaders of the BPWMA saw themselves as Conservative despite their independence from the local Conservative organisation and they were uncomfortable with being referred to as radical. At a BPWMA meeting, one member declared, 'God speed the day when Ultramontanism, Romanism and radicalism will be buried in the same grave, when every thing opposed to our grand old Conservative principles will be buried in the dust, when the old man shall leave the Vatican forever, and when the death knell of Popery shall be tolled, and from out a million voices the gladsome music of a disenthralled, emancipated and Protestant world.' Another member, John Reid, declared, 'it was said that William Johnston was a radical; but if he was, they were all radicals and agreed with him (hear and laughter)'.[55]

In fact, pan-Protestantism was more important in the ideology of the BPWMA than the economic interests of the working class. Johnston and the leaders of the BPWMA always emphasised that they did not advocate class warfare but rather a kind of partnership with capital. Johnston told a crowd during the campaign that although he was the working man's candidate, 'I am proud to tell you that the merchants and shopkeepers of Belfast, in very large proportions, are rallying round the workmen's candidate.' He declared he was 'no leveller and I don't wish to raise class against class (hear, hear)' and that he had the support of men from other classes 'who honour the working men for the stand they have taken'.[56] In politics too, what the BPWMA sought was partnership with the Conservatives. They wanted their wishes to be consulted. They did not like the arrogance of the Conservative candidates who believed they could take their vote for granted. At the nominations, McCormick stressed, 'We are entitled to have labour represented as well as capital in that illustrious assembly. We demand it as an act of political justice, because parliament has recently invested us with political rights and privileges which we are bound to exercise for the benefit of our common country.' The working class could return two members but 'in their discretion they only ask for one and they are the more surprised and indignant that their moderate and just claims should be denied them.'[57] The anti-big business outlook of the BPWMA does not necessarily mean that this organisation was left-wing. Many right-wing groups in Europe in the early twentieth century were similarly hostile towards big business whilst sharing the BPWMA's emphasis on ethnic loyalty. However, the pan-Protestantism of the BPWMA was qualified by the belief in 'Orange democracy'. They were not willing to be led by the local Conservatives and industrialists, who, by not supporting Protestant causes such as the repeal of the party processions act, had abrogated their right to be leaders of society. The composition of the leadership of the BPWMA confirms the importance of pan-Protestantism in the organisation. The leadership was a mixture of middle class property owners such as the president, Thomas Ward, who was a flax buyer, and vice president, William McCormick, who was a glass manufacturer, lower middle class men such as grocers and publicans and master tradesmen and skilled tradesmen.[58] There was little of economic interest binding these sorts of men together.

Did the BPWMA represent a new departure in Belfast politics? It demonstrated a political awareness among Protestant workers and a determination to utilise their newly won right to vote. They were determined to act independently if the Conservative candidates did not take account of their concerns. The widespread support for the BPWMA in Sandy Row and the fact that two of the association's leaders lived in the district shows that Sandy Row Protestants did have the capacity to act independently in political matters. Peter Gibbon's claim that the Sandy Row district produced no political leaders and that they blindly followed Conservative mill owners is not supported by the evidence.[59] In fact, Frank Wright found in Sandy Row the clearest correlation between occupation and voting patterns; 65% of labourers in Sandy Row voted for William Johnston only, whereas shopkeepers voted overwhelmingly for Johnston and one of the other conservative candidates.[60] The labourers were far from being the tools of the Conservative mill owners such as Mulholland. Not only did they vote for Johnston, they decided not to vote for either of the other Conservative candidates.

The philosophy of the BPWMA was less of a new departure than some observers, such as the *Northern Whig*, had hoped.[61] It did not have the potential to develop into a Liberal working men's organisation such as those which existed in Britain. As the speeches quoted above demonstrate, the BPWMA was uncomfortable with the suggestion that they were radical. Although one prominent member of the BPWMA attended a reform meeting and shared a platform with the editor of the Catholic newspaper which resulted in his expulsion from the Orange Order,[62] this willingness to leave aside sectarian prejudices to further the cause of reform was not typical, particularly in Sandy Row. Although an Orange Order master campaigned for the Liberal candidate McClure in one part of Sandy Row which resulted in him receiving a few votes,[63] the general feeling towards McClure was one of hostility. McClure's support for reform and tenant right were not enough to override the perceived Liberal softness towards Catholicism. The Liberals' financing of Johnston had to be kept secret and any suggestions that workers should support McClure as well as Johnston due to his support of tenant right led to uproar. Such a suggestion was made at a Sandy Row Orange soiree and the resulting uproar led Johnston to make a speech repudiating any link with McClure.[64] During the election, a pro-Johnston mob attacked McClure's rooms as well as those of the official Conservative candidates.[65]

Johnston's Sandy Row supporters did not see his victory as marking any new departure in their attitude towards their Catholic rivals. Once Johnston's victory was announced, a crowd gathered in Sandy Row with music and tar barrels and attempted to enter the Pound but the police and a heavy shower of rain discouraged them.[66] Johnston himself, despite his hatred of 'popery', did not dislike Catholics and as a landlord appeared to treat them well. After his victory, he declared, 'my Catholic fellow countrymen have not misunderstood me. My conduct was not an insult or a scorn to them. It was a defence of the Protestants of Ireland.'[67] He may genuinely have believed in equal marching rights for Catholics and Protestants and in 1870, the two Catholic newspapers noted an improvement in community relations which it put down to Johnston and the BPWMA's influence within Orangeism.[68] However, the riots of 1872 showed that enough Protestant workers were not willing to accept equal marching rights and this was enough to destroy the illusion of improved community relations.

The future of the BPWMA and its successor organisations also demonstrates how important pan-Protestantism was for challenging Conservative candidates. Independent candidates representing Protestant workers could only compete with Conservative candidates if they could outbid them on commitment to Protestantism. Advocating the economic interests of workers was never enough. In 1874, Johnston, short of money and suffering from a decline in popularity due to his support of the secret ballot,[69] agreed to be the official Conservative candidate and toned down his radicalism accordingly. In 1878, Johnston left politics to take up the position of inspector of fisheries and the linen baron, William Ewart, easily beat the BPWMA candidate, Robert Seeds QC, with Johnston's support. Johnston himself ran again as the official conservative candidate for South Belfast in 1885 and easily beat Seeds who was again supported by the BPWMA. In 1885, Seeds campaigned on class issues, such as housing, as well as emphasising his commitment to Protestantism but it was not enough to beat a candidate with the impeccable Protestant credentials of Johnston.[70] In the early twentieth century likewise, the Independent Orange Order could only challenge Conservative candidates if pan-Protestantism was combined with class issues.[71]

The defeat of the home rule bill in the House of Commons in 1886 delayed the development of mass Unionist organisation in Sandy Row as elsewhere but there is ample evidence of opposition to home rule in the district. Kane, the minister of Christ Church, was one of the leaders of the Ulster Loyalist Anti Repeal Union, an organisation formed in January 1886 to campaign for Unionist candidates both in Ulster and in Britain.[72] The organisation formed local fund raising committees and although there are no surviving records it can be assumed that Kane ensured that members of his congregation in Sandy Row were involved. The huge number of loyalist bands in the district shows the support for Unionism at the grass roots level. By the late 1870s there were at least ten bands in the district holding regular parades, such as the 'Lily of the North' band, the 'Go in True Blues' and the 'Sandy Row Conservative Flute Band'.[73] The bands all had impressive uniforms and their parading and music undoubtedly inspired the political passions of the inhabitants. Alvin Jackson has shown in his study of mid-Armagh that for the working class 'unionism was more commonly a matter of self-improvement or recreation than formal party activity'[74] and belonging to a band or watching a parade were the ways in which many inhabitants of Sandy Row learnt their political creed. The 1886 riots in Sandy Row demonstrate the degree of opposition to home rule in the district. Like their compatriots on the Shankill, the inhabitants believed that the country police had been sent to Belfast to put down Protestant opposition to home rule. Crowds attacked the police and police stations. Led by Kane, the residents threatened to oppose by force any attempt to build police barracks in the district.[75]

Between 1850 and 1886, the Protestant and unionist character of Sandy Row was consolidated. The revival reinforced the influence of evangelical Protestantism in the district and increased the divisions between working-class Catholics and Protestants. The revival was a phenomenon experienced by the Sandy Row district as a whole, an experience not shared by the Catholic districts of the town except for the few cases of conversion which were viewed with hostility and often caused conflict. The widening of the franchise in 1867 gave some inhabitants the opportunity to play a greater role in electoral politics. The popularity of the Belfast Protestant Working Men's Association and the return of William Johnston demonstrates the capacity of the Sandy Row inhabitants for independent political action. They were not the tools of Conservative mill owners as Gibbon has argued. However, the advent of the BPWMA did not indicate any softening in the inhabitants' attitudes towards Catholicism and nationalism. The pan-Protestantism of the organisation was more important for its success than its advocacy of working class causes as it only managed to beat official Conservative candidates if it could outbid them in this area. In 1886, the Sandy Row district demonstrated its opposition to home rule, an unsurprising development given the history of rivalry and conflict between the Ribbon society and the Orange Order, the influence of evangelical Protestantism and the fear that their hereditary enemies would be in control in any home rule parliament.

Social and economic composition of
Sandy Row and the Pound in 1901

The 1901 census[1] reveals that the Pound and Sandy Row districts were similar in many respects. There were only small differences between the two areas in housing conditions, places of birth and male occupational structure. These differences diminish when the Pound is compared to the Church of Ireland population of Sandy Row. It appears that Catholic and Church of Ireland members occupied a similar social and economic position whereas Presbyterians occupied a somewhat superior position in this working class district. Surprisingly, the Pound had a higher percentage of skilled workers, semi-skilled workers, clerks and teachers, shopkeepers and shopworkers than Sandy Row. The figures for Belfast as a whole, however, show that Protestants, particularly Presbyterians, dominated the skilled trades whereas Catholics were generally under represented. This suggests that many Protestant skilled workers were living in other areas of the city such as East Belfast or the Shankill. Although Sandy Row had a higher proportion of unskilled workers than the Pound, these labourers appear to have enjoyed better paid and more secure labouring work than their counterparts in the Pound. This is evidenced in the higher percentage of Sandy Row wives who did not have to go out to work. The differences between women in the Pound and those in Sandy Row are starker than the differences between the men. Women in Sandy Row had only half the illiteracy rate of the Pound women and were more likely to work in the cleaner, healthier warerooms than in the mills. Overall, however, the advantages enjoyed by the Sandy Row population were of degree not kind. The minimal benefits enjoyed by Protestants and the disadvantages experienced by Catholics may have been enough to confirm their aspirations of unionism and nationalism but not significant enough to create such aspirations. The discrimination against Catholic workers was the result of political and religious division, not the cause of it.

RELIGIOUS COMPOSITION

The 1901 census data shows that both the Pound and Sandy Row were overwhelmingly Catholic and Protestant respectively (see Table 1). The minority of Protestants in the Pound was greater than the Catholic minority in Sandy Row as the shopping streets which formed the border of the Pound, i.e.,

Albert Street, Divis Street and Durham Street were to some degree mixed. In Sandy Row, some of the small numbers of Catholics also lived on the outskirts of the district. Within the heartlands of the two areas, those who 'dug with the wrong foot' were very rare. They were usually lodgers and often from outside Belfast. In a general survey of Belfast Catholics, A.C. Hepburn found that most Catholics who lived in non-Catholic areas were born outside Belfast.[2] The Catholic lodgers in Sandy Row and Protestant lodgers in the Pound lived in boarding houses or with families of the majority religious persuasion. This population was probably highly transitory and few of them would have made a permanent home in the district. The rest of the minorities in both areas were mainly the partners or children of mixed marriages. Such marriages were extremely rare, far fewer appearing in 1901 than the small number in the 1852 Christ Church census. In the Sandy Row district, a few publicans were also Catholic.[3] The minorities in both communities did not put down deep roots in the district and were not self perpetuating. They were therefore unlikely to change the predominantly Protestant and Catholic communities into mixed areas, as indeed they failed to do.

TABLE 1: RELIGIOUS COMPOSITION[3a]

Religion	Sandy Row		Pound	
Catholic	154	1.2%	8033	93.2%
Church of Ireland	6908	53.8%	346	4%
Presbyterian	4202	32.7%	178	2.1%
Methodist	1103	8.6%	32	0.4%
Other	481	3.7%	33	0.4%

HOUSING

The housing conditions in the Sandy Row and Pound districts were very similar. In the 1870s, both districts still suffered from frequent flooding in winter due to bad drainage and people living near the Pound burn stream and the Blackstaff river suffered from zymotic diseases and diseases of the respiratory organs.[4] Both communities lived in crowded homes. The overall ratios of one person per every 0.85 of a room in the Pound and one person per every 0.9 of a room in Sandy Row (see Table 2 below) obscure the extent of overcrowding as it was not unusual for some small houses to contain six, eight or even ten people whilst other houses contained smaller family groups or couples. The types of houses in both areas were quite similar as Table 3 below demonstrates. The majority of the houses in both areas were valued at between one and six pounds. However, the housing in Sandy Row was valued at a somewhat lower rate than that of the Pound with more houses in the one to three pound bracket.

TABLE 2: HOUSING[4a]

	Sandy Row	Pound
Population	12848	8622
Rooms	11447	7271
Rooms per person	0.9	0.85

TABLE 3: GRIFFITH VALUATION COMPARISON[4b]

Housing valuation[5]	Sandy Row		Pound	
Below £1	0	*0*	1	*0.1*
Over £1 and less than £2	195	*15.8*	62	*6.4*
Over £2 and less than £3	278	*22.6*	110	*11.2*
Over £3 and less than £4	171	*13.9*	318	*32.5*
Over £4 and less than £5	230	*18.7*	209	*21.3*
Over £5 and less than £6	157	*12.8*	121	*12.4*
Over £6 and less than £7	73	*5.9*	53	*5.4*
Over £7 and less than £10	80	*6.5*	52	*5.3*
Over £10 and less than £20	38	*3*	43	*4.4*
Over £20	12	*1*	11	*1.1*

Figures in italics are percentages.

PLACES OF BIRTH

As with the population of Belfast as a whole, the majority of the inhabitants of the Pound and Sandy Row were born in Belfast, Antrim or Down (see Tables 4 and 5). However, there were some differences in the origin of the populations of the two areas. The Pound had fewer people from Antrim and Down and more inhabitants from Belfast, the rest of Ulster and the rest of Ireland. The higher number of people in Sandy Row from Antrim and Down reflects the increase in immigration from Belfast's hinterland in the last decades of the nineteenth century.[6] Protestants from these counties were more likely to be Presbyterian as shown by the table of Presbyterian and Church of Ireland birthplaces.

Over 51% of Sandy Row Presbyterians were migrants from Antrim or Down whereas only 33% of Church of Ireland members came from these counties. In fact, when the Church of Ireland birthplaces in Sandy Row are compared to birthplaces for Pound residents there is little difference, apart from the figures for those born in Great Britain and the rest of Ireland. In both groups approximately 40-41% of inhabitants were born in Belfast, 33% of

TABLE 4: BIRTHPLACES OF BELFAST POPULATION, 1901[6a]

Belfast/Antrim/Down	76.7%
Rest of Ulster	12.6%
Rest of Ireland	3.24%
Great Britain	6.64%
Abroad	0.83%

TABLE 5: BIRTHPLACES, SANDY ROW AND POUND[6b]

	Sandy Row		*Co. of I. Sandy Row*		*Presbyt Sandy Row*		*Pound*	
Belfast	492	*37.1*	295	*41.6*	137	*31.3*	761	*40.1*
Antrim/Down	540	*40.7*	234	*33*	226	*51.7*	601	*31.7*
Rest of Ulster	219	*16.5*	143	*20.2*	48	*11*	383	*20.2*
Rest of Ireland	11	*0.8*	4	*0.6*	3	*0.7*	100	*5.3*
UK/Abroad	64	*4.8*	33	*4.6*	23	*5.3*	53	*2.8*

Figures in italics are percentages.

Church of Ireland residents in Sandy Row came from Antrim and Down, not a substantially higher figure than the Pound's 31.7% and just over 20% of people in both groups came from the other counties of Ulster.

The areas were not radically different in the origins of their populations. The Presbyterian element in Sandy Row, predominantly originating in Antrim and Down, accounted for one of the two main differences between the two communities' origins. The other noticeable difference is the higher number of people from the rest of Ireland in the Pound (5.3% compared to 0.8% in Sandy Row) and the higher number of people from Great Britain in Sandy Row (4.8% compared to 2.8% in the Pound). However, as the numbers of these two migrant groups were quite small, they would not have made the two communities noticeably different in language and non-religious customs.

OCCUPATIONAL STRUCTURE

The majority of male workers in both areas were unskilled labourers, such as porters, carters, general labourers, or mill workers (see Tables 6 and 7 below). These workers were, with the exception of the roughers and flax dressers, un-unionised and poorly paid. The hours and pay of unskilled workers depended on the trade in which they worked and whether they were permanent or casual. Those who worked with skilled tradesmen generally did not have to work such long hours whereas other labourers, porters and carters worked a 68 to 72 hour week.[7] Even at the end of the century, the labourers' weekly wage of 16/- to 22/- was often less than half that of a skilled tradesman. For labourers who were permanently employed, wages were low but at least they were regular. The casual labourer seeking work at the docks or building sites had no such guarantee and often his family had to rely on his wife's or children's wages to survive.[8]

The minority of skilled workers, clerks and substantial shopkeepers in the Pound and Sandy Row were able to live a much more comfortable lifestyle. The wages of, for example, a mechanic or a compositor would have covered rent, food and clothing and perhaps have purchased a holiday at the seaside in summer.[9] Their wives were less likely to be compelled to work and their daughters were more likely to work in warerooms rather than in the mills. These families were more likely to live in the newer streets in larger houses. As 'respectable' artisans, shopkeepers or white collar workers, these men and their families could hold their heads high in Victorian society. Unlike their counterparts in Great Britain who often had more contact with the lower middle class than the labouring class,[10] these skilled workers lived in predominantly unskilled districts (although some of them lived in comparatively superior streets) and the sectarian nature of politics ensured that many would have come into contact with labourers, either at the Orange lodge or the Fenian secret meeting.

One of the most interesting findings from the census data is that there is no noticeable increase in skilled workers despite the development of shipbuilding and engineering in the 1850s and 1860s (see Table 6). There is a small increase in the number of semi-skilled workers and the independent weaver class

TABLE 6: SANDY ROW MALE OCCUPATIONS[10a]

Occupation	1852 (Ch. of I. Members)		1901	
Landlord	1	*0.2*	–	–
Skilled workers	78	*14.6*	543	*15.8*
Semi-skilled workers	37	*6.9*	360	*10.5*
Unskilled workers	164	*30.7*	1968	*57.3*
Mill workers	117	*21.9*	193	*5.6*
Weavers	77	*14.4*	–	–
Clerks/Teachers	13	*2.4*	91	*2.6*
Shopkeepers	6	*1.1*	118	*3.4*
Shopworkers	4	*0.7*	67	*1.9*
Army/Police	18	*3.4*	22	*0.6*
Publicans	6	*1.1*	43	*1.2*
None/Unemployed	13	*2.4*	31	*0.9*

Figures in italics are percentages.

TABLE 7: COMPARISON OF MALE OCCUPATIONS:
SANDY ROW AND THE POUND, 1901[10b]

Occupation	Sandy Row[11]		Pound	
Clerk/Teacher	91	*2.6*	100	*3.8*
Shopkeeper	118	*3*	168	*6.5*
Publican	43	*1.2*	69	*2.6*
Shopworker	67	*1.9*	90	*3.5*
Master/Foreman	25	*0.7*	12	*0.5*
Army	22	*0.6*	26	*1*
Mill worker	193	*5.6*	89	*3.4*
Skilled worker	543	*15.7*	408	*15.7*
Semi-skilled worker	360	*10.4*	336	*12.9*
Unskilled worker	1968	*56.9*	1275	*49.1*
Unemployed	31	*0.9*	23	*0.9*

Figures in italics are percentages.

became completely extinct during this period but the overwhelmingly unskilled nature of the district did not change. The small percentage of shop keepers and shop workers in the Church of Ireland census of 1852 probably reflects the Presbyterian dominance of such occupations seen in the 1901 census.[12]

In 1901, the Pound and Sandy Row were remarkably similar in male occupational composition (see Table 7). The development of shipbuilding and engineering in the second half of the nineteenth century did not benefit the Sandy Row area to a greater extent than it benefited the Catholic Pound district. In fact, the percentage of skilled workers in the Pound was the same as in Sandy Row. There appeared to be little difference in the type of skilled workers in the two areas. Both areas had a mixture of traditional trades such as tailors, carpenters, plasterers and bakers and engineering related trades such as iron moulders and fitters. Specifically shipyard trades were rare in both areas. Slaters and plasterers appear to have been more numerous in the Pound. This corresponds to the findings of R.J. Morris who has highlighted the over-representation of Catholics in the building trades in Belfast as a whole in the late nineteenth century.[13] The danger of counting poorly paid low status trades which did not always require an apprenticeship and which had a large supply of potential workers as being 'skilled' has been averted by classifying such trades as semi-skilled. Shoemakers, hairdressers and butchers have been classified as semi-skilled. A slightly higher percentage of the Pound population were involved in semi-skilled employment (12.9% compared to 10.4%) and the Catholic inhabitants seem particularly to have dominated the hairdressing and butchering trades.

The proportion of unskilled workers and mill workers was higher in Sandy Row at 56.9% and 5.6% compared to 49.1% and 3.4% in the Pound. Sandy Row millworkers may have been more likely to work in the more prestigious weaving sections (see Table 9 below) but this is impossible to prove as many census respondents simply classified themselves as 'mill workers'. In any case, the proportion of male mill workers in the two areas was quite low so any status division in the mills would not have had a widespread impact.

The number of clerks, teachers and other professionals was slightly higher in the Pound (3.8%) than in Sandy Row (2.6%). The number of publicans, shop keepers and shop workers was also higher in the Pound reflecting the Catholic dominance in the retail trades;[14] the percentages being 2.6%, 6.5% and 3.5% compared to 1.2%, 3% and 1.9% in Sandy Row. Not all of these publicans, retailers and shop assistants were part of a respectable lower middle class. Indeed, many of the Catholic traders or 'dealers' were illiterate but they were still economically better off than the labourer who had no security and no assets except his own labour. Even excluding Durham Street, which included a substantial number of Protestants and low numbers of unskilled workers (233 of 347, i.e., 67% were Catholics, 33% Protestants and 75.8% were skilled or semi-skilled workers, shop keepers, shop workers or professionals), the percentage of skilled and semi-skilled workers, shopkeepers, shop workers and professionals is still high. Excluding Durham St, these occupations still total 1118 out of a population of 2472, i.e., 45.2% compared to the Sandy Row percentage of 36%.

The census data for Belfast as a whole suggests that, in contrast to this local study, Protestants, particularly Presbyterians were over represented in most skilled trades and Catholics were over represented in unskilled positions.

Table 8 shows that Catholics were over-represented in unskilled positions. They comprised only 23.3% of the male population but held over 29% of the unskilled jobs in Belfast. Catholics were also over-represented in the spinning sector of mills and under represented in the more prestigious weaving sector (see Table 9). Church of Ireland members were also over represented in unskilled positions, comprising over 34% of unskilled workers although they made up only 29.9% of the population. However, Church of Ireland members fared better than Catholics in the mills, being marginally under represented in the spinning sector and slightly over-represented in the weaving sector. Presbyterians, by contrast, were under-represented in the unskilled portion of the working class, occupying only 24.5% of unskilled jobs while comprising over 35% of the population. Presbyterians also occupied the best positions among mill workers, being substantially under represented in the spinning sector and dominant in the weaving sector. Methodists and other Protestant denominations were also under represented in unskilled positions and occupied a higher percentage of weaving than spinning positions in the mills. This data reveals the unskilled working classes to be predominantly Catholic

TABLE 8: UNSKILLED OCCUPATIONS COMPARED TO
PERCENTAGE OF MALE POPULATION – BELFAST, 1901[15]

Catholics	7045	*30.8*	(23.3%)
Church of Ireland	8269	*36.1*	(29.9%)
Presbyterian	5906	*25.8*	(35%)
Methodists	947	*4.1*	(6.1%)
Others	734	*3.2*	(5.7%)

Figures in italics are percentages.

TABLE 9: RELIGIOUS BREAKDOWN OF MALE MILL WORKERS –
BELFAST, 1901[15a]

Occupation	*R.C.*	*C. of I.*	*Pres.*	*Meth.*	*Other*
Flax spinning	985	729	765	111	74
	37	*27.4*	*28.7*	*4.1*	*2.8*
Flax weaving	264	587	727	94	74
	15.1	*33.6*	*41.6*	*5.4*	*4.2*
Other mill work	328	614	781	112	117
	16.8	*31.4*	*40*	*5.7*	*6*

and Church of Ireland with the latter in a somewhat better position. However, the greatest imbalance between Catholics and Protestants is not to be found among unskilled workers but among the skilled tradesmen.

Table 10 shows that most trades were dominated by Protestants, particularly Presbyterians. Church of Ireland members representation in the trades was generally equal to their percentage of the population as a whole whilst Presbyterians were generally over represented. Catholics were under represented in most trades with the exceptions of watchmaking, masonry, plastering, french polishing, coach making and the small numbers of other ship trades such as rigger, chandler and fitter. With the exception of the obscure ship trades, the trades where Catholics were equally represented were in businesses which may have mainly served their own community. The proportion of Catholic tradesmen is very low in large enterprises such as engineering works and ship yards. Catholics comprised only 10% of machine makers, 9.9% of boiler makers, 7.5% of ship builders and 5.7% of shipwrights and shipcarpenters.

The Presbyterians and the other non-conforming denominations were clearly the better off members of the working class. They were under represented in unskilled jobs and generally occupied a proportion of skilled positions equivalent or greater than their numbers in the population at large.

TABLE 10: RELIGIOUS BREAKDOWN OF SKILLED
OCCUPATIONS – BELFAST, 1901[15b]

Occupation	R.C.	C. of I.	Pres.	Meth.	Other
Printer	34	89	102	23	18
	12.8	*33.5*	*38.3*	*8.6*	*6.8*
Engine and machine	63	208	247	54	59
maker	*10*	*33*	*39.1*	*8.6*	*9.3*
Fitter and turner	192	533	736	129	131
	11.1	*31*	*42.7*	*7.5*	*7.6*
Boiler maker	112	415	455	97	56
	9.9	*36.6*	*40*	*8.5*	*4.9*
Watchmaker	48	46	74	21	11
	24	*23*	*37*	*10.5*	*5.5*
Builder	63	94	174	22	38
	16.1	*24*	*44.5*	*5.6*	*9.7*
Carpenter/Joiner	614	895	1967	244	227
	15.6	*22.7*	*49.8*	*6.2*	*5.7*
Mason	63	40	51	12	11
	35.6	*22.6*	*28.8*	*6.8*	*6.2*
Plasterer	172	114	152	23	16
	36	*24*	*31.9*	*4.8*	*3.3*
Plumber	96	241	376	65	52
	11.6	*29*	*45.3*	*7.8*	*6.3*
Cabinet maker	148	189	287	55	64
	19.9	*25.4*	*38.6*	*7.4*	*8.6*
French polisher	75	46	66	11	10
	36	*22.1*	*31.7*	*5.3*	*4.8*
Coach maker	83	97	89	18	16
	27.4	*32*	*29.4*	*5.9*	*5.3*
Baker	222	270	413	78	77
	20.9	*25.5*	*39*	*7.4*	*7.3*
Ship/Boat builder	302	1567	1673	274	224
	7.5	*38.8*	*41.4*	*6.8*	*5.5*
Shipwright/	54	274	492	63	63
Carpenter	*5.7*	*29*	*52*	*6.7*	*6.7*
Other ship trades[16]	17	21	23	7	4
	23.6	*29.2*	*31.9*	*9.7*	*5.5*

Figures in italics are percentages.

Church of Ireland members were, like the Catholics, over represented in unskilled positions but they generally occupied a position in the trades, including the engineering and shipyard trades, equivalent to their percentage of the total population. Catholics clearly occupied the worst position in the Belfast working class, being over represented in the unskilled sector and under represented in most of the trades, particularly engineering and ship building. It is generally accepted that the restrictive, kinship based apprenticeship system which regulated entry into the skilled trades, rather than blatant prejudice on the part of employers, was responsible for the low numbers of Catholics.[17] A.C. Hepburn points out that, unlike textile employers, engineering and shipyard employers had no interest in encouraging a larger, and therefore more mixed, pool of workers. The apprenticeship system suited their needs and an increase in Catholic tradesmen would only have provoked trouble among the workforce. Unlike textile employers who were predominantly liberal, both Edward Harland and Gustav Wolff were Conservatives who represented constituencies with high numbers of Protestant working men. Therefore, politically, it was also in their interests not to disrupt the Protestant hold over trades.[18]

This picture of a Presbyterian elite, a middling Church of Ireland stratum and a mass of unskilled Catholics is not fully reproduced in the data for the Sandy Row and Pound districts. In the sense that Sandy Row is predominantly unskilled and predominantly Church of Ireland, these general trends are reproduced. However, the proportion of skilled and semi-skilled workers in Sandy Row is slightly lower than in the Catholic Pound. This suggests that a substantial number of the Protestant, particularly Presbyterian, skilled worker elite were living elsewhere. These workers, particularly shipyard workers, were probably concentrated in East Belfast near the yards. However, Sandy Row's geographic position alone could not have been a hinderance for shipyard workers as many lived in West Belfast on the Shankill.[19] A few skilled workers may have lived in lower middle class areas such as the Lisburn Road.

One of the significant differences between the two areas is the higher percentage of wives in the Pound who worked. Table 11 shows that over 30% of wives in the Pound district worked compared to 21.5% in Sandy Row. The proportion of Catholic wives in the Pound who worked was even higher than the total Pound figure. One third of Catholic wives in the Pound worked, whereas only one fifth of Sandy Row wives worked. In common with most of the social and economic comparisons between the two areas, the difference between Church of Ireland members in Sandy Row and the Pound inhabitants is less than between the two areas as a whole. By contrast, Presbyterian wives in Sandy Row were much less likely to work than their Church of Ireland neighbours or their Catholic counterparts. Nevertheless, the difference between Catholic wives in the Pound and Church of Ireland wives in Sandy Row was still noticeable (32% compared to 24%). This suggests that Catholic

TABLE 11: PERCENTAGE OF MEN WHOSE WIVES WORK
AT HOME — SANDY ROW AND POUND, 1901[19a]

Wives	Sandy Row		C. of I. Sandy Row		Pres. Sandy Row		Pound		Pound Catholic	
At home	190	*78.5*	90	*75.6*	69	*81.2*	170	*69.1*	152	*67.9*
Working	52	*21.5*	29	*24.4*	16	*18.8*	76	*30.9*	72	*32.1*

Figures in italics are percentages

husbands' labouring work was less secure or less well paid than their equivalents in Sandy Row. The higher ratio of Catholic women to men and the higher rate of Catholic male migration from Belfast also points to a less secure place in the labour market for Catholic men.[20] Another reason for the discrepancy between Catholic and Protestant working wives may be that Protestant husbands were more eager to conform to the respectable norm of being the sole provider for wife and children although this is difficult to prove. Assuming that the main reason was that Protestant labouring jobs were better paid and/or more secure, what political consequences did this economic advantage produce?

Labourers in the Pound may have had their desire for an Irish parliament reinforced by their own experience of discrimination in labouring employment as well as by a general knowledge of Protestant domination of the best trades in Belfast as a whole. A Catholic docker's remark to a Protestant worker that none of his sort would be able to get work under home rule reportedly sparked off the 1886 riots and suggests that Catholics may have expected the employment situation to change once 'they' were in control.[21] If Protestant labourers in Sandy Row felt that they had any economic advantage over their Catholic neighbours, it would have reinforced their unionist beliefs but it was hardly enough to create such beliefs in the first place. Any bias among employers towards Protestant labourers could have occurred without the introduction of heavy industry seen as crucial by some for the development of working class unionism. This bias in employment is, in any case, a reflection of an existing ethnic or religious loyalty, not the cause of such an identity. Discrimination was a result of the existing sectarian division which then acted to reinforce the divide created by political and religious conflict.

Although the economic changes in Belfast in the 1850s and 1860s were not important in initiating or fostering the development of unionism in Sandy Row, such changes did provide the unionist cause with important additional arguments against home rule. The development of heavy industry did give Protestant employers and skilled workers an important additional reason for maintaining the British link. However, the number of such workers in Sandy Row was small and no greater than the equivalent percentage in the Pound. In both areas, many skilled workers were carpenters, masons, blacksmiths and bakers so not even the total number of the small percentage of skilled workers were associated with heavy industry. The development of unionism in Sandy Row before the industrial changes of the 1850s and 1860s and the strength of unionism in the area in the latter half of the nineteenth century, despite the absence of any substantial economic superiority over their Catholic neighbours, demonstrates that economics was not the main motivation for resistance to home rule among these working class Protestants.

WOMEN

TABLE 12: FEMALE EMPLOYMENT – SANDY ROW AND POUND, 1901[21a]

	Sandy Row		Pound	
Total women	4297	*100*	3291	*100*
Clerk/Teacher	25	*0.6*	24	*0.7*
Shopkeeper	43	*1*	98	*3*
Publican	5	*0.1*	5	*0.1*
Shop worker	31	*0.7*	43	*1.3*
Unskilled worker	339	*7.9*	227	*6.9*
Mill worker	1048	*24.4*	1232	*37.4*
Seamstress	907	*21.1*	450	*13.7*
Housekeeper	1891	*44*	1203	*36.5*
Unemployed	8	*0.2*	8	*0.2*

The comparison of female employment structure in the Pound and Sandy Row in 1901 outlined in Table 12 reveals that Protestant women tended to occupy the more prestigious positions. Protestant women clearly dominated the sewing jobs in warerooms (21.1% of Sandy Row women were seamstresses compared to 13.7% of Catholics) whilst Catholic women were over represented in the less prestigious mills (37.4% of Pound women were mill workers compared to 24.4% of Sandy Row women).

The mills were unhealthy; women in the preparation areas suffered from dust inhalation and those in the spinning and weaving departments contracted bronchitis and other diseases due to working in the hot, damp conditions. Often the damage to the lungs from dust inhalation was so chronic that women had to rise half an hour earlier to allow time for a coughing fit. In the oppressive heat of the spinning and weaving rooms, fainting onto the machinery was not uncommon. In the 1870s, mill workers only lived to an average age of between 45 and 48. Their lives were generally more uncomfortable. They had to rise early to be at work by six, taking their breakfast in a tin can to warm up in the mill. Their clothes became wet and smelly in the damp conditions and they suffered from various ailments which they contracted during their walk home in the cold due to the change of temperature.[22]

By comparison, the warerooms were dry and safe to work in. Although the warerooms were generally not covered by the factory legislation relating to minimum hours until 1878, working hours and holidays were often superior to those in the mills. The women usually started work at 8.30 a.m. and finished at 7.00 p.m. and in some establishments the workers received more holidays than the statutory requirements of Christmas day, Good Friday, Easter Monday and three days in the summer.[23] Messers Jaffe gave their workers twelve *paid* holidays a year, including those days required by law and an additional week in the summer so that their workers could go to the seaside.[24] Although they were paid no more than the millworkers, the wareroom workers were considered by themselves and their employers to be more 'respectable' than the mill girls. One employer declared in response to the proposal that the warerooms work the same hours as the mills, 'As people, at least those in the lower classes, improve in social position, they like to lie later in bed; but a stronger objection is that the mills open at 6.00am: independently of the feeling of the girls themselves, their parents would not like their daughters to be coming through the streets to work at the same hour as the mill hands; the class of girls in the warehouses would certainly deteriorate, in fact where the mill and the warehouse are together the warehouse girls are not quite up to the mark of those who work in warehouses unconnected with mills.'[25] The sub-inspector of factories echoed these remarks. The wareroom workers would 'feel their self-respect hurt if they were compelled to be in the streets between 5.00 and 6.00 a.m. when they are thronged with noisy, barefooted factory girls'. Moreover, 'the idea of such respectable females bringing their food in cans, as the factory girls did, was too monstrous to even be thought of'.[26] One young woman declared that if the mills started to open at 8.30, the same time as the warerooms, she 'would rather begin at 7.00 a.m. even than come at the same time as the mill hands'.[27]

The other main difference between the two areas is that fewer Pound women were full time housekeepers reflecting the greater number of working wives in the Pound. As outlined in the section on male employment, this probably indicates better job security for Protestant labourers.

The differences in female employment were presumably substantial enough to be noticed by men and women at the time. As with the differences between the situations of labouring Catholics and Church of Ireland members, these differences between women may have been enough to reinforce their political aspirations of unionism and nationalism but could not alone have produced such aspirations. After all, there were still more Protestant mill workers in Sandy Row than 'respectable' wareroom workers.

LITERACY

There was a considerable difference in the rates of illiteracy, particularly among women, in the two areas. The high rate of literacy in Sandy Row (which was already at an impressive level by the middle of the nineteenth century, see Table 13 below) may have been due to a greater number of school places in the district and a greater emphasis on bible reading among the Protestant denominations. The higher percentage of Pound inhabitants who came from the outlying counties of Ulster, where schools were more likely to be out of reach for many children, may have had an impact on illiteracy rates in the area. The illiteracy rate for women in the Pound was particularly high in comparison with that of Sandy Row women. Perhaps, more Pound women than Pound men came from remote parts of Ulster and unlike their Sandy Row equivalents they had no pressing religious reason to be able to read the bible. The social and economic implications of the different rates of literacy are difficult to ascertain. The difference in the literacy rates among the men may not have been enough to be noticeable. The different levels of literacy appeared to make no impact on the occupational make up of the two areas as both districts were overwhelmingly manual and the proportion of teachers and clerks was actually higher in the Pound. The difference between the women from the two areas was much greater and may have reinforced any feelings of superiority among Protestant women derived from their domination of the warerooms. The literacy rates were high enough in both communities to support a large newspaper reading population so most people would have been able to acquaint themselves with the political issues of the day.

TABLE 13: ILLITERACY: SANDY ROW AND THE POUND[27a]

	Sandy Row, C. of I. 1852	Sandy Row, 1901	Pound, 1901
Illiterate men	40 (7.5%)	139 (4%)	172 (6.6%)
Illiterate women	57 (8.7%)	274 (6.4%)	418 (12.7%)

SOCIAL AND ECONOMIC DIFFERENCES WITHIN THE TWO COMMUNITIES

Within both Sandy Row and the Pound there were surprising variations in the quality of housing, literacy and occupational composition. Some of the older streets in Sandy Row, particularly those in the north of the district bordering the Pound, were comprised predominantly of two room houses. These districts had a higher rate of illiteracy, greater overcrowding, a higher proportion of unskilled workers and a higher percentage of Church of Ireland members than the district as a whole (see Tables 14, 15 and 16).

TABLE 14: HOUSING DIFFERENCES WITHIN SANDY ROW, 1901[27b]

	Sandy Row total	Poorest district[28]
Population	12848	839
Rooms	11447	505
Rooms per person	0.9	0.6

TABLE 15: ILLITERACY IN SANDY ROW, 1901[28b]

	Sandy Row total	Poorest district[29]
Total adults[30]	7743	518
Illiterate adults	413	36
Percentage illiterate	5.3	6.9

Figures in italics are percentages.

The data in Table 16 reinforces the picture of a predominantly Church of Ireland unskilled sector among the Protestant working class. Even within the same street, it appears that Church of Ireland members occupied the worst houses while Presbyterians, Methodists and other Protestants tended to occupy the better houses. In the three room houses in Stanley Street, the percentage of Church of Ireland members was very high at 67.4% while Presbyterians comprised 26.7% and Methodists 5.8%. In the four room houses in the same street, Presbyterian members nearly equalled Church of Ireland members, comprising 38.5% of the population compared to the Church of Ireland percentage of 41.9% while the Methodists were also well represented at 14.2%.

The streets in the Sandy Row district with the highest number of Presbyterian inhabitants tended to be on the outskirts of the district and often comprised better quality housing. There were substantial numbers of

TABLE 16: RELIGIOUS DIFFERENCES IN SANDY ROW, 1901[30a]

	Sandy Row total	Poorest district[31]
Population	12848	839
Church of Ireland	6903 (53.8%)	544 (64.8%)
Presbyterian	4202 (32.7%)	233 (27.8%)
Methodist	1103 (8.6%)	46 (5.5%)
Catholic	154 (1.2%)	5 (0.6%)
Other	481 (3.7%)	14 (1.7%)

Presbyterians in streets such as Albion Street with seven room houses, Combermere Street with four to six room houses, Norwood and Oban Streets with five to six room houses and Donegall Road at the Shaftsbury Square end with eight room houses. Sandy Row itself, being a shopping street, had a majority of Presbyterian inhabitants.

Within the Pound district there were substantial differences between streets in occupational and literacy terms. Some better streets included a substantial minority of Protestants, such as Durham Street, Albert Street and the city end of Divis Street. In order to illuminate economic differences between Catholics in the Pound, the streets with minorities of Protestants will not be examined and instead two overwhelmingly Catholic streets, containing between them only one Protestant, will be analysed. The two streets, Alexander Street West and Derby Street in the heart of the Pound, contained five and six room houses respectively. The inhabitants clearly enjoyed a higher standard of living and status than the majority of Pound inhabitants as Tables 17,18 and 19 demonstrate.

TABLE 17: HOUSING DIFFERENCES WITHIN THE POUND, 1901[31a]

	Pound total	Better streets
Population	8622	422
Rooms	7271	445
Rooms per person	0.84	1.05

TABLE 18: ILLITERACY IN THE POUND[31b]

	Pound total	Better streets
Total adults[32]	5887	324
Illiterate adults	590	2
Percentage illiterate	10.02	0.62

Figures in italics are percentages

The higher percentage of male skilled workers (32.7% compared to 15.7% for the Pound as a whole), shopworkers (6% compared to 3.5%) and clerks and teachers (6.9% compared to 3.8%) is matched by a high proportion of women in higher status positions. More than 3% of women were clerks and teachers (0.7% in the Pound as a whole) and 32.2% were seamstresses (compared to only 13.7% in the entire district). The number of women in low-status positions, such as mill workers (24% compared to 37.4%) and charwomen, washerwomen and factory hands classed as unskilled workers (3.8% compared

TABLE 19: OCCUPATIONAL DIFFERENCES WITHIN THE POUND,
1901[33a]

Male occupations	Pound total		Better streets	
Total men	2596	*100*	115	*100*
Clerk/Teacher	100	*3.8*	8	*7*
Shopkeeper	168	*6.5*	3	*2.6*
Publican	69	*2.6*	1	*0.9*
Shop worker	90	*3.5*	7	*6.1*
Master/Foreman	12	*0.5*	1	*0.9*
Army/Police	26	*1*	4	*3.5*
Mill worker	89	*3.4*	4	*3.5*
Skilled worker	408	*15.7*	38	*33*
Semi-skilled worker	336	*12.9*	13	*11.3*
Unskilled worker	1275	*49.1*	35	*30.4*
Unemployed	23	*0.9*	1	*0.9*

to 6.9%) was much lower than for the district in general. These economic distinctions, together with a better standard of housing and a negligible illiteracy rate, set these streets apart from those around them.

CONCLUSION

In many ways, the Pound and Sandy Row were very similar communities in 1901. The typical man in both communities was likely to be a labourer or other unskilled worker, such as a porter or carter. He was most likely to be literate. If he was married, his wife was probably a housewife. He lived in a four or three room house in a family of five or less members. The typical Pound or Sandy Row man was extremely unlikely to enter into a mixed marriage. He usually only lived with members of his immediate family, i.e., his wife and children. Although the differences between the women of the two areas were greater, the typical woman from both communities was likely to be the same. If she was married, she stayed at home in her three to four room house to look after her family of five or less members. If she worked, she was probably a mill worker although if she came from Sandy Row she was also fairly likely to be a seamstress. The typical woman from both areas was literate. The typical man and woman from both communities were likely to have been born in Belfast, Antrim or Down.

There were differences both within and between the two areas. These differences were not great enough to alter or create new political beliefs among the inhabitants. The skilled tradesmen, such as fitters, who lived in the six room houses in Derby Street in the Pound did not become unionists even though their economic future would have been more secure within the union. The labourer in Sandy Row was not any less of a unionist because he did not hold a skilled job at the shipyard. The Catholicism of the Pound fitter ensured he was a nationalist and the Protestantism of the Sandy Row labourer ensured he was a unionist, even if he was living in a squalid two room house. The most important difference between the two areas was the more secure position of Protestant labourers, evidenced in the higher number of Protestant wives able to stay at home. This advantage, enjoyed by four-fifths of Sandy Row couples compared to two-thirds of Pound couples, may have been enough to reinforce the Unionism of the Sandy Row worker and heighten the sense of alienation among Catholic labourers but it was not responsible for creating their political aspirations.

Riots, 1851–86

During this period, there were countless small scale riots and four very serious riots which lasted much longer and were more violent than the riots in the first half of the century. The increase in the severity of rioting was a result of the escalating tension between nationalism and the Protestant opposition to it. The influence of evangelical preachers such as Hanna and Kane was a contributory factor, particularly in 1857 but also in justifying the violent defence against nationalism in 1872 and 1886. There is no evidence of job competition or competition for housing being the direct causes of riots. The increasing sympathy of the wider Protestant and Catholic community with the aims of rioters is also important in accounting for the severity and longevity of the late nineteenth century riots. The riots themselves then increased the bitterness between the two communities at large. This accords with the literature on British riots which demonstrates that riots are more severe, the higher the degree of support from the wider community.

On 18 occasions between 1851 and 1886, there were violent encounters of some kind on or around the Twelfth of July.[1] These clashes occurred both whilst the party processions act was in place before 1872 and afterwards. In fact, one of the worst riots of the period, that of 1857, occurred whilst the act was in force. Acts of parliament did not stop the celebration of this festival whether the Orangemen attended special church services or simply confined the celebrations to the beating of drums and the firing of shots in the air. The clashes which occurred so frequently on the Twelfth indicate that the celebrations engendered a state of triumphalism among working-class Protestants and a spirit of defiance among their Catholic counterparts. Throughout the nineteenth century, on the occasions when the Twelfth was trouble free, it was often reported that the weather had been bad or that the troubled districts were saturated with police and military due to riots in the previous year.[2]

Before 1872, when the party processions act was in force, riots on the Twelfth usually took the form of rival crowds clashing on the borders of their districts. The tension on the Twelfth was always high as a result of people firing shots in the air in their own districts during the previous night. When crowds congregated along the interface of the two districts, insults and subsequently stones were exchanged and both sides clashed with the police when they attempted to disperse them. In severe instances such as the riots of 1852 and

1857, targets outside the area were also attacked, people of the opposite religion were expelled from their homes and workers were attacked in mills and on their way to and from work when they had to cross enemy territory. Although there were allegations of bias towards Protestant rioters on the part of the authorities prior to the repeal of the party processions act, the authorities did act to prevent processions on the Twelfth and often used force against both sides in order to disperse them.[3] The illegality of processions also made them less acceptable to middle-class Protestants and therefore the wider legitimacy which would have encouraged more riotous behaviour on the part of the Protestant rioters was lacking.

The riot of 1857 began as a particularly severe Twelfth of July riot when Protestants and Catholics clashed after the Orangemen had attended a special Twelfth sermon given by Dr Drew. It was transformed into a serious riot lasting for weeks after street preaching became a central issue. This increased the legitimacy of the rioters within their wider communities and therefore encouraged their respective campaigns.

On the Twelfth, a large congregation of Orangemen, their wives and girlfriends marched to Christ Church to attend a special sermon by Dr Drew. Once inside the church they put on their Orange sashes, which if worn outside would have made their procession to the church illegal. They then listened to a sermon which emphasised the historic persecution of Protestants by the Catholic church and suggested that such persecution was still being practised. 'Of old times, lords of high degree, with their own hands, strained on the rack, the delicate limbs of Protestant women; prelates dabbled in the gore of helpless victims; and the cells of the pope's prisons were paved with the calcined bones of men and cemented with gore and human hair. Would that such atrocities were no longer formidable.' He portrayed a world wide struggle between the Protestantism of the British empire and the United States and the Catholicism of Rome. He encouraged the women of the congregation to ensure that their husbands did not allow business to interfere with the support of Protestantism. 'In a commercial community there is always great danger of compromise. It is not always deemed safe to be recognised as a firm Protestant lest the Romish customer or the ostentatious Liberal should not renew his custom.'[4]

During the service, which was protected by the police, a large crowd from the Pound gathered in opposition to the Orangemen. Whilst the service was still in progress, a man called Loughrey rode into the midst of the Pound crowd waving an orange lily. Loughrey, who was actually a drunk Catholic, was nearly killed by the crowd before the police managed to rescue him. The rest of the day was relatively quiet except for the usual firing of shots in the air which continued through the 13th. By the night of the 13th, the shots were more numerous and large crowds were gathering although not yet actually clashing. The magisterial and police reports do not mention either side as being the aggressor. The riot commissioners stated that evidence was presented by some witnesses in an attempt to attach blame to the Pound combatants but they concluded that it was

> a matter of little moment by whom the first blow was struck, or the first stone was thrown, or by which party the greater degree of violence was exhibited. The material fact is plain enough – that two parties were there assembled, prepared for extreme action against each other; and only wanting the opportunity to bring their conflict to a bloody issue

and, although each side claimed to have acted in defence, it was difficult to tell 'where defence ends and aggression begins.'[5]

By the night of the 14th, large crowds had formed, houses were attacked and shots were fired into the two districts. It was evident

> that further preparations had been made for the battle that was continuing. In the Pound district, the streets had been torn up and the stones were piled up near the entrance to the streets; the lamps there were also extinguished. In the Sandy Row district, preparations were made for the conflict also; a building in the course of erection was loopholed for the occasion, and bricks were placed behind the walls of some of the back yards to give an easy means of firing; so that in all respects on the 14th of July these districts presented the appearance of actual battle being waged between two hostile forces prepared for a deadly encounter.[6]

This 'battle' lasted nearly a week and took the form of stone throwing, exchange of gunfire, wrecking of houses of those belonging to the minority in both areas and sallies into each other's areas to destroy property. Both crowds attacked the police when they attempted to separate them or prevent attacks on people or property. The local police tended to be lenient towards the Sandy Row Protestants and consequently they were attacked with the utmost ferocity by the Pound inhabitants and, by the end of the riots, refused to enter the district without military support.[7]

Between 17 and 19 July, the exchange of gunfire was so constant and shots were being aimed so low that the people in Albert Crescent, the border between the two areas, could not leave home. In Sandy Row, a half built house had been commandeered and a platform of bricks built inside for men to stand on in order to fire into Albert Crescent. The Pound men had a similar arrangement. Despite the fierce-sounding nature of this battle, no gunshot wounds or fatalities resulted from these shoot outs. Indeed, the Resident Magistrate Tracy emphasised that they usually fired at such a distance that fatalities among the combatants were unlikely and one occasion he even maintained that the two parties were glad to be separated by the military. 'I do not think they wanted to get near each other. I think they were glad of our arrival.'[8] The two gunshot injuries resulting from the riots were inflicted in different and more sinister circumstances. A man from Sandy Row crept up on two children playing on the street in the Pound and deliberately shot both of them. The girl was shot in the eye but miraculously survived; the boy was hit in the leg which had to be amputated.[9]

Although the gun battles generally had something of a ritualistic quality about them, the house wrecking and workplace intimidation demonstrate the degree of sectarian bitterness which existed during the riots. William Watson, a wealthy Catholic who owned 80 houses in the Pound, declared that between 40 and 50 had been damaged. Although most of his tenants in Albert Crescent were Protestants, they had been warned to leave by the Sandy Row mob (and most did) as they were 'not allowed to live there because it was Mr Watson's property'.[10] Subsequently a mob of men, women and children from Sandy Row numbering 200-300 attacked Watson's houses in Albert Crescent, threw the furniture and doors, window frames etc. into the street and made a huge bonfire.[11] Attacks on the border streets of the rival district prompted retaliation by the other side and resulted in a spiralling cycle of violence. The Protestant crowd attempted to wreck 'every Papish house in Mary Street' which prompted the Catholic crowd to destroy all the Protestant houses in Lemon Street.[12]

The intimidation of members of the opposite faith within the two districts was a particularly sinister feature of the 1857 riots. Biddy Burke, a young Catholic mill worker who had boarded for four years with a Protestant man in Mary's Place in Sandy Row, told the riots commissioners that the Sandy Row mob demanded of her landlord that he 'throw out the Papish whore or they would throw down his house'.[13] Like many lodgers, she was protected by her landlord but chose to leave the next day. Catholics and mixed marriage couples living in Sandy Row were told to 'rise up and surrender' and subsequently left the district. A widow cow keeper who had lived on some land between the Pound and Sandy Row for some 20 years was attacked by a Protestant crowd and forced to leave.[14] Although it is stated in the riot commissioners report that similar intimidation and expulsion occurred in the Pound district they do not give any examples or interview any victims. Intimidation in the workplace and on the way to and from work was another unpleasant feature of the riots. Catholic girls and women from the Pound who worked in the Sandy Row mills were particularly vulnerable to attacks. According to their statements, they received little protection from the local police force, many of whom sympathised with the Protestant crowd. They had to eat their lunch in the mill rather than returning home for a hot meal as the risk of attack was too great. Margaret McDowell, a reeler in the Tea Lane mill, described to the riot commissioners how she and 50 other girls and 2 boys from the Pound were assaulted by women, young men and children on the Salt Water Bridge on their way home. She alleged the police stood by as the mob attacked them with stones and cried, 'pull the Papist entrails out of them, for bloody Papish whores'.[15]

After over a week of rioting, the arrival of police and military reinforcements and the saturation occupation of the disturbed districts succeeded in restoring normalcy. However, the bitterness resulting from the rioting remained and sectarian animosities were refuelled in August by the controversy surrounding street preaching. In July, during the first stage of the riots, the Revd McIlwaine had announced on placards his intention to preach sermons for Catholics on the errors of Rome at the customs house steps. McIlwaine claimed that he had organised the series of sermons in June prior to the outbreak of the riots and the sermons were not especially arranged because of the riots. In any case, the magistrates regarded it as an injudicious move and, with the help of the bishop of Down and Connor, they succeeded in persuading the reluctant McIlwaine to postpone his sermons.[16] The Resident Magistrate, Tracy, reported to Dublin Castle, 'He is a very zealous minister but he wants judgement and has made himself so unpopular with the Catholic party by his eternal controversies that I am certain the peace of the town would be seriously endangered.'[17]

In late August, McIlwaine and Drew announced that they would now hold their series of sermons at the customs house steps. In response, a placard printed at the printworks of the owner of the Catholic *Ulsterman* appeared on the streets calling on Catholics to gather at the customs house 'and give the Orange bigot [Drew] such a check that he will not attempt open air preaching again'.[18] Again the Church of Ireland ministers were persuaded to abandon their plans. However, the Revd Hugh Hanna, a Presbyterian minister, announced that he would preach instead. Under pressure from the magistrates, Hanna also postponed his sermon. This was not well received by the Protestant crowd 'who hissed and hooted him ... for not having preached on Sunday last.' The Protestant Defence Association, a Sandy Row gun club established in response to the recently established Pound gun club, actually paid a Presbyterian minister who had had his license revoked to preach in a remote part of the town.[19] However, according to the resident magistrate, Hanna was 'looking for the good opinion of the truculent faction who hissed and hooted him some two or three days since for not having preached' and so he did finally proceed with his plans. In a published letter, Hanna requested that a space called 'the pope's pad' be left for those not wanting to listen so they could pass by. He declared that a stand must be made as 'the blood bought and cherished rights have been imperilled by the audacious and savage outrages of a Romish mob'. The report of the riot commissioners concluded that this type of street preaching 'would seem as intended to be a public and marked insult to the Catholic people, and they in passing, would be forced to endure a proclamation made of their inferiority; and this would seem to us to turn street preaching into a new and more taunting celebration of everything most offensive in connection with the Orange festival in July'.[20]

Predictably, the preaching controversy led to a resumption of serious rioting in the Pound and Sandy Row throughout September. Catholics gathered at the customs house to oppose Hanna's sermon and serious clashes took place between them and the ship carpenters who had armed themselves in preparation with staves and other weapons. Assaults, house wrecking and workplace intimidation resumed in Sandy Row and the Pound before the riots were quelled at the end of September.

Why were the riots of 1857 so severe, far surpassing the riots of 1843 and 1835? Drew's sermon is often mentioned both by historians and the riot commissioners as an important factor.[21] His fiery anti-Catholicism was probably a factor in inciting the Protestant crowd but this occurrence was not unique to 1857. Drew had been giving special Twelfth sermons since 1835. The riot commission report declared that the practice of the Orangemen bringing their sashes to wear in church was an innovation in 1857.[22] This could have inspired a greater sense of Orange solidarity, group loyalty and opposition to their Catholic rivals or it may indicate a pre-existing upsurge in sectarian tension prior to the riots.

The relevance of Drew's sermon is downplayed by those witnesses to the commission who maintained that no Orangemen were involved in the riots. Harris Bindon, the sub-inspector of constabulary, saw some of Drew's congregation marching to church. There were about 300 men 'many with women on their arms'. Generally speaking, they were 'all respectably dressed men … and steady looking, above the labouring class'. Many 'wore white kid gloves'. He maintained that the riotous crowd was composed of boys of 18 or 19 and none of Drew's congregation were involved. However, he was forced to admit that 'the Orangemen are considered to be well armed'.[23]

Considering the extensive use of firearms in the riots, it is hard to believe that the main participants were young lads and women from the very lowest social class who presumably could not have afforded firearms. The use of firearms suggests the involvement of Orangemen. Indeed, it would be unusual if they, as defenders of Protestantism, held aloof once their district was under attack from the Catholic enemy. Resident Magistrate Tracy suspected that many in the mob belonged to the Orange society and that they could be called together quickly even without the use of placards.[24] The evidence shows that the crowds contained youths, women and men, some of whom were most probably Orangemen.

Once it is accepted that Orangemen were involved, Drew's sermon becomes very relevant although it still does not explain why such prolonged and serious riots occurred in 1857 and not in any previous years when the Orangemen were also treated to an inspiring anti-Catholic tirade. Tracy suggests that the election violence of April 1857 may have contributed to the bad feeling in the

Pound and Sandy Row. However, the violence does not appear to have exceeded that of an ordinary election and there was no rioting in the Pound or Sandy Row districts.[25] There was also no visible increase in tension in the two districts prior to the twelfth of July so the April election cannot be considered as a major factor.

Considering the fairly regular clashes on the Twelfth since the 1840s, perhaps it was only a matter of time before a more serious riot occurred. Although the Twelfth in 1856 was peaceful, there had been some rioting in July in all the previous years of the decade and in 1852, the rioting was serious, resulting in house wrecking on a large scale and three gunshot injuries and one death.[26] The celebration of the Twelfth, even without parades, arches and banners, always contained the seeds of a potentially serious riot such as that of July 1857. The riot commissioners rejected the notion that the existence of the Orange Order was justified because of the existence of the Ribbon society. Tracy gave evidence to the effect that although Ribbonism had been a force in the town, arrests and clerical denunciation had fatally weakened it.[27] Considering the institutional weakness of the Catholic Church in Belfast before the 1860s, it is doubtful whether clerical denunciation would have had such an overwhelming effect and whether the Ribbon society organised the Catholic rioters or not, they clearly had stores of weapons to use against their rivals. The riot commissioners also rejected the Ribbon society justification argument because Belfast was an overwhelmingly Protestant town in which the Sandy Row population should have felt secure. However, the superiority of the Pound forces at times during the 1864 riots, possibly assisted by the Fenian society, demonstrates that the Sandy Row Protestants faced a formidable rival despite the Protestant nature of the town in general. While the celebration of Orange anniversaries was obviously a cause of riots, the celebrations and the existence of the society were a reflection of the underlying conflict between the two communities, a conflict inspired by fear in both communities, not just within the Catholic community.

The causes of the September riots are clear. The street preaching controversy, occurring as it did after the riots of July, predictably led to a renewal of disturbances. It should be noted that Protestant street preaching per se did not offend Catholics. Non-controversial ministers had been preaching at the customs house for years without disturbance.[28] The announcement that the Orange ministers Drew, McIlwaine and subsequently Hanna were to preach provoked a violent response from the Pound and other Catholics still embittered from the riots of July.

The seriousness and longevity of the September riots can be accounted for by the legitimacy afforded to the aims of the rioters by their wider communities. Hugh Hanna obviously encouraged his supporters to defend with violence if necessary their 'blood bought and cherished rights' to preach the gospel and sections of the Protestant middle class also encouraged the rioters. When the magistrates had persuaded the Church of Ireland ministers not to preach at the customs house, the *Belfast Newsletter* declared that 'Romish mob rule is now triumphant'. Belfast was 'now like any southern city such as Kilkenny or Cork where priests and their mobs are in control' and the gospel cannot be preached.[29]

The unreliability of the local authorities in suppressing disturbances and protecting Catholics was a major factor in creating sympathy for the rioters in the wider Catholic community. There were numerous accounts of mill girls being intimidated in front of the local police and on one occasion they stood by while a Protestant crowd wrecked houses in Albert Street supposedly because they were waiting for military support. Once the military arrived a Catholic crowd had formed in opposition and it was they who were charged rather than the Protestants.[30] Tracy, the Resident Magistrate, admitted to Dublin Castle that the local police were 'of very little use in cases of popular commotion. With the exception of very few of them, their sympathies are strongly with the Orange party, and, for very sufficient reason, they fear to enter the Catholic quarter of the town except where accompanied by the constabulary or the military.'[31]

The perceived bias of the town police led to some support in the wider Catholic community for the use of force in self defence and in riots the dividing line between 'defence' and 'attack' is often hard to define. A letter to the editor of the Catholic *Ulsterman* argued that 'if the Orangeman takes the law into his own hands, he will be slow in his attack if he understands that men are prepared to meet him and not to wait for the delusive protection of lingering magistrates and a tardy police.'[32] This line of thinking led to the establishment of a Catholic gun club supported by the *Ulsterman* in early August. About 300 'boys' of between 17 and 20 attended its first meeting which was chaired by a marine store keeper. They paid in subscriptions to buy the guns and then drew lots to see who would receive a gun. The Resident Magistrate Tracy told Dublin Castle that it was 'intended for dramatic effect' and indeed it was dissolved after the report of the riot commissioners blamed the Orange Order and its celebrations for the riots and the lord lieutenant declared that no Orangemen would be given the commission of the peace.[33] Another example of the legitimacy enjoyed by the rioters was that collections were made to pay for the fines imposed for rioting, amounting to between £80 and £90 in July. After the street preaching riots, over £60 was collected in one day to pay the fines of Catholic rioters.[34]

The report of the commissioners recognised the importance of the street preaching riots for community relations in general.

> The pious and weak minded of the Protestant inhabitants were easily persuaded that the question at issue was whether Protestant worship was to be put down by violence while those of the Catholic inhabitants were as easily persuaded that the question at issue was now whether Belfast

was henceforth to be proclaimed as a Protestant town in which Catholics could barely find sufferance to live in a state of degradation. The former class became, by this teaching, almost the supporters of the mobs of Sandy Row and the latter of the mobs of Pound Street.[35]

The clashes between the rioters not only divided the town in general, the knock-on effect was that this wider support encouraged the combatants by legitimising their cause. It should be noted that the Orange ministers such as McIlwaine and Hanna cannot be credited with implanting extremism amongst the Protestant mob. They legitimised their actions and gave them a cause to fight for which attracted wide support among Protestants. However, Hanna was hooted by the Protestant crowd when he acquiesced in the magistrates' demand not to preach in early September. As Tracy said in his report, Hanna was dancing to the tune of the extreme Protestant faction not the other way around.

In August 1864 serious riots broke out after some Belfast Catholics returned from the foundation stone laying ceremony of the O'Connell statue in Dublin and a crowd of people from Sandy Row attempted to carry a burning effigy of O'Connell into the Pound. The riot involved crowds from Sandy Row and the Pound as well as the navvies working at the docks and the Protestant ship carpenters. Over 12 days, pitched battles were conducted with stones and guns. Churches, schools and a female penitentiary were attacked. Two aspects distinguish this riot from previous riots: the extensive and deadly use of firearms and the involvement of the Fenian society. During the 1864 riots, 98 people were wounded by bullets (and 217 suffered lacerations or stabs) compared to 2 wounded by bullets in 1857.[36] These casualties, along with other evidence, reflect the fact that this riot was most probably a war between the Orange society and the Fenian society, a fact which has not previously been recognised in the literature. The causes of this riot were predominantly political; i.e., the clash between the aspirations of nationalism, represented by the excursion to Dublin for the O'Connell ceremony and the involvement of the Fenian society, and unionism, i.e., the Protestant working-class opposition to the Fenian society and nationalist goals. As with all riots, there was also an element of local rivalry due to Protestant resentment at their rivals being able to attend parades in the south while Orange parades were banned in the north.

The Sandy Row inhabitants made elaborate preparations for their 'ceremony'. Some of the men had made an effigy of O'Connell which the women then dressed in a coat, trousers and a hat. Catholics who saw the effigy also maintained that it had a large cross on its breast and beads around its neck.[37] A drummer marched through the district tapping his drum to bring the people out of their houses and a crowd of around 5-6000 soon gathered around the effigy. As the Dublin train pulled in, the mob set fire to the effigy on the Boyne bridge. They 'kept shouting and drumming [and] commenced to beat the effigy with sticks. Some of the crowd shouted "to hell with the Pope". They halted on the bridge for some time when some persons shouted to "go on" meaning to advance into Durham Street which leads to the Pound.' Only the despatch of large numbers of constabulary prevented the crowd from proceeding into the Pound. The next day, a crowd from Sandy Row proceeded to the Catholic Friar's Bush cemetery with a coffin containing the ashes of the effigy and insisted on 'burying Dan O'Connell'. The gatekeeper succeeded in repelling them with his rifle and the crowd returned to Sandy Row and threw the ashes in the Blackstaff river. A rumour was circulated that Christ Church was to be attacked and some of the Protestants attempted to surge into the Pound but were prevented by the constabulary.[38]

The next day, according to the Resident Magistrate Orme, the Catholic party 'showed a spirit of retaliation'. Preparations had been made to repel any attack from Sandy Row. Stones had been collected and piled up on street corners. The next two evenings crowds clashed in Durham Street, the riot act was read and the police had trouble separating the combatants and themselves sustained injuries from both sides. At 1am when the police thought the rioting had ceased, they heard that the crowds were reassembling and 'that persons were going around the Sandy Row and Pound districts knocking at the doors of the inhabitants and calling on them to turn out'. In these two days, several arrests from both sides were made and the Methodist chapel on the Falls Road was attacked. The next morning at 5.30 a.m., mill girls from both sides were assaulted on their way to work and subsequently houses belonging to the minority in both districts were wrecked, a Protestant crowd attacked the Catholic penitentiary for fallen women and a Catholic crowd attacked the Revd Dr Cooke's church. The resident magistrate visited the Pound district during the day with two priests and found the people 'in a state of great anxiety and alarm and very much afraid of the opposite party'. They said something to the effect of 'however much they might bear themselves, they would never suffer their women to be beaten in the open street'. Mill girls from Sandy Row were also attacked in the Pound on their way to mills on the Falls Road. Work actually had to be suspended in many mills due to the absence of workers 'many of them no doubt having been participators in the disturbances while others were kept away by fear or curiosity'.[39]

The case of Mary Anne Murphy, a Catholic mill worker at Murphy's mill, Tea Lane, provides a typical example of workplace intimidation. After leaving work, she was grabbed by a group of girls and dragged along by her hair. Her clothes were torn off and one girl hit her in the eye with a stone. A local policeman had refused to see her safely over the bridge. The common response to this request appeared to be 'go to hell for a Papist bitch you have not got half enough'. In one girl's case, when the police refused to protect her, two Protestant girls came to her rescue and said, 'that them that would touch me would touch them and they gave me a plaid to put on me and I said God bless them both'.[40]

The Revd Isaac Wilson provided the commissioners with a heart rendering account of residential intimidation.

> The mobs in my neighbourhood not only hunted poor Catholics out of their houses, but I had to go and beseech them to grant as many hours to these poor people to take their furniture out of the place. I had to go and get horses and carts to remove the furniture and I had a great deal to do to repress the violence of the mob … I could have sat down and wept when a poor little girl came with a pet canary in a cage, when the poor people had been driven from their houses, the children in one direction and the father and mother in another. I had to protect a family in whose house there was a dying person and I believe the death had actually taken place in the house when they were obliged to vacate.

This minister also saved two people being chased by a mob with hatchets and bayonets and put up families in his own house after they had been driven from their homes. The unfortunate people who could not call on friends or relatives for help had to sleep under hedges on the outskirts of town.[41]

Intimidation of mill workers appears to have increased the ferocity of the two sides who started to use firearms and rioted that night until 5.30 a.m. The rioting died down in the next couple of days only to be renewed with even more violence on the Catholic holiday, the feast of the assumption, the 15th of August. A large crowd, mainly navvies employed on the new docks, assembled near St Malachy's. After considerable shouting 'a large mob of several hundreds' marched through the main streets to the Protestant Brown's Square district 'armed with firearms and other weapons'. They fired shots while going through the streets and 'caused great terror and alarm. A general wrecking of houses then ensued and shortly after this the mob commenced an attack upon the Brown Street national school in which there were at the time several hundred children.' Several windows were broken and shots were fired. Several children were hurt by stones and one girl was severely injured. The navvies then attacked the houses in the locality. 'The sashes were torn off the windows and the timber was flung about the street or thrown through the open spaces of the houses at the inhabitants. This wrecking of houses which caused the utmost terror to the inmates lasted about 15 minutes.' A group of workmen from a nearby foundry then appeared and drove the navvies away and into the Pound. Here they clashed with Sandy Row inhabitants who had assembled after hearing of the attack on the school. The Sandy Row crowd were heavily outnumbered and surprised by the navvies' widespread use of firearms. A man hoisted an Orange handkerchief on a pole in Willow Street and went around calling on the inhabitants "to rally".' The battle became more equal after the mills closed and the Sandy Row men brought out their firearms. Shots were fired by both sides but eventually the constabulary managed to drive them into their own areas. 'Here they remained shouting defiance to each other, the Pound party clapping stones in their hands.' Raids by small detached parties continued while a crowd from the Pound entered the town centre, throwing stones and causing great terror among the inhabitants, before attacking Dr Cooke's church. A crowd from Sandy Row went to St Malachy's which men from the Pound were defending. 'A regular engagement then took place in which firearms were freely used on both sides.' Several on both sides were wounded by bullets before the military and constabulary dispersed them. Rioting continued in parts of the town throughout the entire night. A Catholic was fatally shot and died two days later. The sub inspector of constabulary told Dublin Castle that if such a large force of military and constabulary had not been present 'so infuriated were the people of different creeds,...scenes of violence would have been witnessed in Belfast without a parallel in the annals of any civilised community'.[42]

The next day, a small group of constabulary protecting Catholic workers going to work in Sandy Row were assaulted by a crowd throwing stones. After they had driven the policemen off the bridge, the crowd shot at them and the reinforcements which had been sent. In self defence, a sub inspector ordered his men to fire. Several people in the crowd were wounded, two fatally. One of those killed, John McConnell, was reported to have been a leading member of the Sandy Row crowd and his wife allegedly dressed the O'Connell effigy. At the same time, crowds were shooting at each other in Millfield and several wounds were sustained before a magistrate ordered the military to fire which succeeded in dispersing the rioters. Several hundred Protestant ship carpenters stopped work and 'rushed through the streets, shouting defiance to the opposite party'. They ran up Brown's Square where 'they were cheered by the inhabitants and here too received a large addition to their numbers'. They marched to High Street and broke into gun shops and hardware stores stealing guns, spades and shovels. Gun shop owners in sympathy with the carpenters were told that the guns would be returned as 'they were the right sort'. The ship carpenters then headed for the docks, presumably in search of the navvies, but troops and police prevented a confrontation. On the same day, a crowd from Sandy Row attacked the Dublin train because they believed the 'Dublin coal porters were coming to Belfast to join the navvies'. According to the constabulary report, 'inoffensive passengers' as well as any Catholic reinforcements were 'attacked in the immediate vicinity of the local police office who took no steps to disperse the mob'.[43]

The next day, military and police reinforcements were heavily deployed in the riotous districts and 'their presence tended in a great measure to keep the unruly spirits of both sides in some degree of subjection'. A meeting of magistrates decided to search the Sandy Row and Pound districts for arms and 'although only a few stands were seized, fewer shots were afterwards heard in the disturbed districts'. The town was, however, deceptively tranquil. In the afternoon, a large crowd of ship carpenters, armed with guns and other weapons, arrived at the docks where the navvies were working. The navvies retreated behind a pile of stones, one of them fired a shot and another went to the entrance and defied the carpenters to come in. The carpenters rushed in, a battle ensued with deadly weapons used by both sides. The navvies were ultimately defeated and forced to retreat into the mud where they were in danger of drowning due to the incoming tide. Eventually the military and constabulary arrived and rescued the navvies from the mud. Both sides received bullet wounds and one navvy, Neil Fagan, later died. The saturation deployment of the military prevented further outbreaks.[44]

The funerals of those killed in the riots provided another potential flashpoint for renewed rioting. The victims on both sides were buried on the same day. Most of the funerals passed over quietly, the Catholic priests refusing to officiate unless the funeral parties were restricted to friends and family of the victims. However, the funeral of John McConnell, the Protestant shot by the police in Sandy Row, was massive and was attended by sympathisers not just from Sandy Row but from middle-class districts. Magistrates told the commissioners that many respectable people were in the parade and many processionists openly carried arms which was a criminal offence. In Donegall Place, described as one of the best streets in Belfast, the residents encouraged the procession to deviate from its route in order to challenge the Catholic crowd which had assembled at Castle Place. Shots were fired by both sides and a fierce riot ensued. The magistrate, Lyons, who was supposed to be supervising the parade, failed to disarm or arrest any of the people in the procession and did not attempt to force the procession to keep to the direct route to the burying ground. Indeed, he was cheered by the procession. The military and constabulary managed to prevent any further outbreaks of rioting but the tension continued and on the following day a Catholic was killed in a sectarian shooting in Smithfield. Resident Magistrate Orme described it as 'the last episode of these tragic events'.[45]

The riots were finally brought to an end because of the exhaustion of the participants and the overtures of the 'peace committee', a cross community group of clerics, employers and local notables. Those with influence were sent to the respective sides, such as Hanna and McKenna, the editor of the Catholic *Ulster Observer*, and convinced them to go home and be quiet with an assurance that the other side would do the same. The committee was also relatively successful in getting workers reinstated in the mills and the shipyard who had left due to intimidation. However, this appeared to only be tolerated by the other workers on the condition that they not give evidence against anyone from the establishment.[46] Grimshaw, one of the local magistrates and a mill owner, stated that the work of the peace committee was made easier by the rioters' exhaustion. 'The people were in a state of perpetual fear, not going to bed at night. They never slept or worked or left their districts'.[47] The magisterial report stated that the 'stress and strain has made the people nervous, sleepless and more prone to diseases.'[48] The formation of the cross community peace committee was possible because the riots were essentially a battle between two working-class secret societies and their supporters with no wider issue such as street preaching to divide the rest of society as in 1857. Although many in the wider Catholic and Protestant communities would have supported the general political views of the combatants (i.e., nationalism and opposition to it), the future of Ireland was not hanging in the balance in 1864 as it was later in 1886 so the Protestant and Catholic middle classes were not so divided that they could not work together to end the riots.

Despite this peace initiative, the rioters, particularly the Protestants, appeared to have enjoyed some middle-class encouragement. The navvies' rampages through the town undoubtedly increased middle-class Protestants' fears of the Catholic mob. As Frank Wright has pointed out, in this situation it is a question of whose violence one fears most and this tends to make people side with their own.[49] The commissioners were astounded at the middle-class participation in McConnell's funeral procession and the support afforded to it by the well off residents of Donegall Place. As McConnell was shot by the authorities suppressing riots in self defence, such a display of sympathy with the mob 'is perfectly astounding in persons of the class of life who are represented to have exhibited it'. The commissioners declared that the procession should never have been allowed. It was especially 'menacing' as 'it was not made merely by people in McConnell's own rank and file, but largely, if not mainly, by persons whose position was such that any supposed sympathy on their part with any section of the rioters, was likely to prove the surest stimulant to further violence'.[50] Fortunately, the rioters' exhaustion and the exertions of the peace committee prevented this display of support from encouraging further violence.

There is strong evidence to suggest that the 1864 riots became a battle between the Fenian and Orange societies. It probably did not start out as such. Although there were men, and presumably Orangemen, involved in the burning of the effigy, many witnesses stated that many of the initial clashes in this, as in many other riots, involved youths or 'boys' and the men joined in subsequently once it had become serious. The Belfast Fenian leader, Francis Roney, states in his autobiography that, although it pained him to be fighting fellow Irishmen, he and the other Fenian leaders decided that the Orangemen were beyond hope as they were convinced supporters of British rule. They decided to teach the Orangemen a lesson and thrashed them.[51] The Fenian involvement probably dates from the day of the attack on the Brown Street school when the Catholics surprised the Protestants with their large numbers and the widespread use of firearms. Roney seems to have forgotten the rout of the navvies, as had the Pound residents when they displayed an arch in the 1880s with the slogan 'Remember 1864'.[52] An episode in the riot which also suggests Fenian involvement is the Sandy Row attack on the Dublin train which they believed to be carrying coal porters coming to help the local Catholics.[53] This network of support outside the Belfast area and the fact that porters were one of the groups most attracted to Fenianism indicates that they may have been Fenian reinforcements. It is strange, however, that there is little reference to the Fenian society in the magisterial and police reports of the riots sent to Dublin Castle or in the 1864 commissioners' report. John Rea, the solicitor who cross-examined witnesses to the commission on behalf of the Catholic community, asked a magistrate whether he had seen a secret document stating that 'these riots were in point of fact, a pitched battle between the Fenian and Orange associations in the streets of Belfast'.[54] If this secret document existed, it unfortunately cannot be found in the Dublin Castle records.

Without more evidence, it cannot be stated unequivocally that the Fenian society was involved. However, by 1865, Fenianism was undoubtedly a strong force among Belfast Catholics so Roney's claims are believable, especially as he admits it pained him to be fighting fellow Irishmen. The arch commemorating the nationalist 'victory' in the 1864 riots is also an indication that it was a Fenian/Orange battle. The local authorities may not have known of the existence of Fenianism in the town in 1864. It was, after all, a secret organisation and Roney states that they had preserved their secrecy well until 1865. Their actions, in engaging in battles with the Orangemen, were not that different, except in the widespread use of guns, from previous Catholic crowd organisers so the Orangemen may not have noticed the hand of this secret society behind the riots. The local authorities in Belfast tended to try to keep any information about Fenianism from the public if possible so if they did suspect Fenian involvement this could account for their silence on the matter.

Although the Pound and Francis Roney regarded the 1864 riots as their victory due to the Pound's success in the gun battles with Sandy Row, the Protestants regarded the ship carpenters' routing of the navvies with equal pleasure and commemorated the occasion with scores of ballads.[55] Perhaps such an equilibrium was necessary for the two sides to be receptive to the overtures of the peace committee.

The 1872 riots were a trial of strength between the local nationalist forces and their working-class Protestant opponents. The party processions act was repealed in this year and, as the Orange party had done, the newly formed Home Rule Association decided to have an impressive parade. There is good evidence that many Fenians, as well as moderate nationalists, were involved in the Home Rule Association[56] and the banners in the parade reflected their influence. The procession consisted of between 20 and 30,000 people with bands and banners with slogans such as 'Remember 1798' and harps without crowns. The police report of the procession stated that the 'most conspicuous object was a boy dressed in green mantle trimmed with white and gold and mounted on a white horse with green trappings'. He was said to represent Ulster.[57]

Such a parade with 'seditious emblems' from the centre of Belfast to Hannahstown was not tolerated by working-class Protestants. Encouraged by Hugh Hanna, who had expressed concern for the safety of his church at Carlisle Circus where the march was to begin, a Protestant crowd gathered at the church and attacked the parade. The parade organisers had failed to follow the advice of the town's Catholic magistrates to begin the march from the Linenhall instead. As the parade passed along the Falls Road, it was again attacked at the brickfields, a no man's land linking the Falls and the Protestant Shankill. The procession eventually made it to Hannahstown where the people were addressed by the home ruler Joseph Biggar. Guns were sent out to the procession as a result of the attacks in the morning and one man accidentally shot himself. Meanwhile a group of Protestant labourers from Harland and Wolff shipyards rampaged through the town with bludgeons and attempted to enter the Catholic Hercules Street district but the police prevented a clash. The home rule procession, proceeded by a band of 'roughs' for protection, made it back to town unmolested and dispersed peacefully. 100 people were arrested during the clashes surrounding the procession and the Protestants' attempted invasion of Hercules Street.[58]

The town was then quiet until 10 p.m. when a Sandy Row mob attempted to roll tar barrels into the Pound. They clashed with police who prevented their invasion but the crowd exacted revenge and succeeded in breaking all the windows in the police barracks. The next day, rioting resumed on a larger scale, particularly in the evening. On Saturday, after the closure of the mills, 'it became apparent that in the interval the opposing parties had organised their forces and two hours later the streets rapidly filled'. By order of the magistrates, the public houses were closed but this had only a limited effect as crowds broke into pubs and distributed alcohol amongst themselves. Rival crowds fought with sticks, stones, spears in the ends of walking sticks, skull crackers, pointed irons, cleavers and bludgeons, aided occasionally by firearms in the brickfields on the Falls Road. By evening, the brickfields was a battle zone with serious clashes between massive crowds. Troops and police repeatedly charged the combatants and eventually succeeded in dispersing them. As the riots became more serious, there were paradoxically fewer arrests as the police and military concentrated on protecting life and property and the increasing violence of the crowds made arrests more difficult.[59]

On Sunday, the funeral of the man accidentally shot at Hannahstown took place. A potential clash was prevented by the priest organising the funeral procession for two hours earlier than had been announced. However, there was a 'most serious' but unrelated clash between two crowds in Lettuce Hill in the

Pound. Firearms were used by both sides and several people were wounded, three seriously, before the police succeeded in separating them. The arrival of military and police reinforcements meant that the rioting ceased to consist of such large scale battles and tended to take the form of smaller, shorter encounters as well as armed gangs roaming their districts, threatening individuals of the opposite religion and wrecking their houses.[60]

It was difficult for the authorities to constantly occupy every single back street in order to prevent house wrecking and intimidation and even when police were on the scene, they often faced determined opposition from the crowds. In one case on the Shankill, the police stationed there to protect a man who had been beaten came under such a concerted attack and had to fire in self defence which resulted in one injury. Most of the house wrecking took place in the mixed streets in the border areas of the Shankill and Falls districts. Sometimes the victims were warned by friendly neighbours, or in the more sinister manner of a threatening notice whilst others were physically evicted and saw their furniture burnt on the street. By the end of the riots, in which 247 houses were damaged and 837 families and 14 lodgers had to flee their homes, these streets had become almost entirely Catholic or Protestant.[61]

By Wednesday, 21 August, the rioting had abated somewhat but intimidation and house wrecking continued and shots were fired during the night. By Friday and Saturday, there was still some excitement in the disturbed districts but the rioting had ceased and normalcy gradually returned. The magisterial and police reports suggest exhaustion and lack of money as the main reasons for the cessation of hostilities along with the deployment of huge numbers of police and military. Many of the combatants had not worked since the outbreak of the riots and they could no longer afford to stay away from their places of employment, some of which had been closed as a result of the riots. By the time the riots had ceased, over 150 people had been wounded, 37 of whom required lengthy stays in hospital, one policeman had been killed, 76 had been wounded, 271 people had been arrested for rioting and 837 families had had to flee their homes.[62]

The immediate cause of the riots was the repeal of the party processions act and the resumption of processions. The Orange parade on the twelfth of July had passed without incident but a significant portion of the Protestant working class were not prepared to afford the same courtesy to the nationalists. Many of the magisterial reports mention Hanna as being 'most injudicious, if not culpable, in his prominent interference relating to the procession on the 15th which must have much tended to excite opposition'.[63] However, behind this tribal trial of strength, the riots represented a wider political conflict. The Belfast nationalists had challenged Sandy Row and the Shankill by matching their Twelfth parade with a home rule procession. Marching was equated with the overall political state of play as it is today. If a home rule parade had been allowed to march unmolested in Belfast, in the eyes of working-class Protestants, it would have indicated Belfast's acquiescence to home rule.[64]

From 1872 onwards, no nationalist parade could take place in Belfast without it being attacked. Although both sides participated in battles, attacks and house wrecking, the Catholics seem to have felt themselves to have been the defeated victims and appeared traumatised and shocked by the experience. In the aftermath of the riots, Belfast Catholics founded the 'Ulster Catholic Association' to secure equal civil rights and privileges, religious freedom and to maintain the public peace. All male Catholics over 16 and of good character could join and the organisation was based on parishes. The *Daily Examiner* editorial emphasised the necessity of such an organisation because royal commissions could not protect Catholics in riots and could not stop employment discrimination. Countless merchants received money from Catholic customers, the paper claimed, who would not employ a Catholic porter. It was hoped that the organisation would 'present a barrier to the system of exclusiveness which now forms the very worst feature of Orange aggression.'[65]

After 1872, the Conservative mayor James Henderson and Catholic clerical leaders agreed to try to keep processions outside the town boundaries.[66] In 1875, this arrangement broke down and party processions were permitted in the town centre but the Catholic community often abstained from parading on St Patrick's day or the 15th of August as it nearly always led to riots as Protestants attempted to attack the parades. However, the Orangemen were in a much stronger position both in terms of numbers and influential local support. The Orangemen mustered in such numbers that it was difficult for the Catholics to mount a challenge, especially when the local authorities did their utmost to protect the procession.[67] The legality of processions made them increasingly acceptable even to Protestant Liberals. In 1883, for example, the *Northern Whig* suggested that Catholics should not be offended by the Twelfth parade although its size and pageantry had grown to such an extent that most of the town was engulfed by it.[68] There were still clashes on the Twelfth but the positions of the crowds had changed since 1872. Previously both sides had been in opposition to the authorities but after 1872 the law protected the right of Orangemen and their supporters to parade. The law gave the same right to Catholics but the reality of the opposition of the Protestant majority meant that Catholic leaders generally dissuaded their followers from exercising this right.

On some occasions, Protestant and Catholic workers were able to temporarily put aside their political and religious differences to further their economic goals. During the linen workers strike of 1874, the Orangemen appeared to have celebrated in a particularly sensitive way and Catholics appeared readier to tolerate the Orange display. The magisterial report declared that the day 'presented a marked contrast to former years'.[69] Over

20,000 workers comprising 'Protestants, Catholics, Orangemen and Fenians' were reported to have attended strike meetings. During the previous linen strike in 1872, the strike leaders also emphasised the need for unity. One declared, 'religion is very good for the soul, but in the meantime we must have unity in our ranks in order to provide for the wants of the body'.[70] However, this solidarity was unable to flourish or develop into a political alliance as the depression in the linen industry made trade union activity difficult[71] and the intensification of the conflict between nationalism and unionism left little room for the development of socialist politics. Indeed, despite the display of solidarity in May 1872, terrible riots broke out three months later, dispelling any hopes of an end to working-class sectarianism.

The 1886 riots were the worst of the nineteenth century. They lasted sporadically from early June until late September and claimed the lives of 32 people; 371 others were injured, and countless numbers were expelled from their jobs or their homes. The severity of the riots reflected the fact that Gladstone's conversion to home rule meant that the future of Ireland and that of the two communities in Belfast hung in the balance. These riots differed from previous riots in that they were essentially a battle between Protestant crowds and the constabulary. There was a general belief among working-class and some middle-class Protestants that the government had sent police reinforcements from the south to Belfast to 'put down the Protestants' and crush their opposition to home rule. Although there were some clashes between Protestant and Catholic crowds and the usual intimidation and house wrecking, the Catholics were comparatively passive during the riots, allowing the constabulary and the Protestant crowds to fight it out. In their campaign, the Protestant rioters received widespread sympathy, and even support, from respectable people in their own areas, clergymen such as Hanna and Kane, conservative newspapers such as the *Belfast Newsletter*, members of parliament such as de Cobain and some local magistrates. The extensive legitimacy enjoyed by the Protestant rioters and the critical political situation account for the longevity and seriousness of the riots which were unparalleled in the nineteenth century.

The 1886 riots erupted during the excitement surrounding the general election and the first home rule bill. During a fight between a Protestant and a Catholic dock labourer, the Catholic told the Protestant that none of 'his sort' would get work once the home rule bill had passed. The ship carpenters on nearby Queen's Island heard of this incident and about 100 of them launched a massive attack on the navvies who were taken by surprise and routed. Many had to take to the water and one lad of 17 called Curran drowned. The ship carpenters had to be protected from Catholic crowds by police escort on their way home to the Shankill. The funeral for Curran was attended by thousands and the police had to keep back Protestants intent on attacking the procession.[72]

Over the next two days, crowds on the Shankill clashed with police who had been stationed in the district to protect Catholic pubs. On the second evening, the 8th of June, a small party of police protecting a Catholic public house were forced to retreat. Reinforcements were sent but they came under attack from 'a mob of some hundreds of people'. The riot act was read, the police fired and 'due to great confusion' some policemen misunderstood and kept firing. As the crowd yelled, 'Murder the Fenian whores', the police managed to retreat and have their wounds attended to. On the following day, the Protestant workmen of Coombe foundry were charged by the police as they left work in a group although there was some doubt as to whether they were a 'mob' or not. This heightened the ill feeling against the police. In the evening, another Catholic pub on the Shankill was attacked as were the police endeavouring to defend it.[73]

Revd Dr William Johnston described how he and Hanna attempted to control the crowd on the Shankill. They addressed the crowd of 2000 on some vacant land and 'told them of the folly and wickedness of fighting the police. They heard us most patiently but at the same time when our presence was gone, they occupied their position on the Shankill Road again'. He and Hanna took one crowd each and tried to keep them calm but 'they were a very riotous and ill disposed set, and were particularly anxious for the enjoyment of stone throwing'. Hanna and Dr Johnston tried to calm the crowd and negotiated with the magistrates that the police should return to their barracks. This apparently encouraged the crowd who then attacked the barracks. A district inspector who was present recalled, 'they thought we were retiring before them and rushed on us'.[74] The police fired on the crowd, killing one boy and two women who, the evidence suggests, were not rioters but onlookers. Johnston believed the police were justified in firing at first but not subsequently once the crowd had dispersed.[75] The commission report concluded that not every shot was necessary but the police were forced to fire or the crowd would have wrecked the barracks and endangered the lives of the police inside. In Sandy Row, the Albert Street barracks were attacked and the police were also forced to fire. An executive committee of magistrates decided to withdraw the police from patrolling duties in the Shankill and other disturbed Protestant districts and use the military instead until the decision was changed in early August.[76]

Rioting continued the following day. Windows of houses were smashed in Great Victoria Street and Dublin Road, public houses were attacked in York Street and the police barracks on the Shankill was attacked again. Several Protestant clergymen and two local gentlemen formed what they called 'a living wall' between the crowd and the barracks until the military arrived. It should be pointed out that the Protestant crowd had no problem with the military and did not attack them and on occasions even walked behind them singing patriotic songs such as 'Rule Britannia'.[77]

The town was then comparatively quiet until July when there were minor disturbances when rival bands clashed in Ballymacarrett on the 7th and on the

12th slight disturbances occurred following the parade. On the 13th, serious rioting again erupted when bands clashed on the Grosvenor Road. Massive crowds soon assembled in the brickfields, in Durham Street, and on the Grosvenor Road. They fought each other and the Protestants also fought the police, the Catholics generally complying with the requests of their clergy and the police to disperse. One policeman was deliberately shot and killed by a Protestant on the brickfields. The excitement continued the following day on the Falls and the Shankill but the Catholic crowd was 'kept well in check' by the local priest, Father Magee, to whom, according to the commission report, 'much praise is due for his conduct'.[78]

The hostility between the two parties and 'the still more bitter feeling of the Protestant rioters against the police' continued but nothing of note occurred until 31 July. On that date, Hanna's annual excursion for his Sunday school children took place. He agreed with the magistrate's request not to allow bands to accompany the excursion but in the evening, two bands met the children at the station and played them through the town. This provoked serious rioting at Carrick Hill and another Catholic pub was attacked on the Shankill. Two days later, a Catholic schoolchildren's excursion was attacked upon its return despite having no bands or banners. This led to a two-hour riot in York Street between crowds numbering over 1000 and involved several hand-to-hand encounters.[79] This was followed by days of rioting against the police on the Shankill and in Ballymaccarret and between Protestant and Catholic crowds in Sandy Row and the Pound.

On 8 August, the Revd Kane chaired a meeting of residents in the Sandy Row hall which resolved not to allow the constabulary into Sandy Row and that peace would never be re-established until the police were deprived of their firearms 'which they had made such cowardly use of'. He then went to the executive committee of magistrates and told them that if they attempted to establish a police barrack in Sandy Row (which apparently they had no intention of doing), he would hold a protest meeting in the brickfields and a Catholic magistrate present insisted that he threatened that 4000 armed Orangemen would prevent a barrack being erected.[80] On 13 August, one of the few remaining Catholic workmen at Harland and Wolff was attacked by Protestant workmen and covered with tar. This atrocity caused an upsurge in rioting and the following day, a battle between crowds armed with guns took place at the brickfields. The last serious incident of the riots took place in Divis Street when a Catholic crowd attacked the police barracks after a drunk had been arrested. The police fired on the crowd, killing one person and injuring others. Paradoxically, this incident served to convince the Protestants that the police had not come there to put them down and so, tragically, the firing on a Catholic crowd helped to end the riots.[81]

The riots were accompanied by extensive and severe workplace intimidation, the tarring incident at the shipyards being one of the worst examples. Most of the Catholic workmen at Harland and Wolff were attacked or left for fear of attack. One old holder up, Newtown O'Malley, was told to 'get up, there was a girl beat last night on the Falls.' He replied, 'What's that to me. I don't even live on the Falls'. A mob of 30 men then attacked him. He had thought, 'I was so long among them that I thought they would never beat me at all, because I bore a good name.' The holder up, who had a wife and four children, could not find work elsewhere because he had prosecuted one of his attackers. Unlike in 1864, the Harland and Wolff management did not make any serious attempt to reinstate the Catholic workmen and known mob leaders were not dismissed.[82] In other establishments, such as Ewart's mill, there was also workplace intimidation which was tolerated by the management. A police head constable told the riot commissioners that the management refused to allow the police to enter the mill so that those attacking the Catholic women could be identified. When the police appeared outside the mill in order to protect workers arriving or leaving work, they were pelted with bolts, coal cinders and stones by people inside the mill. The police officer considered the women to be particularly vicious. 'We could have managed the men well enough, only for the girls. The girls were by far the worst.'[83] In contrast to Ewarts, other employers were praised by the representatives of the Catholic community for doing all in their power to stamp out intimidation.[84] The Catholic workers who lost their jobs were supported by their community through the St Vincent de Paul society.[85]

There were also cases of Catholics intimidating Protestants, particularly those who had to pass through the Falls Road on their way home from the mills to the Shankill. The congregation of the Albert Street Presbyterian church in the Pound was also attacked and the church had to be closed for two weeks and services were held elsewhere. Despite the fact that the minister had a good relationship with many local Catholics and had never experienced any rudeness or hostility in the past, his church and his sexton were targeted. His sexton was only saved by the intervention of a friendly Catholic neighbour who helped him to escape over a wall. Young men coming from near the Shankill to a meeting of communicants were attacked, as was a bridal party, the groom being splattered with mud. Once the riots had ended, the church was re-opened and some of the Catholic residents came along to wish the minister well and to help ensure that there was no trouble: an unusually happy ending to a riot saga.[86]

Obviously the conflict over home rule formed the background to the riots. The excitement surrounding the defeat of the first home rule bill on the 8th of June and the general election, which was a close fought contest in West Belfast between the nationalist Sexton and the unionist Haslett with Sexton emerging victorious, raised the tension between the Protestant and Catholic working class in Belfast. The victories and defeats of this period were extravagantly celebrated by both parties. After Sexton's victory, there were 25 to 30 bonfires in Smithfield alone and after the defeat of the home rule bill, the Protestant areas were just as demonstrative.[87] The mayor, Sir Edward Harland, declared that the nationalist party was disappointed at not getting home rule but pleased at the return of Sexton and vice versa for the Protestants 'so that the two parties had all the mental elements ready when an opportunity of their coming into contact offered itself'.[88]

There is no doubt that the Protestants in the Sandy Row and Shankill districts believed that the constabulary had been sent to Belfast to put down Protestant opposition to home rule. One of the additional magistrates sent to Belfast, Henry Keogh, RM from Louth, emphasised to the riot commission that 'this was not in my view an ordinary riot, it was more in the nature of an insurrectionary movement, there was no opposing mob. It was only against the forces of the state that the crowd were opposed. Of course, it only wanted the element of a treasonable object to make it an insurrection.'[89] The Revd Richard Irvine was told by people on the Shankill, 'It is very easy for you to reason with us but if you saw our friends shot at for doing nothing, you would understand our feelings. Sir, Mr Morley [the chief secretary] is trying to experiment on the Belfast people to see how he will be able to put down any agitation that may arise out of home rule.'[90] Another minister, Samuel McCombe, declared that

> these people, who were looked upon as ignorant people on the Falls and the Shankill Road are not at all so unintelligent or illiterate as you or other people might be disposed to think of them. I believe these people are well informed on political matters and they have an opportunity of reading the newspapers and making themselves up on all matters of political purposes.

The commissioners found this claim of intelligence hard to believe as they maintained intelligent men would not believe such rumours about the police. However, such claims were appearing in the newspapers and were supported by notables such as Hugh Hanna and the Belfast MP de Cobain. The Protestant crowds also had experienced what was probably unnecessary firing by the police and this tended to give the rumours some weight. McCombe maintained,

> the people are not so irrational as some people are disposed to believe. If the police had really shot rioters on the road, they would have said nothing ... but the idea was that the police had injured innocent people and that persons who had taken no part in the riots were riddled with bullets and many persons otherwise injured who were perfectly innocent.[91]

Many Protestant witnesses gave evidence to the commission of the police standing by as Protestant mill workers were attacked on the Falls Road and during clashes between crowds, always charging or shooting at the Protestants regardless of who the aggressors had been.[92] It is always difficult to establish what really happened in such cases but the important thing is that the Protestants believed the police were against them.

Politicians and some Protestant clerics encouraged Protestant crowds to view the police with hostility. After the defeat of the home rule bill, Hanna told his congregation,

> We stand for right and truth and liberty against the forces of error and tyranny and are resolved to resist them in whatever form they may appear. The safety for every interest that is dear to us lies in the union existing with the sister kingdoms ... It was right that the loyalty of the land should celebrate as it did the victory that God has given us through men in the House of Commons faithful to their high trust as the conservators of a great empire. But that celebration has cost us dear. It incurred the wrath of a government that has been traitorous to its trusts. And it was necessary that the government should show that the metropolis of loyal Ireland could be subdued, reduced to obedience to a rebel parliament and its rule in Ireland. The armed servants of that government are sent to repress rejoicing loyalty by the sanguinary slaughter of a people resolved to resist a wicked policy and to maintain their full relationship to the British nation and crown. The alleged offences were trivial as compared with the savage retribution resorted to by the government ... The people of the north have effective means of resistance but the time has not come to employ them. It may please God to give us the victory in an easier way. Seven martyrs to loyalty have already fallen. Their names we will devoutly cherish.

This sermon was published in full in the *Belfast Newsletter* on 14 June.[93]

The Belfast MP de Cobain added further weight to the conspiracy theories during a speech to the Belfast Constitutional Club which was also reported in the press. He maintained that he had received information from certain gentlemen in the south that the police had indicated that 'their intention in coming northwards was to carry on a war against a certain class of the inhabitants (hear, hear).' He 'deeply regretted' that any Protestants had been involved in disorder but 'the forbearance of the Protestant people of the town was taxed to the very uttermost (hear, hear) by the system of brutality and outrage, by the identification of the force of law and order with crime and provocation.[94] de Cobain also referred to the police as 'liveried assassins' because they allegedly threw a drunk man from Sandy Row into a cell on his head as a result of which he subsequently died. He also alleged that 'a considerable number of the force were in sympathy with the Land League'.[95] The minister of Christ Church in Sandy Row, Kane, also declared against the 'foreign police'. He led the opposition to any attempt to establish a barrack in Sandy Row and, according to a visiting Magistrate, during a riot told the crowd the police were keen to shoot them. Kane borrowed a policeman's stick and 'drove the mob up the street before him – his flock'. He yelled at them that 'the police were very anxious to shoot them and I told him that was not true. I was very angry myself and used very strong language to Dr Kane.'[96]

Even among some of the local magistrates there was 'a great deal of irritation about the foreign police'[97] which was reflected in their withdrawal of the police from patrols on the Shankill. Not until early August was there an official statement released affirming that the chief secretary had not chosen police from Catholic districts to come to Belfast and in fact it was the constabulary inspector who chose where reinforcements should come from and he made the decision based on the needs and resources of districts alone. The commissioners recognised in their report the importance of the absence of public support among the executive committee of magistrates for the police. Additionally, Hanna, Kane and de Cobain were chastised in the report. 'Certain persons having great influence in Belfast indulged in language written and spoken well calculated to maintain excitement.'[98]

The degree of legitimacy enjoyed by the rioters in the wider Protestant community accounts for the severity and longevity of the 1886 riots. This accords with the literature on British riots which claims that severe riots usually only occurred when the rioters believed that they enjoyed 'the wider consensus of the community' which was occasionally endorsed 'by some measure of licence afforded by the authorities.'[99] Rioters often had the sympathy of local magistrates during eighteenth century food riots and, in the case of the anti-Catholic Gordon riots in London in 1778, a degree of sympathy was shown by the city authorities. Rioters knew there was some chance of their aims being achieved and the risk of punishment was low. In some cases, such as the Gordon riots, the ambiguous attitude of the authorities was then exploited by a criminal element who felt free to run amok which increased the number of casualties and property damage.[100]

The degree of legitimacy afforded to the campaign against the police in 1886 meant that 'respectable people' such as shop keepers and shop assistants joined in the rioting. The commission report emphasised 'the sympathy with which, at certain stages, the well to do classes of Protestants regarded the proceedings of the rioters. At one stage of the riots, it seemed as if the greater part of the population of the Shankill district were united against the police.'[101] One of the magistrates stated, 'in the beginning of the riots the respectable portion of the people of the Shankill were, as a body, against the police just as much as the lower classes'. 'They took part against the police?' the magistrate was asked by the commissioner to which he replied 'yes'. The commissioner exclaimed, 'Respectable people!'[102] These people left their houses open so that the rioters could retreat and continue to attack the police.[103] Whereas shopkeepers would help the police in connection with ordinary crimes, such as drunkenness, in 'times of excitement, they would not' and generally the police would not ask for their help on such occasions.[104] During the 1886 riots, the support of these 'respectable' people was more active than during other disturbances. Col. William Forbes, Resident Magistrate, declared that after Hanna's school excursion, he saw 'a good many respectable persons throwing stones at the police. They were either belonging to the trip or friends of the trip. I went over to try to prevent them doing it, and as soon as I did, I received two blows on the head and one on the side of the face. They looked like shop assistants ... and were well dressed.'[105] Major General Moore, the commanding officer of the northern district based in Belfast, explained,

> on all these occasions, there is a residuum that comes forward. The roughs and corner boys, especially when looting is to be done, come to the front, and I think the crowd was largely composed of the members of that class; but at the same time, I think that in the attacks on the police, they had the moral support of the respectable people who live in the neighbourhood and have houses there.

He claims to have heard respectable people talking of their relatives being shot and using expressions like 'Morley's murderers'. Concerning Hanna's school excursion, he declared, 'I do not consider that the mob on this occasion was composed of roughs. I think they were largely composed of people living in the district ..., [that is] people who in ordinary times would conduct themselves.'[106]

Ministers such as Johnston and Hanna claimed none of their congregations were involved in the rioting and that the crowds were composed of the lowest classes and drunks. This is difficult to accept as it contradicts the magistrates' descriptions of the crowds, even those magistrates sympathetic to Orangeism. Johnston maintained that the crowds were composed of 'drunken, reckless, worthless, rowdy characters. A large portion of them were boys from 14 to 17 with a sprinkling of drunken men and, I am sorry to say, drunken women.' No respectable or well dressed people were in the crowd at any stage, he claimed, unless they were trying to restrain the others. He maintained, as did Hanna, that although the crowds listened to him, he did not know any of them and so could not give any names to the police. The denial of the involvement of any respectable, church going people was probably made in order to avoid having to give evidence against any of them, an offence for which their congregations would never have forgiven them.[107] Shopkeepers who gave evidence against rioters were boycotted; workers who gave evidence found it hard to keep their job or find a new one. Even an Orange publican, who gave shelter to a Catholic shopkeeper's family when his shop was attacked, was boycotted and had to sell his pub.[108] It is doubtful whether ministers would have been immune to the same social pressures. Henry Keogh Resident Magistrate from Louth, maintained that as Orangemen were 'respectable' and 'prayed in their lodges', they would not have been involved in the riots. The crowd, he believed, was composed of the same sort of people who formed the rag tail of Orange processions. These people were in sympathy with the Orange Order but not members. However, he had to admit that there were some respectable men in the crowd, people in 'the position of foreman or something of that kind'. He was then asked if 'those so called respectable persons who go on procession on the Twelfth of July, did they correspond very much with the class of persons you saw in the crowd?' – 'Yes, some of them. I saw in the crowd several respectable persons.'[109] The conclusion drawn must be that it was very probable that there were Orangemen in the crowd, as well as a higher proportion of shop assistants, foremen etc. than would usually have participated in riots.

Between the major riots of the mid to late nineteenth century there was frequent rioting surrounding school excursions and band parades as well as the periodic outbreaks of rioting on the Twelfth. A special report commissioned for Dublin Castle on band parades in Belfast identified school excursions as a frequent occasion for rioting. School excursions were usually accompanied by banners and bands which often had a political as well as a religious meaning. The processions of children to Belfast's railway stations were guarded by 'roughs' to ensure that the procession could be defended if attacked. The effect was, of course, that the procession proved a tempting target for 'roughs' of the other persuasion hanging about street corners. Once the rioting started, which usually involved breaking the windows of houses and pubs of those of the opposite persuasion as well as brawls and stone throwing, other people often joined in.[110] Resident Magistrate Colonel Forbes described Hanna's annual excursion as being 'far worse than the twelfth. There is a bodyguard that follows it and this bodyguard generally kicks up disturbances.' On one occasion, when his procession was passing, 'he stood up on a car in Royal Ave and called on the bodyguard "to do their duty".' His excursion always resulted in a riot at Carrick Hill. Either the Protestants attacked the Catholic pub or the Catholics attacked the Protestant houses or both.[111]

Impromptu band parades were also frequently the cause of rioting, particularly from the mid 1870s onwards. The number of nationalist and unionist bands increased dramatically during this period, reflecting the increasing disposable income for recreation purposes among the working class and the increasing political tension. These bands had politically poignant names such as Grattan Flute Band, Sandy Row True Blues etc. and usually had special uniforms for their members. The green uniforms of the Emmet Flute Band were described as being particularly provocative to their Protestant rivals. These bands would suddenly, without warning, start parading the streets, often provocatively marching outside their own areas and into the town centre or some other mixed district. The spectacle quickly collected a following of supporters, children, interested onlookers and 'roughs'.[112] Judging by the band parades of today, the stirring nature of the music and the political symbolism of the bands' banners and uniforms would have stirred the people's emotions and caused them to rally round. Sometimes two or even three bands would coincidentally collide and rioting was the inevitable result. In the late 1870s and early 1880s, the problem became so severe, particularly in summer, that the local authorities were requested to prepare special weekly reports for Dublin Castle. The local authorities were reluctant to accede to Dublin Castle's request that band parades be made illegal in the town and instead insisted that any law should govern the whole of Ireland. The town council believed it would be politically unpopular to stop 'loyal' bands parading in Belfast while 'disloyal' bands were permitted to parade elsewhere in Ireland. The council was only prepared to suppress the parades once a breach of the peace had been committed.[113]

In dealing with riots, the constabulary and resident magistrates were often hampered by the local magistrates who together with the mayor formed a decision making body to deal with the riots. Up to 40 local magistrates attended these meetings, often making irrelevant speeches despite the fact that few ever ventured into a riotous area. Those local magistrates who did attempt to help put down the riots sometimes exacerbated the situation as they were perceived as being biased. After the 1872 riots, one resident magistrate declared that the local magistrates admit that they would not fire on the rioters even when necessary. He emphasised that one could not expect men pursuing commercial pursuits to command the military or to fire on rioters who may well be their employees. There were also no set rules for sentencing those convicted of rioting. There was a general belief that many local magistrates were biased in their judgements. Even in cases where no bias was intended, decisions could be 'extremely various, following no given rule or principal' which one resident magistrate described as being 'injurious to peace'.[114]

The composition of riotous crowds did not change markedly in the mid to late nineteenth century. Despite the claims of some witnesses to riots that the participants were generally the lowest scum of the town, a claim that was also mistakenly made about food rioters in Britain,[115] the rioters were fairly representative of their districts. They were generally, with the exception of 1886, mill and factory workers, labourers and semi-skilled and skilled workers, men, women and children. They were not all unemployed or from a criminal underclass. The literature on British riots suggests that rioters were usually fairly representative of their communities.[116] This indicates a tacit legitimacy within their districts for their actions which was probably necessary for a serious riot to exist. The occupations of those victims of rioting in 1864 who could be identified (i.e., those treated in hospital) give an indication of the composition of the crowds. They included 36 labourers, 11 mill workers, 8 mechanics, 8 carpenters, 6 porters, 3 carters, 3 linen lappers, 3 shoe makers, 3 dealers, 3 shop keepers, 2 butchers, 2 carriers, 2 tailors, 1 sweep, 1 sexton, 1 stone cutter, 1 tin smith, 1 clerk, 1 cooper, 1 engineer, 1 horse shoer, 1 jeweller, 1 painter, 1 pipe maker, 1 printer and 1 sawyer. The magisterial report states that some were 'from their social position, unlikely to be involved in riots'.[117] However, even allowing for the probability that some were bystanders, the occupations still appear to be very representative of the districts. During a riot in the meadows adjacent to the Pound and Sandy Row which broke out while people were collecting special flowers for May day in 1865, seven people were arrested whose occupations were representative of the districts. There was one carpenter, one labourer, one hairdresser, one tobacco spinner, one butcher and two women mill workers.[118]

The magisterial report of the 1872 riot stated that the rioters were 'confined chiefly to the very lowest of the Orange and Catholic parties' including 'men, women and children of all ages'. Much of the wrecking was done by 'mobs consisting of boys and girls who are employed in mills but the hand to hand encounters took place between mobs composed chiefly of men employed in the same establishments and labourers but from the arrests which have been made it is apparent that occasionally persons of a grade superior to those indicated have taken part'. This description suggests that, apart from shopkeepers, the rioters were representative of the Sandy Row and Pound districts. In 1886, the Protestant crowd included more of those groups thought to be generally respectable, such as shopkeepers, shop assistants and foremen, because of the widespread belief that the police were deliberately attacking the Protestant community.

Apart from the addition of the navvies and ship carpenters, the composition of the crowds did not change throughout the nineteenth century. The rioting between the navvies and the ship carpenters did add a new and dangerous element to Belfast rioting, the acts of one or the other inflaming the situation in 1864 and 1886, but much of the rioting continued to involve crowds which included men of the occupations described above, women, youths and children.

Peter Gibbon argues that men became more important in riots after 1864, initiating clashes which would then draw in youths and women whereas previously riots were initiated by women and children. This forms part of his theory that prior to the 1860s, when Protestant skilled workers realised that their economic future depended on the British link, riots had local origins and the participants had no sense of a wider ethnic Catholic or Protestant identity. In fact, magistrates continued to stress the importance of clashes between children or youths in initiating skirmishes which would then become full scale riots once the men joined in. Alderman William Mullan, one of the initiators of the peace committee in 1864, emphasised to the commissioners that boys and girls in Belfast, from the fact of their getting wages and employment, will become sooner independent of their parents than in other places; and, being under their own control, they frequently act impulsively and unwisely. I know no other feature in the character of Belfast which requires to be more carefully investigated with regard to the origin of riots than the peculiar character of the boys and girls of Belfast, arising from the fact that their parents have less control over them than in other places.[119]

Charles Lanyon, the architect, local politician and magistrate, also told the 1864 commissioners that clashes begin with boys and girls collecting together and adult men do not join in 'until they assume a serious aspect'.[120] In 1886, boys were prominent in the early attacks on the police on the Shankill. One of the local magistrates giving evidence in 1886 declared, 'very often it begins with boys. From 10 to 14 years of age and then it gets up, and then the class of stone throwers and rioters are young men of from 18 to 22 or 23 years of age.'[121]

Women also continued to be involved as they had been in the earlier nineteenth century. In all the major riots in the mid to late nineteenth century, they were involved in workplace beatings and intimidation, in collecting stones for the men to throw, and sometimes throwing them themselves. David Taylor, a local magistrate, was asked by the commission in 1864, 'In these riots, as far as your experience goes, do women and children take part ? They do. – And the women are as bad as the men, I suppose ? – I think they are.'[122] One of the arguments used for not firing on the mob during a serious riot on the brickfields in 1872 was the large number of women and boys in the crowd.[123] During riots on the twelfth in 1885, twenty people, 'including several women, were charged with stone throwing or otherwise participating in the riots'.[124] In 1886, the women prised paving stones out of the street with pokers and filled their aprons with the ammunition and carried it to the men at the 'front'. They also continued to be prominent in workplace beatings and attacks on mill workers crossing enemy territory, the 'Falls Road dogs' being particularly feared by the Protestant women workers of the Broadway mill and the viciousness of the Protestant women in Ewart's mill being notorious among Catholic workers.[125]

Gibbon tries to claim that the targets of rioting changed after the 1860s from fighting in 'shatter zones' and wrecking houses to attacks on institutions.[126] In fact, both occurred throughout the nineteenth century. Institutions, such as the diocesan seminary and O'Connell's hotel, were attacked in the 1830s and 1840s and in the 1870s and 1880s there was fighting in 'shatter zones' and houses were still being wrecked. Gibbon also maintains that riots became less frequent but more serious as the nineteenth century progressed. They certainly became more serious but, if anything, they also became more frequent as the number of band parades increased.[127]

CONCLUSION

The increasing political tension between nationalism and the Protestant opposition to it was the main cause of the serious rioting in Belfast between 1851 and 1886. This political division had existed between the Pound and Sandy Row since the repeal campaign of the early 1840s. The rise of Fenianism in the 1860s and the home rule movement in the 1870s drew Pound Catholics into Irish nationalist movements and encouraged them to assert their religious and political identity and, in so doing, they threatened the sense of security of working-class Protestants. In responding to this challenge, the Protestant workers were encouraged by ministers such as Hanna and Kane and serious rioting was the result. The importance of political tension for the increase in rioting in the mid to late nineteenth century in Belfast becomes even more obvious when a comparison is made with British cities. Riots between Catholics of Irish origin and Protestants in British cities declined in the late nineteenth century as did the degree of residential segregation whereas in Belfast the opposite was the case.[128]

The rise of Irish nationalism in the 1860s and 1870s gave the battles between the two districts increased importance and urgency and this was reflected in longer, more serious riots involving the deadly use of firearms. The ritualistic exchange of gunfire described in the 1857 riots became a thing of the past as did the unofficial rules or constraints which had governed the early nineteenth-century riots. The sympathy for the aims of the rioters in their wider communities was also important for the longevity of riots, particularly in 1857 when middle-class Protestants and Catholics took their rioters' sides on the street preaching issue and in 1886 when the Protestant crowd had the sympathy of certain ministers, sections of the middle class and some local magistrates in their battle with the police. The increased legitimacy enjoyed by the rioters in their wider communities was also a reflection of the escalating tension between unionism and nationalism in Belfast society in general.

There is no evidence in magisterial reports to suggest that job competition was an immediate cause of riots and the influence of any employer bias towards Protestant workers in the development of sectarianism in the long term is difficult to assess. Hepburn's claim that ethnic conflict was 'greatly exacerbated after 1850 by competition over a limited number of skilled male jobs'[129] does not hold true for the districts where much of the rioting took place. Although the trades were predominantly Protestant and this was resented by Catholics in general, the vast majority of workers in Sandy Row and the Pound were unskilled or semi-skilled and there was little or no difference in occupational composition of the two districts according to census data and contemporary descriptions. Protestant labourers probably tended to enjoy more secure employment (see Chapter Six) but this favouritism was a result of the existing religious and political divisions in Belfast society rather than the cause of the divide. However, this favouritism may then have reinforced the division caused by religious and political differences. Certainly after the 1872 riots, the Ulster Catholic Association complained that many Protestant merchants who took money from Catholic customers would not employ a Catholic porter. The association also claimed that in some mills and workshops, less than 2% of the workforce were Catholic and 'this system of exclusiveness ... now forms the very worst feature of Orange aggression'.[130] Favouritism towards Protestant workers probably did fuel Catholic resentment which reinforced the attraction of nationalist movements. However, against this must be balanced the evidence of working-class solidarity displayed during the linen workers' strikes in 1872 and 1874. Protestant and Catholic linen workers obviously felt their economic interests were identical (rather than competitive) although their political outlooks always remained opposed. To complicate the picture, there is evidence that, to some extent, employment became tied up with the national question in some workers' minds. An example of this is the incident at the start of the 1886 riots when the Catholic dock worker told the Protestant dock worker that none of his sort will get work once home rule was granted. However, this seems to have been as much a stick with which to beat the enemy rather than a genuine expectation that jobs would be created for themselves or others in their own community. The relationship between the favourable position of Protestant workers, class conflict and sectarian attitudes is complex. The most that can be said is that the favourable position of Protestant workers, particularly their domination of skilled trades, caused a degree of resentment among Catholics which may have increased the attraction of nationalism and therefore reinforced the political and religious divide among the working class. However, during riots, the Catholics were often fighting Protestants who were as poor as themselves.

Workplace intimidation during riots appears to have been politically motivated, i.e., Catholics were expelled from the shipyards and some mills not primarily in order to provide more Protestants with jobs but to expel and punish individuals who did not share the political convictions of the majority. In times of political tension, Protestant gangs in workplaces expelled Catholics because they were seen as belonging to the other side and they did not want to work with them. Distrust and hatred were the cause of the expulsions. This was a symptom of rioting which could then fuel the feelings of hostility but it was not the cause of rioting.

The same motivation lay behind residential intimidation. Shortage of housing is never mentioned as a motivating factor for rioting in magisterial reports. Riots did not generally begin with residential intimidation of the minority in both areas. Riots began with the battles between rival stone throwing crowds and then the residential and workplace intimidation followed. Once rioting had commenced, the minority were regarded with hatred and distrust by the rioters and were commanded to leave. It would be misleading to refer to this as 'ethnic cleansing' as the rioters were not attempting to carve out ethnically pure, viable states. Although the rioting in Belfast in the mid to late nineteenth century was politically motivated, the actions of rioters did not always have an obvious political aim. Residential intimidation and the wrecking of houses did not make home rule any more or less likely during the riots of 1872 and 1886. It could be argued that violence in general, such as residential intimidation, had a political message, i.e., that the group committing the violence could not be trifled with and that the government and the group's opponents should be made aware of that fact. There is some truth in this argument. When rioters wanted an easy target for violent protest, they needed to look no further than the minority in their own areas. Once a full scale riot existed, a criminal element usually took advantage of the situation to loot and steal, particularly from public houses, and this was also a reason for house wrecking. However, often members of the minority were informed, either by friendly neighbours or by ultimatum, that they should leave by a certain time. The process then occurred without violence so, in these cases, residential intimidation was not part of a desire to make a violent political protest. The explanation must be that once rioting has commenced, the hatred and distrust of the rioters towards the other side is also directed at the minority in their midst. In many cases, the minority were saved from actually being attacked by warnings from friendly neighbours or by the vestiges of humanity possessed by the rioters who chose not to kill or injure them.

Rioting in Belfast throughout the nineteenth century was the result of religious and political division among the working class. Riots erupted on occasions of political excitement and were not caused by job or housing competition. The composition of the rioters and their targets did not change much. Riots continued to involve men, women and children who fought in 'shatter zones', wrecked houses and attacked institutions. What transformed the semi-ritualistic riots of the early nineteenth century into the long, bloody battles of 1864, 1872 and 1886 was the rise of Irish nationalism and the Protestant determination to fight against it.

Conclusion

From the early 1840s, the conflict between working-class Catholics and Protestants in areas like the Pound and Sandy Row was political. It was not a local conflict centred around competition for housing or jobs. It was a political conflict surrounding Irish nationalism which had been grafted onto an older ethnic divide based on nominal religious allegiance. Widespread support for the Fenian society and the home rule movement among working-class Catholics in the second half of the nineteenth century and the continual opposition of working-class Protestants to Irish nationalism confirmed the political division evident during the campaign for the repeal of the union in the early 1840s. Irish nationalism developed much earlier among Belfast Catholics than has previously been assumed and the Protestant working-class hostility towards it dates from the same period and had little to do with any economic advantage over their Catholic rivals (at least as far as Sandy Row Protestants were concerned). The arguments of historians, such as A.C. Hepburn and Brian Walker, that Ulster politics could have developed around something other than a unionist/nationalist divide before the 1880s must be called into question in the light of these findings.

The Repeal Association had a much greater influence among the Catholic working-class than has previously been acknowledged. The weekly meetings of the association were often attended by 2000 people, mainly from the working-class, and the introduction of special penny-a-month subscriptions for the poor meant that more people were touched by the work of the association than an examination of the total amount of rent would suggest. The nationalist ideology of the Repeal Association transcended the simpler sectarian outlook of working-class Catholics but at the same time it gave a political legitimacy to hostility towards Protestants as they were generally opponents of repeal. Moreover, whilst sectarianism was denounced by the local repeal leaders, they did not hesitate to ally the association with purely Catholic causes which intensified the association between Catholicism and nationalism. The fact that some of the repeal wardens and many members of the society were also members of the Ribbon society demonstrates that nationalism had been grafted onto existing sectarian attitudes. The tendency of historians to only consider the amount of 'repeal rent' collected in Ulster as a whole and the fact that no 'monster meetings' were held in Belfast (which was due to the risk of them provoking sectarian violence) has obscured the influence of the Repeal Association in the town.

In the 1830s and 1840s, working-class Protestants also became politicised due to their contact with evangelical ministers who mobilised them in support of Protestant causes and in opposition to repeal. Ministers such as Cooke and Drew did not have to work hard to persuade working-class Protestants that repeal would result in a Catholic ascendancy in Ireland and the persecution of Protestants. Whilst Catholic workers were becoming involved in the repeal campaign, the Protestants of Sandy Row were listening to lectures on the errors of Catholicism and the dangers of repeal in the Belfast Protestant Operatives' Association.

However, the Repeal Association and evangelical ministers did not create the divisions among the working class. The rioting of the 1820s shows that an ethnic division based on nominal religious adherence existed in the town prior to any contact with politicians or ministers. The conflict was a working-class conflict, imported into Belfast by migrants from the Ulster countryside and reflected in the establishment and growth of the Orange Order and the Ribbon society. These secret societies were nearly in a state of war with each other in parts of Ulster, particularly in the early 1820s when the circulation of Pastorini's prophecies exacerbated the fears of Protestants. The campaign for Catholic emancipation in 1828-9 re-ignited tension in Ulster generally, including Belfast where there was an upsurge in rioting on the Twelfth of July and on other occasions such as funerals.

There is no evidence of job competition or economic advantage being the cause of sectarian tension in the 1820s and 1830s. Both Sandy Row and the Pound were poor districts, populated by weavers, labourers, mill workers and a few skilled tradesmen. Weavers were particularly prominent in Sandy Row and other Orange districts such as Brown's Square and Ballymaccarret, suggesting that their social and economic decline in the early nineteenth century may have exacerbated sectarian tension. Even after the introduction of heavy industry in Belfast in the 1860s with the consequential rise in skilled trade positions, Sandy Row continued to be as unskilled in occupational make-up as the Pound. The chapter analysing the census data for the two areas in 1901 shows that the only advantage enjoyed by Sandy Row workers was that fewer of their wives had to work, suggesting that their labouring employment was probably more secure. One third of Pound wives worked compared to one fifth of Sandy Row wives. However, this minimal advantage could not have been the reason why Sandy Row Protestants supported the union. It was their Protestantism which made them support the union just as it was the Catholicism of the few skilled tradesmen in the Pound which made them support home rule despite the fact that their prosperity probably rested with the British link.

Throughout the nineteenth century, sectarian conflict was exacerbated by the absence of an impartial system of law and order. Even after the introduction of stipendiary magistrates in 1835-6, who were appointed by Dublin castle and were relatively unbiased, the behaviour of the nearly entirely Protestant town police and the local magistrates, who continued to assist the stipendiary magistrates, ensured that the justice system was not considered impartial. Although the situation improved in 1865 with the replacement of the town police by the constabulary, the influence of local magistrates was still strong enough to ensure that the Protestant crowd was often favoured during riots. This state of affairs encouraged violent action by both Catholic and Protestant crowds. Favourable treatment of the Protestant crowd, seen most clearly in the riots of 1886 when the local magistrates withdrew the mainly Catholic constabulary from the Shankill at the behest of the Protestant crowd, increased the legitimacy of rioting. Whereas Catholics believed that they were justified in using violence in confrontations with Protestants because they could not always rely on the forces of the state to protect them.

The religious distinctiveness of the Sandy Row and Pound districts increased as the influence of the respective churches became greater. This process had begun in Sandy Row in the mid 1830s when the district acquired its first church, Christ Church. The Protestant churches serving Sandy Row were all evangelical and therefore emphasised the differences between Protestants and Catholics and regarded tolerance of religious differences as a denial of true faith. The gains of the evangelical churches were consolidated during the Ulster revival of 1859 and the district acquired three new churches, two of which were served by ministers who were chaplains in the Orange Order. Although by no means all the inhabitants of Sandy Row were 'converted' during the revival, it was a phenomenon experienced by the district as a whole which was not experienced by the Catholic districts of the town. The revival could be seen as conferring God's blessing upon Ulster Protestants, even by those who were not leading evangelical lifestyles or attending church. The revival probably increased the confidence of the district, as it did for Ulster Protestants in general, by confirming their Protestantism in the face of the religious and political challenges which Catholicism was mounting in Ireland.

Meanwhile, in the early 1860s, the people of the Pound were increasingly becoming practising Catholics as opposed to nominal Catholics. Bishop Dorrian, a strong supporter of Ultramontanism, increased church attendance dramatically among Belfast Catholics and introduced Italianate devotional practises which widened the gulf between Catholicism and Protestantism. The increasingly Catholic (in religious terms) nature of the Pound strengthened its association with the rest of Ireland and heightened the appeal of nationalism whereas the Protestant workers' sense of a separate identity must have been strengthened when they encountered what they considered to be foreign religious practices.

The churches in both areas began to have an impact on popular entertainment and to some extent new 'respectable' forms of entertainment made inroads into rough working-class culture. These new respectable forms of entertainment such as young men's improvement societies and church picnics necessarily increased segregation in leisure time for working-class Protestants and Catholics. However, it is by no means certain that this respectable culture became more popular than the traditional rough forms of entertainment such as drinking in the pub or attending the singing saloon or bawdy penny theatre. The complaints about 'bullet throwing' matches in the town in the early 1880s show that new forms of non-respectable entertainment were being introduced into the town so rough working-class culture was at least holding its own. In painting a picture of two increasingly divided working-class districts, it should not be forgotten that rough working-class culture united sections of the Protestant and Catholic working-class against the values of the middle class and the respectable people in their own districts.

The importance of the Fenian society in Belfast has been overlooked by many historians, partly because of its secretive nature and partly because there is a general assumption that nationalism was not a force in Belfast until later in the century. The Dublin Castle records show that Belfast was one of the main Fenian strongholds in Ireland with over 1000 members in the mid 1860s. The local Fenians drilled, manufactured ammunition and recruited soldiers in the Belfast garrison in preparation for the intended uprising throughout Ireland. The composition of the Belfast Fenians does not fit the description of an artisan elite organisation as outlined by Comerford. Many of those arrested in Belfast were labourers or from the poorer class of artisans such as shoemakers and tailors and meetings were held in some of the poorest streets in the Pound. The fact that the Fenian society in Belfast appears to have taken over some of the functions of the Ribbon society and was led by men with long standing commitments to Irish nationalism suggests that it should be seen in the Irish context of the merged tradition of Ribbonism, constitutional nationalism and republicanism rather than in the British context of Victorian artisan organisations.

The success of the Belfast Protestant Working Men's Association in 1868 demonstrated the political independence of Sandy Row Protestants from mill owners and the local Conservative organisation but it also confirmed the virility of their anti-Catholicism which ensured they would continue to oppose Irish nationalism. Although the organisation was to some degree hostile towards big business and favoured electoral reform, it did not have the potential to evolve into a Liberal working men's association such as existed in Britain because of the importance of pan-Protestantism in its ideology. The upper classes were criticised but more for their refusal to support Protestant causes such as the repeal of the party processions act than for the exploitation of workers. However, by returning their own candidate, William Johnston of Ballykilbeg, in opposition to the conservative candidates, the Protestant workers demonstrated their political independence. The Sandy Row Protestants were not simply the tools of Conservative mill owners as some have suggested. Rather than mill owners using Orangeism to deliberately divide the working-class, the Protestant workers demonstrated by their espousal of pan-Protestantism in 1868 that they were more 'orange' than their social superiors.

The strong support for Fenianism and the early home rule movement in Belfast prove that Belfast Catholics were among the most nationalistic in Ireland and there was no possibility of them developing a regional Ulster identity prior to the 1880s or 1890s as Hepburn and Walker have suggested. The Belfast Home Rule Association was one of the earliest branches of the organisation. It was an early and enthusiastic supporter of obstructionist tactics at Westminster and in some areas of policy, most notably in its support of land nationalisation, it was more progressive than the movement as a whole. The support enjoyed by the 'real nationalists' in the 1870s is further confirmation of the strength of nationalism in Belfast. The proliferation of nationalist bands whose members paraded regularly in uniform with banners and music through the Catholic districts of the town also testifies to the degree of nationalisation of the Catholic population. The home rulers and the 'real nationalists' were motivated by the desire for Irish independence, not reform, and their speeches show that they could not have been bought off by a reforming British government sensitive to Ireland's needs.

An ethnic conflict between Catholic and Protestant workers existed prior to the development of heavy industry in Belfast. The conflict was not 'local' as Peter Gibbon has claimed. This study has found no evidence of a paternalist relationship between Sandy Row workers and mill owners which Gibbon claims is the reason for the workers' support of Orangeism. In fact, workers regarded mill owners with a degree of class antagonism and in 1868 demonstrated their political independence by voting in William Johnston.

The analysis of Belfast riots shows that the nature of rioting did not change as Gibbon has argued to reflect a change from a local to an ethnic conflict. In the first half of the nineteenth century institutions outside the 'shatter zones' were attacked and in the mid to late nineteenth century, house wrecking and rioting in 'shatter zones' continued to be a feature of Belfast rioting. The participants in riots did not change over time as Gibbon has maintained. Rioters continued to be representative of the working people in their districts and women, whom Gibbon considers to have a more limited capacity for political understanding than men, continued to participate in late nineteenth century riots.

Riots did become more serious in the latter half of the nineteenth century due to the increasing political tension in Ireland. Guns were used more widely and rioting lost its ritualistic quality which was apparent during some of the earlier riots. As the tension between nationalism and the Protestant opposition to it escalated throughout the nineteenth-century, Protestant and Catholic rioters increasingly received some sympathy from their respective middle classes. This increased legitimacy afforded to rioting is also important in accounting for the severity and longevity of the late nineteenth century riots. This accords with the literature on British riots which demonstrates that riots are more severe, the higher the degree of support from the wider community

This book ends with the riots surrounding the first home rule bill in 1886. These riots were primarily a war between working-class Protestants and the constabulary, who the Protestants believed had been sent to Belfast to put down opposition to home rule. Since the riots surrounding repeal in 1841 and 1843, opposition to Irish nationalism had been the main motivating factor behind Protestant rioting. In 1886, Protestants feared that their nightmare of being governed by their hereditary enemies was about to come true and this was reflected in the large numbers of casualties, exceeding those of all previous riots combined. The 1886 riots provide the final, overwhelming confirmation that the conflict between working-class Catholics and Protestants was political and in the Protestant attacks on the police, can be seen the precursor of the more organised unionist resistance of 1912.

Notes

INTRODUCTION

1 A.C. Hepburn, *A past apart*, pp 147-8
2 B. Walker, *Ulster politics*, p. 265.
3 P. Gibbon, *Origins of Ulster unionism*, pp 81-5.
4 F. Wright, *Two lands on one soil*.

CHAPTER 1

1 A.T.Q. Stewart, *The narrow ground*, p. 144.
2 G. McAteer, *Down the Falls*, p. 2.; *Report ... into the origin and character of the riots in Belfast in July and September 1857*, PP, 1857-8 [2309] xxvi, p. 28.
3 *Second report of the commissioners of Irish education inquiry*, PP, 1826-7 [12] xii, pp 234-9.
4 *Belfast Street Directory*, 1820, 1836-7, 1841, 1846-7, 1852; Christ Church Baptismal Records, 1837-50 (P.R.O.N.I., T679/284-5); Brown Street Sunday School Register, 1819-25 (P.R.O.N.I., SCH 580/1/1).
5 John Burrow, *A tour round Ireland*, p. 33.
6 I. Budge and C. O'Leary, *Belfast; approach to crisis*, p. 27.
7 During the famine, Catholic cottiers and small holders from poorer parts of Ulster and some from elsewhere in Ireland streamed into Belfast in the hope of finding employment. Some Catholics from the south of Ireland were employed during the famine in public works such as widening the quays in Belfast. In evidence submitted to the Riot Commissioners in 1857, a chief constable of constabulary testified that many of these Catholic workers from the south had settled permanently in Belfast, some of them in the Pound. Despite this southern migration, the census of 1861 shows that 75.2% of the Belfast population were born in Antrim, Down or Belfast, 15.8% were born elsewhere in Ulster and only 3.3% were born in the rest of Ireland. The same witness to the Riot Commission, while categorically stating that some of the Pound inhabitants came from outside Ulster, refused to give any estimate as to what proportion. Clearly the population of the Pound were not generally regarded as southerners in the way that navvies in other parts of Belfast, such as Pinkerton's Row, were. The inhabitants of the Pound were generally from Ulster. More were probably from the outlying counties than were the Protestant migrants to Belfast and some came from the south but many must also have come from Antrim and Down. Budge and O'Leary, *Belfast: approach to crisis*, p. 27; *Report of commissioners of inquiry, Belfast riots 1857*, p. 70.
8 Christ Church baptismal register 1837-50 (P.R.O.N.I., T679/284-5); Townsend Street Presbyterian Church baptismal register 1835-50 (P.R.O.N.I., MIC 1P/336A/1); Fisherwick Place Presbyterian Church list of communicants 1833-9 (P.R.O.N.I., MIC 1P/92/2); Census of Christ Church district, 1852 (P.R.O.N.I., CR1/13/D1).
9 Christ Church census 1852, (P.R.O.N.I., CR13/D/1); Christ Church baptismal register 1837-50 (P.R.O.N.I., T679/284-5) ; Townsend Street Presbyterian Church baptismal records, 1835-50 (P.R.O.N.I., MIC 1P/336A/1); Fisherwick Place Presbyterian Church list of

communicants, 1833–39 (P.R.O.N.I., MIC 1P/92/2)

10 1837 valuation (PRONI, Val. 1B/79); A. Malcolm, *The sanitary state of Belfast*, pp 5–7, 10, 26–7.

11 See below, p. 17.

12 George Benn, *A history of the town of Belfast*, pp 555–6.

13 This is according to an official guide at the Ulster Folk and Transport Museum at Cultra where the Tea Lane houses are now on display.

14 R.M. Sibbett, *For Christ and crown*, p. 26.

15 Census of Christ Church district, 1852 (P.R.O.N.I., CR1/13/D1).

16 Methodist baptismal register, Belfast circuit, 1815–43 (P.R.O.N.I., MIC 429/1).

17 D. Hempton and M. Hill, *Evangelical Protestantism*, p. 34.

18 *Belfast Newsletter*, 14 July 1825; *Northern Whig*, 15 July 1825.

19 *Vindicator*, 26 July 1843; *Report of commissioners of inquiry, Belfast riots 1857*, p. 138, 124–5.

20 *Report of commissioners of inquiry, Belfast riots 1857*, pp 138, 124–5.

21 *Belfast street directory*, 1820, 1835, 1840–1, 1846–7; Methodist baptismal register, Belfast circuit, 1815–43 (P.R.O.N.I., MIC 429/1); Christ Church baptismal register (P.R.O.N.I., T679/284–5); Brown Street Sunday school register (P.R.O.N.I. SCH 580/1/1).

22 1837 valuation (P.R.O.N.I., Val. 1B/79).

23 Malcolm, *Sanitary state of Belfast*, pp 26–7, 29; Christ Church baptismal register (P.R.O.N.I., T679/284–5).

24 See, for example, P. Gibbon, *Origins of Ulster unionism*, p. 85.

25 1837 valuation (P.R.O.N.I. Val. 1B/79).

26 *Report of commissioners of inquiry, Belfast riots 1857*, p. 21.

CHAPTER 2

1 'Ethnic' in the sense that poor Protestants and Catholics felt that they belonged to two distinct, opposing groups identified by (in some cases, nominal) religious allegiance.

2 A.T.Q. Stewart, *The narrow ground*; D. Miller, *Queen's rebels*; F. Wright, *Two lands on one soil*.

3 Wright, *Two lands on one soil*, pp 17, 25–6, 33–5.

4 Ibid., p. 26.

5 *Belfast Newsletter*, 13 July 1813.

6 W.A. Maguire, *Belfast*, p. 50.

7 Sovereign Thomas Verner's report, 10 Jan. 1814 (National Archives of Ireland, SOC 1565/1).

8 *Belfast Newsletter*, 11 January 1814, 25 February 1814, 20 June 1815, 27 August 1815.

9 D. Hempton and M. Hill, *Evangelical Protestantism*, pp 82–3.

10 D. Bowen, *The Protestant crusade in Ireland 1800–70*, p. 63.

11 Letter from Thomas Carlen and threatening notice, 8 December 1819 (N.A.I., SOC 2084/7).

12 M.R. Beames, 'The Ribbon societies', pp 134, 136.

13 State of the country reports 1822–24 (N.A.I., SOC 2358/10, 17–18, 21, 27, 32, 34, 37, 41, SOC 2360/7, 29, 36, 41, 45–6, SOC 2520/8–9, 35–41, SOC 2622/17–19, 23, SOC 2623/2, 5–6, 8–9, SOC 2623/14, 17, SOC 2623/20, 24, 30–2).

14 *Reports brought from the Lords viz. minutes of evidence on the state of Ireland*, PP, 1825 [181] ix, p. 20.

15 Stewart, *The narrow ground*, p. 144.

16 Memo on the origin and development of Ribbonism from W. Hagan (CO 904/7; P.R.O.N.I., MIC 448/1).

17 Beames, 'Ribbon Societies', p. 129.

18 Report of Ribbon informer, 8 November 1839 (CO 904/8, MIC 448/2 in P.R.O.N.I); Report of W. Maloney, RM, to Dublin Castle, 31 January 1842 (CO 904/9, MIC 448/3 in P.R.O.N.I.).

19 See Chapter 3.

20 Grand Lodge Registry of Warrants, 1823, 1828–9, 1856.

21 Both the conservative *Belfast Newsletter*, the liberal *Northern Whig* and the Catholic *Vindicator* describe districts such as Brown's Square, Sandy Row and Ballymaccarret as being main Orange areas. *Belfast*

Newsletter, 14 July 1829; *Northern Whig*, 2 June 1825, 19 July 1825; *Vindicator*, 7 February 1844, 5 February 1845. A sympathetic source, *The repealer repulsed*, an anonymous contemporary pamphlet, refers to the main opponents of O'Connell's visit to Belfast as being 'the loyal opposition of the sons of Brown Street, Sandy Row and Ballymaccarret': *The repealer repulsed!*, p. 151.

22 *Report from the select committee appointed to inquire into the nature, character, extent and tendency of Orange lodges, associations or societies in Ireland*, PP, 1835 [377] xv, p. 113; *Minutes of evidence on the state of Ireland*, p. 269.

23 The sovereign, Thomas Verner, acted as the chief magistrate before the appointment of resident magistrates. He was appointed by the Donegall family who owned much of the land in Belfast. The other justices of the peace appear to have been land owners from the surrounding countryside such as Sir Robert Bateson Bart, MP, JP, deputy lord lieutenant for County Down: *Northern Whig*, 23 April 1832.

24 *Belfast Newsletter*, 14 July 1825, *Northern Whig* 15 July 1825, 23 April 1832, 3 May 1832; Memorial of special constables to lord lieutenant (N.A.I., CSORP/1833/Private Index/277).

25 *Report of the select committee on Orange lodges*, p. 183.

26 Letter from Thomas Carlen and threatening notice, 8 December 1819 (N.A.I., SOC 2084/7).

27 R. Harris, *Prejudice and tolerance in Ulster*, pp 77-8, 81-2, 141-3.

28 Hepburn, *A past apart*, p. 232.

29 Sybil Baker, 'Orange and green', p. 795; J.C. Beckett, 'Belfast: a general survey', pp 187-8.

30 Baker, 'Orange and green', p. 795.

31 *Vindicator*, 20 May 1843.

32 Report of resident magistrate, 11 Nov. 1835 (N.A.I., Outrage Papers, County Antrim, 1835).

33 Report of resident magistrate, 31 May 1837 (N.A.I., Outrage Papers, County Antrim, 1837).

34 *Belfast Newsletter*, 21 July 1825, 14 July 1835.

35 *Reports from assistant hand loom weavers' commissioners*, PP, 1840 [43.-II] xxiii, pp. 634, 717, 773-6.

36 E.P. Thompson, 'Time, work-discipline and industrial capitalism', p. 85.

37 *Belfast Newsletter*, 23 September 1814, 18 October 1814, 28 April 1815, 2 May 1815.

38 *Belfast Newsletter*, 4 April 1815.

39 *Northern Whig*, 2 June 1825, 19 July 1825. The ritual parading and execution of the effigy in this case is very similar to a rural practice in England called 'skimmington' or 'stang ride' used when someone offends against a custom or an unwritten moral code. A classic English example is the case of a woman fined by a sheriff for allowing her geese to stray. The population regarded this as unfair because the sheriff, who was in his sixties, had numerous illegitimate children who had to be supported by the parish. A mob gathered with an effigy of the sheriff and a baby and paraded through the village accompanied by music played on primitive instruments before gathering outside his house: J. Stevenson, *Popular disturbances in England*, p. 48.

40 *Report from commissioners, hand loom weavers*, pp 674-5.

41 Gibbon, *Origins of Ulster unionism*, p. 85.

42 *Report from commissioners, hand loom weavers*, pp 674-5.

43 1837 valuation (P.R.O.N.I., val 1B/79); Belfast poll book, 1832-7 (P.R.O.N.I., D2472/1).

44 *Report from commissioners, hand loom weavers*, p. 718.

45 H. Patterson, *Class conflict and sectarianism*, pp 143-4.

46 *Northern Whig*, 21 July 1825.

47 On 12 July 1821, the sovereign, Thomas Verner, reported to Dublin Castle, 'I ineffectually endeavoured to prevent an Orange procession here yesterday ... [and] there was an angry

appearance for a short time of a large gathering of mob.' However, he managed to keep the peace: Report of Sovereign Thomas Verner, 12 July 1821, (N.A.I., SOC 2298/3); *Belfast Newsletter*, 14 July 1818, 13 July 1819, 14 July 1820, 13 July 1821.

48 *Belfast Newsletter*, 14 July 1825, *Northern Whig*, 15 July 1825.

49 *Belfast Newsletter*, 15 July 1828, *Northern Whig*, 13 July 1826, 13 July 1827.

50 Statement of Outrages, County Armagh, September 1828, (N.A.I., SOC 2882/7), Statement of Outrages, County Down, September 1828 (N.A.I., SOC 2882/20), Statement of Outrages, County Monaghan, November 1828 (N.A.I., SOC 2882/69).

51 Statement of Outrages, County Antrim, September 1828 (N.A.I., SOC 2882/2).

52 Statement of Outrages, County Tyrone, September 1828 (N.A.I., SOC 2882/72).

53 Statement of Outrages, County Londonderry, December 1828 (N.A.I., SOC 2882/30).

54 *Belfast Newsletter*, 15 July 1828, *Northern Whig*, 13 July 1826, 13 July 1827.

55 Herewald Senior, *Orangeism in Britain and Ireland*, p. 225.

56 *Belfast Newsletter*, 14 July 1829, 9 July 1830.

57 Maguire, *Belfast*, p. 50; Budge and O'Leary, *Belfast; approach to crisis*, p. 75.

58 *Northern Whig*, 18 March 1830.

59 *Northern Whig*, 23 April 1832.

60 Ibid.

61 *Northern Whig*, 23 April 1832, 3 May 1832.

62 Memorial to lord lieutenant, 28 April 1832 (N.A.I., CSORP/1832/Private Index/859).

63 Report of chief constable, 19 May 1832 (N.A.I., CSORP/1832/Private Index/893), Report of chief constable, 24 May 1832 (N.A.I., CSORP/1832/Private Index/930).

64 *Belfast Newsletter*, 19 March 1833.

CHAPTER 3

1 *First report of commissioners for inquiring into the condition of the poorer classes in Ireland*, PP, 1835 xxx, pp 2-7.

2 *First report of commissioners for inquiring into the condition of the poorer classes in Ireland*, PP, 1836 [369] xxxii, pp 31-48, 65-7, 91, 97-100, 168-87, 262-8, 450, 706-11.

3 Revd McIntyre's diary, 1854 (P.R.O.N.I., D1558/4/1), p. 163.

4 S.J. Connolly, *Priests and people in pre-famine Ireland 1780-1845* (Dublin, 1982), pp. 153-6.

5 *First report of commissioners for inquiring into the condition of the poorer classes in Ireland*, PP, 1836 xxx, pp. 21-2 (my italics).

6 Harris, *Prejudice and tolerance in Ulster*, p. 79.

7 W.M. O'Hanlon, *Walks among the poor of Belfast*, pp. 35-6.

8 Revd McIntyre's Diary, 1854, (P.R.O.N.I., D 1558/4/1), p. 163.

9 Sibbett, *For Christ and crown*, p. 37.

10 *Northern Whig*, 26 May 1825.

11 J. Gray, 'Popular entertainment', p. 103.

12 Gray, 'Popular entertainment', p. 103.

13 *Vindicator*, 3 April 1847.

14 *Belfast Newsletter*, 6 July 1868.

15 Gray, 'Popular entertainment', p. 99; E. Black, *The people's park* (Belfast, 1988), p. 42.

16 Census of the Christ Church district, 1852 (P.R.O.N.I., CR1/13/D1).

17 *Second Report of the Commissioners of Irish Education Inquiry*, pp 234-9.

18 Annals of Christ Church (P.R.O.N.I., T1075/11), pp. 89-92.

19 A. Macauley, *Dr William Crolly*, p. 103.

20 *Report from the select committee appointed to inquire into the progress and operation of the new plan of education in Ireland*, PP, 1837 [485] ix, p. 585.

21 G. McAteer, *Down the Falls*, p. 3.

22 County Antrim national schools register (P.R.O.N.I., ED6/1/2).

23 Annals of Christ Church, (P.R.O.N.I., T1075/11), pp. 31-4.

24 Ibid., p. 87.

25 *Vindicator*, 15 April 1846.

26 *Vindicator*, 3 October 1846; *Report*

from the select committee on inquiry into drunkeness, PP, 1834 [559] viii, p. 66.

27 Report of resident magistrate, 23 March 1842 (N.A.I., Outrage papers, County Antrim, 1842); *Report of the commissioners of inquiry, Belfast riots 1857*, p. 31.

28 *Report of the commissioners of inquiry, Belfast riots 1857*, pp 123–9.

29 Revd McIntyre's diary, 1855 (P.R.O.N.I., D1558/4/1), p. 198.

30 *Report of the commissioners of inquiry, Belfast riots 1857*, p. 2.

31 Annals of Christ Church (T1075/11, P.R.O.N.I.); Revd James Morgan, *Recollections of my life and times*; Townsend Street Presbyterian Church, history of the congregation, 1833-1933 (P.R.O.N.I., CR3/27).

32 Annals of Christ Church (P.R.O.N.I. T1075/11,), pp 139-41, 145-9.

33 Ibid., pp. 160-3, 179-80.

34 Census of Christ Church district, 1852 (P.R.O.N.I., CR1/13/D1).

35 K. Inglis, *Churches and the working class in Victorian England*, p. 335.

36 Census of Christ Church district, 1852 (P.R.O.N.I., CR1/13/D1); Inglis, *Churches and the working class*, p. 333.

37 *Northern Whig*, 13 July 1848.

38 Reports of resident magistrate, 4 April 1843, 5 April 1843 (N.A.I., Outrage papers, County Antrim, 1843).

39 *Vindicator*, 3 January 1844, 5 February 1845; Alderdice was arrested during riots on the Twelfth in 1834. *Belfast Newsletter*, 18 July 1834.

40 Reports of sub-inspector of constabulary, 21 June 1843, 27 June 1843 (N.A.I., Outrage papers, County Antrim, 1843); *Vindicator*, 24 June 1843, 26 June 1843.

41 *Belfast Newsletter*, 14 July 1835.

42 *Belfast Newsletter*, 14 July 1835, 17 July 1835, 24 July 1835.

43 Ibid.

44 *Belfast Newsletter*, 13 July 1824, 14 July 1825, 16 July 1822, 23 July 1822, 14 July 1829, *Northern Whig*, 15 July 1824, 21 July 1825, 4 August 1825, *Vindicator*, 27 September 1843.

45 *Belfast Newsletter*, 20 January 1835.

46 *Belfast Newsletter*, 14 July 1829.

47 *Belfast Newsletter*, 24 July 1835.

48 *Belfast Newsletter*, 15 July 1836, 14 July 1837, *Northern Whig*, 13 July 1839, 14 July 1840.

49 Report of resident magistrate, 13 July 1842 (N.A.I., Outrage Papers, County Antrim, 1842).

50 Report of resident magistrate, 9 May 1837 (N.A.I., Outrage Papers, County Antrim, 1837).

51 Report of head constable, 16 August 1838 (N.A.I., Outrage Papers, County Antrim, 1838).

52 Report of sub-inspector, 28 August 1840 (N.A.I., Outrage Papers, County Antrim, 1840).

53 Reports of resident magistrate, 4 April 1843, 5 April 1843 (N.A.I., Outrage Papers, Country Antrim, 1843.

54 Reports of resident magistrate, 23 March 1842, 27 March 1842 (N.A.I., Outrage Papers, County Antrim, 1842).

55 Macauley, *Dr William Crolly*, p. 282.

56 *The repealer repulsed!*, p. 20.

57 Maura Cronin, paper on 'Ballads and politicisation in pre-famine Ireland' presented to post-graduate seminar, QUB, 10 November 1995.

58 *The repealer repulsed!*, pp 147-8.

59 Ibid., pp 36-39.

60 Police reports, 20 January 1841, 23 January 1841 (Outrage papers, County Antrim, 1841, P.R.O.N.I., T3280/1); *Belfast Newsletter*, 22 January 1841; *The repealer repulsed*, pp 44-6.

61 *The repealer repulsed*, p. 151.

62 *Vindicator*, 31 May 1843, 7 June 1843. Although the *Vindicator* may have exaggerated the numbers attending repeal meetings, a report from the mayor sent to Dublin castle estimates a crowd of over 1000 attending a normal weekly meeting in 1845 so the claims of 2-2500 do not seem extreme for the heyday of the movement in 1843. Report of the mayor of Belfast, Charles Mulholland, 14 May 1845 (N.A.I., Outrage papers, County Antrim, 1845).

63 *Vindicator*, 18 October 1843.

64 *Vindicator*, 4 September, 1844.

65 *Vindicator*, 1 March 1843.

66 S.J. Connolly, 'Catholicism in Ulster, 1800-50', p. 168.
67 *Vindicator*, 8 October 1842.
68 Connolly, 'Catholicism in Ulster', p. 168.
69 *Vindicator*, 6 November 1844.
70 *Vindicator*, 1 February 1845.
71 *Vindicator*, 11 September 1844.
72 See below, p. 61.
73 *Vindicator*, 4 February 1846.
74 *Vindicator*, 18 September 1844.
75 Only those repeal wardens whose identity in the street directories could be established beyond reasonable doubt have been included in this list. If the surname and christian name were very common or if there were more than one entry for a particular name, these individuals have not been listed. *Belfast Street Directory*, 1843-42, 1843-4, 1846-47; *Vindicator*, 1 March 1843, 1 April 1843, 31 May 1843, 13 September 1843, 19 June 1844, 31 July 1844, 4 September 1844, 11 September 1844, 18 September 1844, 25 September 1844, 16 October 1844, 7 May 1845, 23 September 1846.
76 *Vindicator*, 31 July 1844.
77 *Vindicator*, 24 December 1845.
78 *Vindicator*, 15 November 1843, 11 September 1844.
79 *Vindicator*, 22 February 1843.
80 K.T. Hoppen, *Elections, politics and society in Ireland*.
81 *Vindicator*, 16 December 1843.
82 *Vindicator*, 28 October 1846.
83 In October 1843 the government proclaimed a 'monster meeting' due to be held at Clontarf near Dublin. O'Connell acquiesed in the banning of the meeting which showed the government he would not resist direct suppression of the repeal movement except in the law courts.
84 *Vindicator*, 23 October 1844, 13 November 1844.
85 *Vindicator*, 13 May 1846.
86 *Vindicator*, 29 March 1843.
87 *Vindicator*, 15 February 1845.
88 *Vindicator*, 8 May 1844.
89 *Vindicator*, 3 April 1844.
90 *Vindicator*, 8 May 1844.
91 *Vindicator*, 17 December 1842.

92 *Vindicator*, 20 December, 1843.
93 *Vindicator*, 24 February 1847, 27 February 1847, 3 March 1847, 6 March 1847, 10 March 1847, 17 March 1847, 20 March 1847, 24 March 1847 and 31 March 1847.
94 *Vindicator*, 4 January 1845.
95 *The repealer repulsed*, p. 94; J.C. Beckett, *The making of modern Ireland*, pp 328-9.
96 Connolly, 'Catholicism in Ulster', p. 171.
97 *Vindicator*, 17 September 1845, 24 September 1845.
98 *Vindicator*, 20 September 1845, 4 October 1845.
99 D.G. Boyce, *Nationalism in Ireland*, pp 154-69.
100 *Vindicator*, 1 August 1846.
101 *Vindicator*, 1 August 1846.
102 *Vindicator*, 1 July 1846.
103 *Nation*, 19 September, 1846.
104 Report taken from the *Northern Whig*, quoted in the *Nation*, 26 September 1846.
105 *Nation*, 26 September 1846.
106 *Vindicator*, 23 September 1846.
107 *Nation*, 10 October 1846.
108 *Nation*, 19 September 1846.
109 *Nation*, 10 October 1846.
110 *Vindicator*, 23 September 1846, *Belfast street directory 1843-44*.
111 R. Davis, *The Young Ireland movement*, pp 135-7.
112 *Nation*, 20 November 1847.
113 *Nation*, 20 November 1847.
114 *Nation*, 27 November 1847.
115 *Nation*, 27 November 1847.
116 *Nation*, 20 November 1847.
117 *Nation*, 20 November 1847, 27 November 1847.
118 Davis, *Young Ireland movement*, pp 134-5.
119 *Nation*, 1 July 1848.
120 Ferguson belonged to a group of writers who contributed to the *Dublin Penny Journal*. They were cultural nationalists, interested in the history and literature of ancient Ireland and its surviving Gaelic culture in the west. Most of this group were unionists in politics, including Ferguson except for the brief period

in 1848 before the rising. See Thomas Flanagan, 'Literature in English, 1801–91', pp 500–1.

121 Davis, *Young Ireland movement*, p. 228.
122 Ibid., p. 219.
123 Ibid., pp 227–8; *Nation*, 15 July 1848.
124 Davis, *Young Ireland movement*, p. 165.
125 *Nation*, 22 July 1848.
126 *Vindicator*, 3 April 1847.
127 *Vindicator*, 28 June 1843.
128 *Belfast Newsletter*, 7 July 1843.
129 *Belfast Newsletter*, 14 July 1843, *Vindicator*, 15 July 1843.
130 *Vindicator*, 15 July 1843.
131 *Belfast Newsletter*, 18 July 1843.
132 *Vindicator*, 19 July 1843.
133 *Belfast Newsletter*, 18 July 1843.
134 *Vindicator*, 19 July 1843, 2 August 1843.
135 *Vindicator*, 22 July 1843.
136 *Vindicator*, 26 July 1843.
137 *Vindicator*, 26 July 1843, 12 August 1843.
138 *Vindicator*, 22 July 1843, 20 September 1843, 2 August 1843, 13 September 1843, 11 November 1846.
139 *Vindicator*, 2 August 1843.
140 Baker, 'Orange and green', pp. 795–6.
141 Reports of resident magistrate, 16 July 1843, 18 July 1843, 24 July 1843 (N.A.I., Outrage Papers, County Antrim, 1843).
142 *Belfast Newsletter*, 17 July 1846.
143 *Belfast Newsletter*, 17 July 1846, *Northern Whig*, 16 July 1846.
144 J. Stevenson, *Popular disturbances in England 1700–1870*, pp 277–8; *Vindicator*, 18 July 1846.
145 Report of resident magistrate, 12 July 1849 (N.A.I., Outrage Papers, County Antrim, 1849).
146 *Northern Whig*, 13 July 1848.
147 *Belfast Newsletter*, 14 July 1848.
148 *Northern Whig*, 13 July 1848.
149 *Belfast Newsletter*, 14 July 1848.
150 *Northern Whig*, 13 July 1848.
151 Ibid.
152 Ibid.
153 *Northern Whig*, 14 July 1849.
154 Report of resident magistrate, 13 July 1849 (N.A.I., Outrage Papers, County Antrim, 1849).
155 *Northern Whig*, 14 July 1849.

156 *Northern Whig*, 13 July 1850.
157 *Northern Whig*, 11 July 1850.
158 Belfast poll book, 1832–37 (P.R.O.N.I., D.2472).
159 Macauley, *Dr William Crolly*, p. 50.
160 *Northern Whig*, 20 December 1832, 24 December 1832.
161 K.T. Hoppen, *Elections, politics and society in Ireland, 1832–85*, pp 401–7.
162 *Belfast Newsletter*, 18 December 1832.
163 *Northern Whig*, 20 December 1832, 24 December 1832.
164 *Northern Whig*, 24 December 1832, 27 December 1832.
165 *Belfast Newsletter*, 20 January 1835, 23 January 1835.
166 *Northern Whig*, 7 August 1847.
167 *Belfast Newsletter*, 1 August 1837.
168 *Northern Whig*, 13 July 1841, 15 July 1841.
169 In December 1846, a crowd of 100 or so raided three bakeries demanding bread. See Report of resident magistrate, 18 December 1846 (N.A.I., Outrage Papers, County Antrim, 1846); *Belfast Newsletter*, 22 December 1846; *Northern Whig*, 19 December 1846.
170 Report of resident magistrate, 22 August 1838 (N.A.I., Outrage Papers, County Antrim, 1838).
171 *Northern Whig*, 23 August 1838.
172 Report of resident magistrate, 22 August 1838 (N.A.I., Outrage Papers, County Antrim, 1838).
173 *Northern Whig*, 25 August 1838, 14 March 1839.
174 E.P. Thompson, 'The moral economy of the English crowd in the eighteenth century', pp 76–9.
175 *Belfast Newsletter*, 2 May 1837 (my italics).
176 *Northern Whig*, 28 May 1842.
177 Thompson, 'Moral economy', pp 128–31.
178 Stevenson, 'Popular disturbances', pp. 309–13.
179 *Belfast Newsletter*, 14 July 1835, 17 July 1835; Report of resident magistrate, 16 July 1843 (N.A.I., Outrage papers, County Antrim, 1843).

180 *Belfast Newsletter*, 13 July 1813, 14
     July 1829; *Northern Whig*, 18 March
     1830, 14 July 1849.
181 *Report of the commissioners of inquiry,
     Belfast riots 1857*, p. 24.
182 *Vindicator*, 26 July 1843; *Northern
     Whig*, 13 July 1848.
183 C. Townsend, *Political violence in
     Ireland*, pp 41, 45.
184 Townsend, *Political violence*, p. 45.
185 Baker, 'Orange and green', p. 806;
     Townsend, *Political violence*, p. 46.
186 Stevenson, *Popular disturbances*,
     p. 302.
187 *Northern Whig*, 13 July 1848; *Belfast
     Newsletter*, 14 July 1848.
188 See Chapter 7.
189 Budge and O'Leary, *Belfast*, p. 27.
190 *Minutes of evidence on the state of
     Ireland*, p. 213.
191 P. Gibbon, *The origins of Ulster
     unionism*, pp 80-5.
192 Belfast Poll Book, 1832-37
     (P.R.O.N.I., D.2472); *Report of the
     commissioners of inquiry, Belfast riots
     1857*, p. 28.
193 Gibbon, *Origins of Ulster unionism*,
     p. 75.
194 Ibid., p. 75.

CHAPTER 4

 1 A. Macaulay, *Patrick Dorrian*, p. 30.
 2 Ibid., p. 92.
 3 Ibid., p. 29.
 4 Ibid., p. 117.
 5 P. Rogers, *St Peter's pro-cathedral,
     Belfast 1866-1966*, p. 17.
 6 Macauley, *Patrick Dorrian*, p. 90.
 7 Ibid., p. 372.
 8 *Irish Catholic directory, 1887*, p. 136.
 9 Macauley, *Patrick Dorrian*, p. 373; E.
     Larkin, 'The devotional revolution in
     Ireland 1850-75', pp 644-5.
10 Rogers, *St Peter's pro-cathedral*, pp
     18-19.
11 Macaulay, *Patrick Dorrian*, p. 118.
12 Rogers, *St Peter's pro-cathedral*, p. 10.
13 *26th Report of the commissioners of
     national education*, PP, 1860 [2706]
     xxvi, pp 378-91.
14 *Reports from commissioners: primary
     education (Ireland): educational census,
     returns showing number of children
     actually present in each primary school,
     25 June 1868*, PP, 1870 [C.6-V] xxviii,
     part V, pp 12-14; Macaulay, *Patrick
     Dorrian*, p. 285.
15 Macaulay, *Patrick Dorrian*, p. 284.
16 Ibid., p. 299.
17 Hepburn, *A past apart*, pp. 147-8.
18 *50th Report of the commissioners of
     national education in Ireland*, PP, 1884
     [C.4053] xxv, pp. 271, 286, 288-9,
     366-73.
19 *Report of the inter departmental
     committee on the employment of children
     during school age especially in street
     trading in the large centres of population
     in Ireland*, PP, 1902 [Cd. 1144] xlii,
     p. 113.
20 Macaulay, *Patrick Dorrian*, p. 30; F.
     Roney, *Frank Roney*, p. 22.
21 Rogers, *St Peter's pro-cathedral*, p. 11.
22 *Belfast Morning News*, 18 June 1878.
23 *Belfast Morning News*, 2 March 1885.
24 *Belfast Morning News*, 3 June 1878, 29
     January 1885.
25 Reports of resident magistrates, Bands
     file (N.A.I., CSORP/1882/20,807);
     Belfast Morning News, 3 June 1878, 18
     June 1878.
26 *Belfast Morning News*, 18 June 1878, 3
     June 1878, 29 January 1885.
27 *Belfast Morning News*, 6 January 1873;
     R.V. Comerford, 'Patriotism as
     pastime', p. 250.
28 A. Buckley, 'On the club', p. 53.
29 *Belfast Morning News*, 18 March 1884.
30 A. Buckley, 'On the club', p. 48, 58.
31 *Belfast Morning News*, 16 August
     1884.
32 *Belfast Morning News*, 2 March 1885.
33 *Belfast Morning News*, 23 February
     1885, 11 March 1885; *Belfast street
     directory* 1887.
34 Macaulay, *Patrick Dorrian*, pp 140-1.
35 Memorandum of association of the
     Belfast Catholic Institute Association
     Ltd. and List of shareholders of the
     Belfast Catholic Institute (P.R.O.N.I.,
     D1905/2/205A); *Belfast street
     directory* 1865.
36 R. Gray, *The labour aristocracy in
     Victorian Edinburgh*, pp 108-10, 141-2;
     G. Crossick, *An artisan elite in
     Victorian society*, pp 130-1.

37 Macaulay, *Patrick Dorrian*, p. 207.
38 Ibid., p. 150.
39 Wright, *Two lands on one soil*, p. 299.
40 Macaulay, *Patrick Dorrian*, p. 150.
41 Ibid., pp 128–9.
42 R.V. Comerford, *The Fenians in context*, pp 124–5.
43 Budge and O'Leary, *Belfast: approach to crisis*; F. Wright, *Two lands on one soil*, p. 359; W.A. Maguire, *Belfast*.
44 Comerford, *Fenians in context*, p. 208.
45 Report of resident magistrate, 5 May 1866 (N.A.I., CSORP/1866/9687).
46 Roney, *Irish rebel*, p. 57.
47 Report of resident magistrate, 6 May 1867 (N.A.I., Fenian papers 564R); *Northern Whig*, 1 January 1867, 18 January 1878.
48 Report of resident magistrate, 5 May 1866 (N.A.I., CSORP/1866/9687).
49 Roney, *Irish rebel*, p. 72.
50 Report of resident magistrate, 5 May 1866 (N.A.I., CSORP/1866/9687).
51 *Northern Whig*, 1 January 1867, 18 January 1867.
52 Roney, *Irish rebel*, p. 154.
53 Reports of resident magistrate, 6 May 1867, 24 January 1868 (N.A.I., Fenian papers, 564R, 706R); *Ulster Observer*, 17 September 1867.
54 Roney, *Irish rebel*, pp 163–6.
55 The police found a subscription card for a William Harbison memorial on a man they arrested for yelling 'Hurrah for the harp without the crown' in Divis Street. The secretary and treasurer of the fund were both Fenians who had been arrested under the HCSA. Report of resident magistrate, 5 January 1868 (N.A.I., Fenian papers 284R); Police report, 1 November 1869 (N.A.I., Fenian papers 4677R).
56 Comerford, *Fenians in context*, p. 222.
57 *Belfast Morning News*, 16 October 1879.
58 Reports of resident magistrates, Fenian papers, 6 May 1867, 24 January 1868, 5 January 1868, 1 January 1867, 1 April 1867, 11 January 1868 (564R, 706R, 284R,1920R, 3114R, 2261R); Report of resident magistrate, 25 February 1866 (CSORP/1866/17917); *Belfast Street Directory* 1865-6, 1870;

Northern Whig 1 January 1867, 18 January 1867; *Ulster Observor* 31 March 1866.
59 Comerford, 'Patriotism as pastime', p. 241.
60 Ibid., pp 244–5.
61 Gray, *Labour aristocracy*, pp 108-10, 141-2; Crossick, *Artisan elite*, pp 130-1.
62 Report of resident magistrate, 5 January 1868 (N.A.I., Fenian papers 284R).
63 Comerford, 'Patriotism as pastime', p. 245.
64 Roney, *Irish rebel*, p. 69.
65 W.F. Mandle, *The Gaelic Athletic Association and Irish nationalist politics*, pp 68, 192-3.
66 Roney, *Irish rebel*, p. 76.
67 *Northern Whig*, 1 January 1867.
68 Comerford, *Fenians in context*, p. 113.
69 Gray, *Labour aristocracy*, pp 141-2; Crossick, *Artisan elite*, p. 137.
70 Comerford, 'Patriotism as pastime', p. 250.
71 Comerford, *Fenians in context*, p. 112.
72 J. Newsinger, *Fenianism in mid-Victorian Britain*, p. 88.
73 Report of resident magistrates, 5 May 1866, 25 February 1866 (N.A.I., CSORP/1866/9687; CSORP/1866/17917); Fenian photo files (N.A.I., FP60; FP199; FP149).
74 S.J. Connolly, *Priests and people in pre-famine Ireland*, pp 276-7.
75 Roney, *Irish rebel*, p. 87.
76 Report of resident magistrate, 25 February 1866 (N.A.I., CSORP/1866/17917). In his article on Ribbonism, M.R. Beames, speculating about the possible links between Ribbonism and Fenianism, mentions that it would be interesting to find evidence of the mutual aid function in Fenianism. M.R. Beames, 'The Ribbon societies', p. 142.
77 Roney, for example, refused to join the Ribbon society in Britain although he was told this would facilitate the organisation of Fenianism there: Roney, *Irish rebel*, p. 102.
78 Beames, 'The Ribbon societies', p. 142.
79 Police report, 21 July 1873 (N.A.I., CSORP/1873/10,008).

80 Roney, *Irish rebel*, pp 52-3.
81 Roney, *Irish rebel*, pp 12-13.
82 Ibid., p. 69.
83 Ibid., p. 13.
84 Ibid., pp 56, 65.
85 Beames, 'The Ribbon societies', p. 137.
86 Roney, *Irish rebel*, p. 97.
87 See below, pp 106-7.
88 Reports of magistrates and police, 19 October 1872 (N.A.I., CSORP/1873/1022).
89 Roney, *Irish rebel*, p. 52.
90 Comerford, *Fenians in context*, p. 137.
91 Ibid., p. 249.
92 Ibid., pp 146, 154.
93 Ibid., p. 147. However, he is wrong to compare Harbison's funeral with that of another Fenian before the rising as this prisoner had been transferred to Belfast from Dublin and was not a local and the matter was dealt with in a secretive manner by the authorities so people were unaware of his death at the time: *Ulster Observer*, 27 March, 1866.
94 Report of resident magistrate, 13 December 1867 (N.A.I., Fenian papers F4932).
95 Wright, *Two lands on one soil*, p. 360; Macaulay, *Patrick Dorrian*, p. 188.
96 Comerford concedes that these pamphlets were 'the very stuff of popular nationalism' but then goes on to say that this did not really mean anything in political terms and that people only wanted a fair deal for Ireland which they believed Gladstone would give them: Comerford, *Fenians in context*, p. 146.
97 Macaulay, *Patrick Dorrian*, pp. 224-5.
98 *Belfast Morning News*, 21 June 1872.
99 *Belfast Morning News*, 17 April 1872.
100 *Belfast Morning News*, 17 April 1872.
101 *Belfast Morning News*, 21 June 1872.
102 Roney, *Irish rebel*, p. 59. I cannot be certain that the two John Griffiths were the same man. However, it was not a common name. There were only three John Griffiths in the street directory of 1870, two were manual workers and one was a clerk living in Leeson Street just outside the Pound. There is no evidence in the Dublin Castle records that the Fenian John

Griffith went to America and the fact that the Belfast Home Rule Association held a testimonial for John Griffith suggests that he had an illustrious career behind him and was probably the ex-Fenian leader. The Fenian Griffith was a Young Irelander in his youth and the fact that the Home Ruler Griffith quoted Thomas Davis also suggests he was the same person. Given the mercantile and retail composition of the Home Rule leadership in Belfast, I suspect that Griffith was the clerk listed in the 1870 directory and that by 1880 he had aquired his own spirit business as the clerk is no longer listed and there is a new listing for a spirit dealer. See *Belfast street directory*, 1870, 1880; *Belfast Morning News*, 21 June 1872.
103 Reports of resident magistrate, 25 February 1866 (N.A.I., CSORP/1866/17917), 6 May 1867 (N.A.I., Fenian papers 564R); Police report, 1 November 1869 (N.A.I., Fenian papers 4677R).
104 *Belfast Morning News*, 6 May 1882, 26 October 1885.
105 *Belfast Morning News*, 25 January 1876.
106 *Belfast Morning News*, 25 January 1876.
107 *Belfast Morning News*, 16 August 1876.
108 *Belfast Morning News*, 27 September 1877.
109 *Belfast Morning News*, 27 September 1877.
110 *Belfast Morning News*, 27 September 1877.
111 An understanding between the IRB's John Devoy and Parnell, the details of which are somewhat hazy. It basically allowed individual Fenians to become involved in the land agitation and to give support to the advanced section of the Home Rule party. See F.S.L. Lyons, 'Fenianism 1867-1916', p. 41.
112 *Belfast Morning News*, 16 October 1879.
113 *Belfast Morning News*, 16 October 1879.

114 *Belfast Morning News*, 6 May 1882, 26 October 1885.

115 *Belfast Morning News*, 18 December 1884, 9 January 1885, *Belfast street directory* 1880.

116 *Belfast Morning News*, 30 July 1884.

117 *Belfast Morning News*, 18 December 1884.

118 Macaulay, *Patrick Dorrian*, p. 362; *Belfast Morning News*, 30 December 1884.

119 *Belfast Morning News*, 9 January 1885.

120 *Belfast Morning News*, 24 January 1885, 2 March 1885.

121 *Belfast Morning News*, 1 June 1886.

122 *Belfast Morning News*, 10 November 1885.

123 *Belfast Morning News*, 25 November 1885.

124 *Belfast Morning News*, 21 September 1885, 10 November 1885.

125 Budge and O'Leary, *Belfast, approach to crisis*, p. 103.

126 *Belfast Morning News*, 7 December 1885.

127 *Belfast Morning News*, 18 May 1886.

128 Macaulay, *Patrick Dorrian*, p. 230.

129 *Belfast Morning News*, 21 June 1872.

130 *Belfast street directory*, 1870, 1878 and 1880; *Belfast Morning News*, 17 April 1872, 16 August 1873, 18 March 1874, 16 August 1876, 27 September 1877, 16 October 1879, 18 November 1880, 19 February 1881, 15 October 1881, 29 October 1881, 6 May 1882, 18 December 1884, 30 December 1884, 10 November 1885, 24 November 1885.

131 Hepburn, *A past apart*, p. 149.

132 Macaulay, *Patrick Dorrian*, p. 232.

133 *Belfast street directory*, 1870, 1878 and 1880; *Belfast Morning News*, 17 April 1872, 16 August 1873, 18 March 1874, 16 August 1876, 27 September 1877, 16 October 1879, 18 November 1880, 19 February 1881, 15 October 1881, 29 October 1881, 6 May 1882, 18 December 1884, 30 December 1884, 10 November 1885, 24 November 1885.

134 *Belfast Morning News*, 16 October 1879.

135 *Belfast Morning News*, 10 August 1885; Rogers, *St Peter's pro-cathedral*, p. 23.

136 Membership cost five shillings per annum, a sum which some Catholic working men could not have afforded. *Belfast Morning News*, 17 April 1872.

137 Police report, 21 July 1873 (N.A.I., CSORP/1873/10,008).

138 Police report, 21 July 1873 (N.A.I., CSORP/1873/10,008).

139 Report of resident magistrate, 26 February 1879 (N.A.I., CSORP/1882/20807).

140 Police report, 18 October 1872 (N.A.I., CSORP/1873/1022).

141 *Ulster Examiner*, 2 August 1877 included in magistrate's report, 3 August 1877 (N.A.I., CSORP/1877/12,217).

142 *Ulster Examiner*, 2 August 1877 included in magistrate's report, 3 August 1877 (N.A.I., CSORP/1877/12,217); *Belfast Morning News*, 7 August 1877.

143 *Belfast Morning News*, 6 August 1877.

144 Report of resident magistrate, 7 August 1877 (N.A.I., CSORP/1877/12,217).

145 *Belfast Morning News*, 6 August 1877, 7 August 1877.

146 Report of resident magistrate, 7 August 1877 (N.A.I., CSORP/1877/12,217); *Belfast Morning News*, 7–11 August 1877.

147 Police report, 21 July 1873 (N.A.I., CSORP/1873/10,008).

148 Presumably the drink trade considering the dominance of spirit merchants and spirit grocers in the Home Rule leadership in Belfast.

149 *Belfast Morning News*, 18 March 1879.

150 Report of resident magistrate 17 March 1879 (N.A.I., CSORP/1879/5161).

151 *Belfast Morning News*, 18 March 1879.

152 *Belfast Morning News*, 18 March 1879.

153 Report of resident magistrate, 17 March 1879 (N.A.I.,

CSORP/1879/5161); *Belfast Morning News*, 18 March 1879.

154 *Belfast Morning News*, 18 March 1879.

155 Comerford, *Fenians in context*, p. 194.

156 *Belfast Morning News*, 16 August 1873.

157 *Belfast Morning News*, 27 September 1877.

158 *Belfast Morning News*, 6 May 1882.

159 *Belfast Morning News*, 18 March 1874.

160 Comerford, *Fenians in context*, p. 194.

161 *Belfast Morning News*, 16 August 1876.

162 Band file (N.A.I., CSORP/1882/20807).

163 *Belfast Morning News*, 18 March 1885.

164 Hepburn, *A past apart*, pp 147–8. (my italics)

165 Ibid., pp 154–5.

166 Ibid., p. 155.

167 See p. 72 above.

168 Macauley, *Patrick Dorrian*, pp 224, 227, 362.

169 Brian Walker, *Ulster politics*, p. 46.

170 Wright, *Two lands on one soil*, p. 475.

171 Walker, *Ulster politics*, p. 265.

172 Ibid., p. 265.

173 Ibid., p. 28.

174 *Belfast Morning News*, 6 May 1882.

CHAPTER 5

1 D. Hempton and M. Hill, *Evangelical protestantism*, p. 147.

2 Hempton and Hill, *Evangelical protestantism*, p. 149.

3 Janice Holmes, 'Lifting the curtain on popular religion', p. 35; Hempton and Hill, *Evangelical protestantism*, p. 146.

4 M. Hill, 'Ulster awakened', pp 459–60.

5 *Banner of Ulster*, 21 May 1859.

6 *Banner of Ulster*, 2 June 1859, 4 June 1859.

7 *Banner of Ulster*, 4 June 1859.

8 *Banner of Ulster*, 23 June 1859

9 *Banner of Ulster*, 2 July 1859.

10 *Banner of Ulster*, 23 June 1859.

11 *Banner of Ulster*, 23 June 1859.

12 *Banner of Ulster*, 4 June 1859.

13 Holmes, 'Lifting the curtain', p. 83.

14 Gibbon, *Origins of Ulster unionism*, p. 62.

15 *Banner of Ulster*, 4 June 1859.

16 Holmes, 'Lifting the curtain', p. 68.

17 Ibid., pp 85–6.

18 Ibid., p. 35.

19 Ibid., pp 78–83.

20 *Banner of Ulster*, 9 June 1859, 21 June 1859, 6 August 1859, 15 November 1859.

21 Hill, 'Ulster awakened', p. 460.

22 Hempton and Hill, *Evangelical protestantism*, p. 148.

23 Hempton and Hill, *Evangelical protestantism*, pp 159–60.

24 *Banner of Ulster*, 9 February 1860; *Belfast Newsletter*, 16 January 1861.

25 *Banner of Ulster*, 16 October 1860.

26 *Belfast Newsletter*, 6 October 1868.

27 *Reports from commissioners: primary education (Ireland): educational census*, pp 12–14; *26th report of commissioners of national education in Ireland*, pp 378–9.

28 *Belfast Newsletter*, 6 October 1868.

29 *Belfast Newsletter*, 6 July 1868.

30 *Banner of Ulster*, 12 April 1860.

31 *Banner of Ulster*, 16 February 1860.

32 Belfast street directories 1870, 1878; Grand Lodge of Ireland register of warrants Jan 1875, 1856, 1823, 1828–9.

33 Patterson, *Class conflict and sectarianism*, p. xv.

34 See Chapter 7.

35 *Belfast Newsletter*, 14 November 1868.

36 *Banner of Ulster*, 14 July 1859.

37 *Banner of Ulster*, 23 June 1859.

38 *Banner of Ulster*, 23 June 1859.

39 *Banner of Ulster*, 23 June 1859, 16 July 1859.

40 *Banner of Ulster*, 22 November 1859.

41 *Banner of Ulster*, 31 December 1859.

42 *Banner of Ulster*, 21 June 1860, 26 June 1860; *Northern Whig*, 17 September 1867.

43 J. Gray, 'Popular entertainment', pp 103–4; *Banner of Ulster*, 28 April 1860.

44 Police report, 17 December 1881 (N.A.I., CSORP/1881/45199).

45 *Belfast Newsletter*, 5 March 1868.

46 *Belfast Newsletter*, 4 March 1868.

47 *Belfast Newsletter*, 5 March 1868.

48 William Johnston's diary, 15 September 1868, 10 October 1868, 19 October 1868 (P.R.O.N.I., D/880/2/19).

49 *Belfast Newsletter*, 16 September 1868.
50 *Belfast Newsletter*, 14 October 1868.
51 *Belfast Newsletter*, 14 October 1868.
52 *Belfast Newsletter*, 21 October 1868.
53 A. McClelland, *William Johnston of Ballykilbeg*, pp 51-2.
54 *Belfast Newsletter*, 5 March 1868.
55 *Belfast Newsletter*, 5 November 1868.
56 *Belfast Newsletter*, 19 September 1868.
57 McClelland, *William Johnston*, pp 54-5.
58 Ibid., pp 47-8.
59 Gibbon, *Origins of Ulster unionism*, p. 90.
60 Wright, *Two lands on one soil*, p. 330.
61 Ibid., p. 325.
62 Ibid., pp 288-9.
63 Ibid., pp 330-1.
64 *Belfast Newsletter*, 14 November 1868.
65 *Belfast Newsletter*, 19 November 1868.
66 *Belfast Newsletter*, 21 November 1868.
67 Wright, *Two lands on one soil*, p. 328.
68 The *Northern Star* declared that on the 12th of July 1870 'the conduct of the Belfast Orangemen was better than it was wont to be; they were exceptionally sober and kept within the usual limits of traditional offence.' The *Ulster Examiner* noted 'the very credible feelings of tolerance and forebearance which for some time past have distinguished the brethren of Belfast in their relations with their Catholic fellow citizens.' See Wright, *Two lands on one soil*, p. 351.
69 The Orange Order, including many members of the BPWMA, in Belfast was opposed to the introduction of the secret ballot because they feared that while Protestant landlords would lose their influence, Catholic priests would continue to exercise an influence through the confessional: McClelland, *William Johnston*, p. 79.
70 McClelland, *William Johnston*, pp 79, 96.
71 Patterson, *Class conflict and sectarianism*, p. 45.
72 D.C. Savage, 'The Origins of the Ulster Unionist Party 1885-86', pp 193-5.
73 Bands file (N.A.I., CSORP/1882/20807).
74 A. Jackson, 'Unionist politics and Protestant society in Edwardian Ireland', p. 866.
75 See Chapter 7.

CHAPTER 6

1 This is the earliest census for which detailed records still exist.
2 A.C. Hepburn, *The Catholic community of Belfast, 1850-1940*, pp 44-5.
3 Census of Christ Church district, 1852 (P.R.O.N.I., CR1/13/D1); Census returns, 1901 (P.R.O.N.I., MIC 354/1/79/87, 92, 100-1, 108).
3a Source: Census returns, 1901 (P.R.O.N.I., MIC 354/1/79-87, 92, 100-1, 108).
4 C.D Purdon, *The longevity of flax mill and factory operatives* (Belfast, 1875), p. 27.
4a Source: Census returns, 1901 (P.R.O.N.I., MIC 354/1/79, 87, 92, MIC 100-1, 108).
4b Source: *General valuation of rateable property in Ireland: union of Belfast, Counties Antrim and Down*, 1860.
5 Includes houses and shops but not industrial property.
6 Hepburn, 'Catholic Community', p. 43.
6a Source: I. Budge and C. O'Leary, *Belfast*, p. 27.
6b Source: Census returns, 1901 (P.R.O.N.I., MIC 354/1/79, 87, MIC 92, MIC 354/1/100-MIC354/1/101, MIC 354/1/108). Based on a selection of representative streets: Sandy Row district: Cullingtree Street, Fox's Row, Hutchinson Street, Leeds Street, Mary's Place, North Queen Place, Stanley Street, Wylie Place, Wylie Street, Rowland Street, Sandy Row, Schomberg Street, Scott Street. Pound district : Albert Street, Cullingtree Road, Brook Street, Crane Street, Pound Street, Quadrant Street, Scotch Street, Derby Street and Durham Street.
7 S. Gribbon, *Edwardian Belfast*, p. 20.
8 Collins, 'Edwardian City', p. 176.
9 Gribbon, *Edwardian Belfast*, pp 16-17.

10 Gray, *Labour aristocracy*, pp 108-10, 141-2; Crossick, *Artisan elite*, pp 130-1.

10a Source: Census of Christ Church district, 1852 (P.R.O.N.I., CR1/13/D1) Census returns, 1901 (P.R.O.N.I., MIC 354/1/79, 87, 92, MIC 354/1/100-MIC354/1/101, MIC 354/1/108).

10b Source: Census returns, 1901 (P.R.O.N.I., MIC 354/1/79, 87, 92, MIC 354/1/100-MIC354/1/101, MIC 354/1/108).

11 Durham Street has not been included as it was mainly Catholic. Grosvenor Street has not been included as most of the street is outside the district. Turin, Naples and Pisa Streets are considered to be in the Roden Street district and have also been omitted.

12 Presbyterians particularly dominated the grocery business; they comprised over 50% of the grocers in Belfast in 1901 whereas members of the Church of Ireland comprised only 17.89%: *Census of Ireland, 1901*, PP, 1902 [cd. 1123] cxxvi, vol. 126, p. 21.

13 R.J. Morris, 'Inequality, social structure and the market in Belfast and Glasgow, 1830-1914', p. 199.

14 Catholics comprised over 51% of the male general shopkeepers and dealers, 18.62 % of the grocers, 54% of the green grocers and 80% of the publicans and innkeepers in Belfast although their percentage of the population was only 23.26: *Census of Ireland, 1901*, pp 21, 24.

15 Unskilled occupations include domestic servants, carters, porters, messengers, coal heavers, road labourers, general labourers, factory labourers, machinists, machine workers and chimney sweeps. Even if domestic servants are excluded from these calculations, the numbers of Church of Ireland members is still high at 35.6%, Catholics formed 31.35%, Presbyterians 25.62%, Methodists 4.16% and Other denominations 3.26%: *Census of Ireland, 1901*, pp 17-25.

15a Source: *Census of Ireland, 1901*, PP, 1902 [cd. 1123] cxxvi, p. 22.

15b Source: *Census of Ireland, 1901*, PP, 1902 [cd. 1123] cxxvi, pp. 17-25.

16 Including riggers, chandlers and fitters.

17 Hepburn, 'Catholic Community', p. 49; H. Patterson, *Class conflict and sectarianism*, p. xv.

18 Hepburn, 'Catholic Community', p. 49.

19 The report of the 1886 riot commissioners mentions that the shipyard workers had to be guarded by the police on their way home to the Shankill: *Report*, PP, 1887 [C.4925], xviii, pp 4-6.

19a Based on a selection of representative streets: Sandy Row district: Fox's Row, Hutchinson Street, Stanley Street, Wylie Place, Wylie Street, Sandy Row, Schomberg Street, Scott Street. Pound district: Albert Street, Cullingtree Road , Brook Street, Crane Court, Pound Street, Derby Street, Durham Street, Quadrant Street and Scotch Street. Source: Census returns, 1901 (P.R.O.N.I., MIC 354/1/79, 87, 92, MIC 354/1/100-MIC354/1/101, MIC 354/1/108).

20 Hepburn, *Catholic community*. However, the ratio of sexes in the two areas was very similar (80 men to every 100 women in Sandy Row and 78 men to every 100 women in the Pound) unlike those for Protestants and Catholics in Belfast as a whole (64 Catholic men to every 100 Catholic women and 79 Protestant men to every 100 Protestant women).

21 See Chapter 7.

21a Source: Census returns, 1901 (P.R.O.N.I., MIC 354/1/79, 87, 92, MIC 354/1/100-MIC354/1/101, MIC 354/1/108).

22 C.D. Purdon, *The mortality of flax mill and factory worker*, p. 7.

23 *Fifth report of the children's employment commissioners*, PP, 1866 [3678] xxiv, p. 196.

24 Ibid., p. 196.

25 Ibid., p. 175.

26 Ibid., p. 175.

27 Ibid., p. 174.

27a Source: Census of Christ Church district, 1852 (P.R.O.N.I., CR1/13/D1); Census returns, 1901 (P.R.O.N.I., MIC 354/1/79, 87, 92, MIC 354/1/100–MIC 354/1/101, MIC 354/1/108).

27b Source: Census returns, 1901 (P.R.O.N.I., MIC 354/1/79, 87, 92, MIC 354/1/100–MIC354/1/101, MIC 354/1/108).

28 Defined as streets with a majority of two to three room houses. The streets included are Isaac Court, Leeds Street, Mary's Place, North Queen Place, Wylie Place, Stanley Street, Faulkner Street, Scott Street, St Andrew's Square West, Sturgeon Street, Watson Street and McFarlane's Court.

28a Source: Census returns, 1901 (P.R.O.N.I., MIC 354/1/79, 87, 92, MIC 354/1/100–MIC 354/1/101, MIC 354/1/108).

29 Defined as streets with a majority of two to three room houses. The streets included are Isaac Court, Leeds Street, Mary's Place, North Queen Place, Wylie Place, Stanley Street, Faulkner Street, Scott Street, St Andrew's Square West, Sturgeon Street, Watson Street and McFarlane's Court.

30 'Adults' includes children in employment.

30a Source: Census returns, 1901 (P.R.O.N.I., MIC 354/1/79, 87, 92, MIC 354/1/100–MIC 354/1/101, MIC 354/1/108).

31 Defined as streets with a majority of two to three room houses. The streets included are Isaac Court, Leeds Street, Mary's Place, North Queen Place, Wylie Place, Stanley Street, Faulkner Street, Scott Street, St Andrew's Square West, Sturgeon Street, Watson Street and McFarlane's Court.

31a Source: Census returns, 1901 (P.R.O.N.I., MIC 354/1/79, 87, 92, MIC 354/1/100–MIC 354/1/101, MIC 354/1/108).

31b Source: Census returns, 1901 (P.R.O.N.I., MIC 354/1/79, 87, 92,

MIC 354/1/100–MIC 354/1/101, MIC 354/1/108).

32 'Adults' includes children in employment.

33a Source: Census returns, 1901 (P.R.O.N.I., MIC 354/1/79, 87, 92, MIC 354/1/100–MIC 354/1/101, MIC 354/1/108).

CHAPTER 7

1 *Northern Whig*, 15 July 1852, 14 July 1853, 16 July 1863, 15 July 1878, 14 July 1879, 14 July 1882, 14 July 1884, 14–15 July 1885; *Belfast Newsletter*, 17 July 1854, 14 July 1866, 13–14 July 1868, 13 July 1871, 14 July 1873, 14 July 1881; Reports of resident magistrates, 19 July 1855, 13 July 1857, 17 July 1857, 15 July 1864 (N.A.I., CSORP/1855/6655, CSORP/1858/16743, CSORP/1864/17343); *Report of the Belfast riot commissioners, 1886*, p. 10.

2 See for example *Northern Whig*, 13 July 1858, 14 July 1879.

3 Report of resident magistrate, 19 July 1855 (N.A.I., CSORP/1855/6655).

4 *Report of the commissioners of inquiry, Belfast riots 1857*, pp. 248–51.

5 Ibid., p. 6. In giving an account of what happened during riots, there is always the problem of the biased nature of many sources such as the evidence given by participants and the accounts of newspapers. The reports compiled by the riot commissioners in 1857, 1864 and 1886, after hearing evidence from all sides, are probably the sources which are the least biased. For factual information, the reports have been used. For information regarding the attitudes of participants and observers, the minutes of evidence have been used as well as newspapers. The minutes of evidence have also been used on occasions for factual information subject to cautious scrutiny. In the cases of smaller scale riots where no riot commission was appointed, the reports of resident magistrates have been used as the most reliable sources.

6 *Report of the commissioners of inquiry, Belfast riots 1857*, p. 5.

7 Report of resident magistrate, 23 July 1857 (N.A.I., CSORP/1858/16743).

8 *Report of the commissioners of inquiry, Belfast riots 1857*, p. 24.

9 Ibid., p. 6.

10 Ibid., pp 26, 126.

11 Ibid., p. 7.

12 Ibid., p. 133.

13 Ibid., pp 124-5.

14 Ibid., pp 86, 138.

15 Ibid., pp 123-4.

16 Ibid., p. 13.

17 Report of resident magistrate, 26 July 1857 (N.A.I., CSORP/1858/16743).

18 Report of resident magistrate, 29 August 1857 (N.A.I., CSORP/1858/16743).

19 Report of resident magistrate, 13 September 1857 (N.A.I., CSORP/1858/16743).

20 *Report of commissioners of inquiry, Belfast riots 1857*, p. 13.

21 Budge and O'Leary, *Belfast; approach to crisis*, pp 79-80; *Report of commissioners of inquiry, Belfast riots 1857*, p. 9.

22 *Report of commissioners of inquiry, Belfast riots 1857*, p. 3.

23 Ibid., pp 49, 57-8.

24 Ibid., p. 31.

25 Ibid., pp 32, 49.

26 *Northern Whig*, 15 July 1852.

27 *Report of commissioners of inquiry, Belfast riots 1857*, p. 11.

28 *Ulsterman*, 10 September 1857 in report of resident magistrate, 13 September 1857 (N.A.I., CSORP/1858/16743).

29 *Belfast Newsletter*, 5 September 1857.

30 The commissioners found this incident particularly regrettable. *Report of commissioners of inquiry, Belfast riots 1857*, p. 7.

31 Report of resident magistrate, 23 July 1857 (N.A.I., CSORP/1858/16743).

32 *Ulsterman*, 3 August 1857.

33 Report of resident magistrate, 12 August 1857 (N.A.I., CSORP/1858/16743).

34 *Report of commissioners of inquiry, Belfast riots 1857*, p. 26; Report of resident magistrate, 8 September 1857 (N.A.I., CSORP/1858/16743).

35 *Report of commissioners of inquiry, Belfast riots 1857*, p. 13.

36 Ibid., p. 6; Report of resident magistrate, 2 December 1864 (N.A.I., CSORP/1864/22,222).

37 *Report of the Commissioners of Inquiry 1864 respecting the magisterial and police jurisdiction arrangements and establishment of the borough of Belfast*, PP, 1865 [3466-I] xxviii, p. 32.

38 Report of resident magistrate, 19 August 1864 (N.A.I., CSORP/1864/20438).

39 Report of resident magistrate, 19 August 1864, report of sub-inspector of constabulary, 19 August 1864 (N.A.I., CSORP/1864/20438).

40 *Report of commissioners of inquiry 1864, magisterial and police jurisdiction*, pp 37-40, 49.

41 Ibid., pp 16, 272.

42 Report of sub-inspector of constabulary, 19 August 1864 (N.A.I., CSORP/1864/20438).

43 Ibid.

44 Report of resident magistrate, 19 August 1864 (N.A.I., CSORP/1864/20438).

45 Ibid., *Report of commissioners of inquiry 1864, magisterial and police jurisdiction*, pp 14-15.

46 *Report of commissioners of inquiry 1864, magisterial and police jurisdiction*, pp 58, 120.

47 Ibid., pp 58, 255.

48 Report of resident magistrate, 2 December 1864 (N.A.I., CSORP/1864/22,222).

49 Wright, *Two lands on one soil*, p. 269.

50 *Report of commississioners of inquiry 1864, magisterial and police jurisdiction*, pp 14-15.

51 See Chapter 4.

52 *Northern Whig*, 13 July 1885.

53 Report of sub-inspector of constabulary, 19 August 1864 (N.A.I., CSORP/1864/20438).

54 Rea was contesting the view of this magistrate that the navvies were the cause of the riots and argued that the riots 'were caused by the animosity of these rival secret societies.' This seems a strange claim to make considering

Rea was representing the Catholic community and that he later went on to defend most of the Belfast Fenian suspects in court. His only possible motive could have been to deflect blame away from Catholics in general. See *Report of commissioners of inquiry 1864, magisterial and police jurisdiction*, p. 155.

55 Ballads sent to chief secretary's office, September 1864 (N.A.I., CSORP/1864/19263).

56 See chapter four.

57 Report of sub-inspector of constabulary, August 1872 (N.A.I., CSORP/1873/1022).

58 Report of resident magistrate, August 1872 (N.A.I., CSORP/1873/1022).

59 Ibid.

60 Ibid.

61 Reports of resident magistrate and sub-inspector of constabulary, August 1872 (N.A.I., CSORP/1873/1022).

62 Ibid.

63 Ibid.

64 One can see the same connection in the minds of people today. Orangemen have told me that if they acquiesce in a decision to ban their march down the Garvaghy Road, there will be a united Ireland tomorrow. This attitude is probably due to Protestant distrust of British governments. They feel it is necessary to make a stand otherwise the British will sell them out.

65 *Daily Examiner*, 23 September 1872.

66 Wright, *Two lands on one soil*, p. 481.

67 Report of resident magistrate, 26 February 1879 (N.A.I., CSORP/1882/20807).

68 *Northern Whig*, 14 July 1883.

69 Report of resident magistrate, 14 July 1874 (N.A.I., CSORP/1874/9808).

70 E. Boyle, 'The linen strike of 1872', pp 12-13.

71 Boyle, 'Linen strike of 1872', p. 13.

72 *Report of the Belfast riot commissioners, 1886*, pp 4-6.

73 Ibid., pp 6-8.

74 Ibid., pp. 4-9; *Report of the Belfast riot commissioners, 1886, minutes of evidence*, PP, 1887 [C.4925-I], xviii, p. 81.

75 *Report of the Belfast riot commissioners, 1886, minutes of evidence*, pp 214-16.

76 *Report of the Belfast riot commissioners, 1886*, pp 16, 20.

77 Ibid., pp 4-9, 25 and *minutes of evidence*, pp 71-2.

78 *Report of the Belfast riot commissioners, 1886*, p. 10.

79 Ibid., *minutes of evidence*, p. 159.

80 Ibid., pp. 224, 298.

81 *Report of the Belfast riot commissioners, 1886*, pp 9-16 and *minutes of evidence*, p. 67.

82 *Report of the Belfast riot commissioners, 1886, minutes of evidence*, pp 493, 507.

83 Ibid., pp 490, 493-4.

84 Ibid., p. 509.

85 Ibid.

86 Ibid., pp 371-4.

87 Ibid., p. 63.

88 Ibid., p. 264.

89 Ibid., p. 207.

90 Ibid., p. 375.

91 Ibid., p. 370.

92 Ibid., pp 414, 447, 458-9 and 462.

93 *Belfast Newsletter*, 14 June 1886.

94 *Belfast Newsletter*, 18 August 1886.

95 *Report of the Belfast riot commissioners, 1886, minutes of evidence*, pp 333-4.

96 Ibid., p. 340.

97 Ibid., pp 176-8.

98 *Report of the Belfast riot commissioners, 1886*, p. 17.

99 E.P. Thompson, 'The moral economy of the English crowd in the eighteenth century', p. 78.

100 J. Stevenson, *Popular disturbances in England, 1700-1870* (London, 1979), p. 86.

101 *Report of the Belfast riot commissioners, 1886*, p. 17.

102 *Report of the Belfast riot commissioners, 1886, minutes of evidence*, p. 40.

103 Ibid., p. 61.

104 Ibid., p. 159.

105 Ibid., p. 131.

106 Ibid., p. 176.

107 Ibid., pp 217-19, 352.

108 Ibid., p. 298.

109 Ibid., p. 205.

110 Band file (N.A.I., CSORP/1882/20807).

111 *Report of the Belfast riot commissioners, 1886, minutes of evidence*, p. 134.
112 Band file (N.A.I., CSORP/1882/20807).
113 Ibid.
114 Report of resident magistrate, August 1872 (N.A.I., CSORP/1873/1022); *Report of the Belfast riot commissioners, 1886, minutes of evidence*, p. 64.
115 Thompson, 'Moral economy', pp 79-84.
116 Ibid., pp 80-84; Stevenson, *Popular disturbances*, p. 2.
117 Report of resident magistrate, 2 December 1864 (N.A.I., CSORP/1864/22,222).
118 *Belfast Newsletter*, 1 May 1865.
119 *Report of commissioners of inquiry 1864, magisterial and police jurisdiction*, p. 253.
120 Ibid., pp 274-5.
121 *Report of the Belfast riot commissioners, 1886, minutes of evidence*, p. 57.
122 *Report of commissioners of inquiry 1864, magisterial and police jurisdiction*, p. 135.
123 Report of resident magistrate, August 1872 (N.A.I., CSORP/1873/1022).
124 *Northern Whig*, 15 July 1885.
125 *Report of the Belfast riot commissioners, 1886, minutes of evidence*, pp. 61, 460.
126 Gibbon, *Origins of Ulster unionism*, pp 80-5.
127 Band file (N.A.I., CSORP/1882/20807).
128 D. Hempton, 'Belfast: the unique city?', p. 147.
129 Hepburn, *A past apart*, p. 231.
130 *Daily Examiner*, 23 September 1872.

Bibliography

MANUSCRIPT SOURCES

Public Records Office of Northern Ireland, Belfast.
Annals of Christ Church, 1833-59 (T1075/11)
Autobiography of Robert McElborough, a Belfast workman (D770)
Belfast poll book, 1832-7 (D2472/1)
Belfast valuation 1837 (Val. 1B/79)
Brown Street Sunday school register, 1817-50 (SCH 580/1/1)
Census of Christ Church district, 1852 (CR1/13/1D)
Census returns, 1901 (MIC 354/1/79-84)
Chief Secretary's office registered papers relating to O'Connell's visit to Belfast, 1841 (T3280/1)
Christ Church baptismal register, 1833-50 (T.679/262)
Colonial Office records on Ribbonism 1798-1867 (MIC 448/1-3)
County Antrim national schools register, vol. 2 (ED6/1/1/2-3)
Fisherwick Presbyterian list of communicants, 1833-9 (MIC 1P/92/2)
Linen Hall Street Presbyterian baptismal register, 1831-50 (MIC1P/57/2)
Linen Hall Street Presbyterian marriage register, 1831-50 (MIC 1P/57/3)
May Street Presbyterian baptismal register, 1836-50 (MIC 1P/9/1)
May Street Presbyterian marriage register, 1835-50 (MIC 1P/9/2)
Memorandum of association of the Belfast Catholic Institute (D1905/2/205A)
Methodist baptismal register, Belfast circuit, 1815-43 (MIC 429/1)
National board grant aid applications, 1838-50 (ED1/1/1-100, ED1/2/41-181)
Reports of the committee of Belfast ladies industrial national school, 1851-4 (SCH 361/8/7/1)
Reverend McIntyre's diary (D1558/4/1)
Rosemary Street Presbyterian marriage register, 1820-46 (MIC 1P/7/1)
Townsend Street Presbyterian baptismal register, 1835-50 (MIC1P/336A/1)
Townsend Street Presbyterian Church, history of the congregation, 1833-1933 (CR 3/27)
Townsend Street Presbyterian marriage register, 1836-50 (MIC 1P/336A/1)
William Johnston's diary (D/880/2/19)

House of Orange, Belfast
Grand lodge register of warrants (GLOI/1/23, GLOI/1/28-9, GLOI/1/56, GLOI/1/75)

National Archives of Ireland, Dublin.
Chief secretary's office registered papers, 1852-86.
Fenian papers.
Outrage papers, County Antrim, 1832-1852.
State of the country papers, Belfast and Ulster counties, 1805-1831.

PRINTED PRIMARY SOURCES

Parliamentary papers
Second report of the commissioners of Irish education inquiry, PP, 1826-7 [12] xii.
Report from the select committee of inquiry into drunkeness, PP, 1834 [559] viii.
*Report from the select committee appointed to inquire into the nature, character, extent and
    tendency of Orange lodges, associations or societies in Ireland*, PP, 1835 [377] xv.
First report of the commissioners of public instruction, Ireland, PP, 1835 [45] xxxiii.
*First report from His Majesty's commissioners for inquiring into the state of the poorer classes in
    Ireland*, PP, 1835 [369] xxxii.
*Report from the select committee appointed to inquire into the progress and operation of the new
    plan of education in Ireland*, PP, 1837 [485] ix.
Fourth report of the commissioners of national education in Ireland, PP, 1837-8 [447] xxviii.
Fifth report of the commissioners of national education in Ireland, PP, 1839 [160] xvi.
Reports from assistant hand loom weavers' commissioners, PP, 1840 [43-II] xxiii, part iii.
Eighth report of the commissioners of national education in Ireland, PP, 1842 [398] xxiii.
Sixteenth report of commissioners of national education in Ireland, PP, 1850 [1231] xxv.
Report from the select committee on outrages (Ireland), PP, 1852 [438] xiv.
*Report from the select committee of the House of Lords appointed to inquire into the practical
    working of the system of national education in Ireland*, 1854 [525] xv, part ii.
*Report of the commissioners of inquiry into the origin and character of the riots in Belfast in July
    and September 1857*, PP, 1857-8 [2309] xxvi.
Twenty sixth report of the commissioners of national education in Ireland, PP, 1860 [2706] xxvi.
*Report of the commissioners of inquiry 1864 respecting the magisterial and police jurisdiction
    arrangements and establishment of the borough of Belfast*, PP, 1865 [3466-I] xxviii.
Fifth report of children's employment commissioners, PP, 1866 [3678] xxiv.
*Reports from commissioners: primary education (Ireland), educational census returns showing
    number of children actually present in each primary school, 25 June 1868*, PP, 1870 [C.6-V]
    xxviii, part v.
*Report of the commissioners appointed to inquire into the working of the factory and workshop acts
    with a view to their consolidation and amendment*, PP, 1876 [C.1443-I] xxx.
Fiftieth report of the commissioners of national education in Ireland, PP, 1884 [C.4053] xxv.
Report of the Belfast riot commissioners, 1886, PP, 1887 [C.4925] and minutes of evidence
    [C.4925-I] xviii.
Census of Ireland 1901, PP, 1902 [Cd. 1123] cxxvi.
*Report of the inter-departmental committee on the employment of children during school age
    especially in the large centres of population in Ireland*, PP, 1902 [Cd. 1144] xlix.

Newspapers
Banner of Ulster   *Nation*
Belfast Morning News   *Northern Whig*
Belfast Newsletter   *Ulster Observer*
Daily Examiner   *Vindicator*
Irishman

Other printed sources
*General valuation of rateable property in Ireland (Griffith valuation), 1860, union of Belfast,
    Counties Antrim and Down.*
Belfast street directory, 1819, 1820, 1831-2, 1835-6, 1840-1, 1846, 1860, 1865-6, 1870, 1878,
    1880.
Irish Catholic directory, 1887.

SECONDARY SOURCES

Aunger, E., 'Political violence in Canada: the case of New Brunswick' in Darby, J., Dodge, N. and Hepburn, A. (ed.), *Political violence. Ireland in a comparative perspective* (Belfast, 1990)

Adams, J., *The printed word and the common man: popular culture in Ulster, 1700-1900* (Belfast, 1987)

Akenson, D.H., *Between two revolutions: Islandmagee, County Antrim, 1798-1920* (Dublin, 1979)

—— *The Irish education experiment* (London, 1970)

Allen, R., 'Henry Montgomery, 1788-1865' in Cronne, H., Moody, T.W. and Quinn, D. (ed.), *Essays in British and Irish history in honour of James Eadie Todd* (London, 1949)

Anon., *The Repealer repulsed!* (Belfast, 1841)

Armstrong, D., 'Social and economic conditions in the Belfast linen industry, 1850-1900' in *Irish Historical Studies*, vol. 7 (Sept. 1951), pp 235-69

Baker, S., 'Orange and green, Belfast, 1832-1912' in Dyos, H. and Wolff, M. (ed.), *The Victorian city*, vol. 2, (London, 1973)

Beames, M., 'The Ribbon societies: lower class nationalism in pre-famine Ireland' in *Past and Present*, vol. 97 (1982), pp 128-43

Beckett, J.C., *The making of modern Ireland, 1603-1923* (London, 1981)

—— et al. (ed.), *Belfast: the making of the city* (Belfast, 1983)

—— 'Belfast: a general survey' in Beckett and Glasscock (ed.), *Belfast: the origin and growth of an industrial city*

Beckett, J.C. and Glasscock, R.E. (ed.), *Belfast: the origin and growth of an industrial city* (London, 1967)

Benn, G., *A history of the town of Belfast from the earliest times to the close of the eighteenth century* (London, 1877)

Bentley, M., *Politics without democracy: Great Britain, perception and preoccupation in British government* (Oxford, 1984)

Bew, P., 'Politics and the rise of the skilled working man' in Beckett, et al. (ed.), *Belfast: the making of the city.*

—— *Ideology and the Irish question* (Oxford, 1994)

Black, E., *The people's park: the Queen's Island, Belfast, 1849-1879* (Belfast, 1988)

Bowen, D., *The Protestant crusade in Ireland, 1800-70* (Dublin, 1978)

Boyce, D.G., *Nationalism in Ireland* (London, 1982)

Boyce, D.G. and O'Day, A. (ed.), *The making of modern Irish history; revisionism and the revisionist controversy* (London, 1996)

Boyd, A., *Holy war in Belfast* (Tralee, 1970)

Boyle, E., 'Linenopolis: the rise of the textile industry' in Beckett, J.C., *Belfast: the making of the city* (Belfast, 1983)

—— 'The linen strike of 1872' in *Saothar*, vol. 2 (1976), pp 12-22

Boyle, J., 'The Belfast Protestant Association and the Independent Orange Order, 1901-10' in *Irish Historical Studies*, vol. 13 (1962-3), pp 117-52

Brock, M., *The great reform act* (London, 1973)

Brook, P., 'Religion and secular thought, 1800-75' in Beckett et al. (ed.), *Belfast: the making of the city.*

Buckland, P., *Irish unionism two: Ulster unionism and the origins of Northern Ireland, 1886-1922* (Dublin, 1973)

Buckley, A., 'On the club: friendly societies in Ireland' in *Irish Economic and Social History*, xiv (1987), pp 39-58

Budge, I. and O'Leary, C., *Belfast, approach to crisis: a study of Belfast politics, 1613-1970* (London, 1973)

Burrow, J., *A tour round Ireland* (London, 1836)

Clarkson, L., 'The city and the country' in Beckett, et al. (ed.), *Belfast: the making of the city*

Collins, B., 'The Edwardian city' in Beckett, et al. (ed.), *Belfast: the making of the city*

Comerford, R., *The Fenians in context: Irish politics and society, 1848–82* (Dublin, 1985)

—— 'Patriotism as pastime: the appeal of Fenianism in the mid-1860s' in *Irish historical studies*, lxxxvii (March 1981), pp 239–250

Connolly, S.J., 'Catholicism in Ulster 1800–50' in Roebuck, P. (ed.), *Plantation to partition: essays in honour of J. L. McCracken* (Belfast, 1981)

—— *Priests and people in pre-famine Ireland, 1780–1845* (Dublin, 1982)

—— *Religion and society in nineteenth century Ireland* (Dundalk, 1985)

Crossick, G., *An artisan elite in Victorian society: Kentish London, 1840–1880* (London, 1978)

Daly, M., *Dublin, the deposed capital: a social and economic history 1860–1914* (Cork, 1984)

Davis, R., *The Young Ireland movement* (Dublin, 1987)

Doyle, M., 'Belfast and Tolpuddle: attempts at strengthening a trade union presence 1833–34' in *Saothar*, vol. 2, pp 2–11.

Elliott, M., *Watchmen in Sion: the Protestant idea of liberty* (Derry, 1985)

Evans, E., *The forging of the modern state: early industrial Britain, 1783–1870* (London, 1983)

Flanagan, T., 'Literature in English, 1801–91' in Vaughan, *A new history of Ireland*, vol. 5

Gallagher, C., *All around the Loney-O* (Antrim, 1978)

Garvin, T., 'Defenders, Ribbonmen and others: underground political networks in pre-famine Ireland' in *Past and Present*, xcvi (1982), pp 133–55

Gibbon, P., *The origins of Ulster unionism* (Manchester, 1975)

Gray, J., 'Popular entertainment' in Beckett et al. (ed.), *Belfast: the making of the city*

Gray, R., *The labour aristocracy in Victorian Edinburgh* (Oxford, 1976)

Green, E., *The Lagan valley, 1800–50* (London, 1949)

Gribbon, S., *Edwardian Belfast: a social profile* (Belfast, 1982)

—— 'The social origins of Ulster unionism' in *Irish Economic and Social History*, iv (1977), pp 66–72

Hanson, R., 'Is it a religious issue?' in *Encounter*, lv, no. 4 (Oct. 1980), pp 11–20

Harris, R., *Prejudice and tolerance in Ulster: Neighbours and strangers in a border community* (Manchester, 1972)

Harrison, B., 'Traditions of respectability in British labour history' in Harrison, B. (ed.), *Peaceable kingdom: stability and change in modern Britain* (Oxford, 1982)

—— 'Religion and recreation in nineteenth century England' in Harrison, B. (ed.), *Peaceable kingdom: stability and change in modern Britain* (Oxford, 1982)

Heatley, F., 'Community relations and the religious geography, 1800–86' in Beckett, J.C., *Belfast: the making of the city* (Belfast, 1983)

Hempton, D., 'Belfast: the unique city?' in McLeod, H. (ed.), *European religion in the age of great cities* (London, 1995)

—— *Religion and political culture in Britain and Ireland* (Cambridge, 1996)

Hempton, D. and Hill, M., *Evangelical Protestantism in Ulster society, 1740–1890* (London, 1992)

Hepburn, A.C., *A past apart: studies in the history of Catholic Belfast, 1850–1950* (Belfast, 1996)

—— *The Catholic community of Belfast, 1850–1940* (Dartmouth, 1992)

Hepburn, A.C. and Collins, B., 'Industrial society: the structure of Belfast, 1901' in Roebuck, P. (ed.), *Plantation to partition: essays in Ulster history in honour of J.L. McCracken* (Belfast, 1981)

Heslinga, M., *The Irish border as a cultural divide: a contribution to the study of regionalism in the British isles* (Utrecht, 1962)

Hill, M., 'Ulster awakened: the '59 revival reconsidered' in *Journal of Ecclesiastical History*, xli (July 1990), pp 443–62

Holmes, F., *Henry Cooke* (Belfast, 1981)

Holmes, J., 'Lifting the curtain on popular religion: women, laity and language in the Ulster revival of 1859', MA thesis, Queen's University, Kingston, Ontario, 1991.

Hoppen, K.T., *Elections, politics and society in Ireland, 1832-85* (Oxford, 1984)

Hughes, M., *Nationalism and society in Germany, 1800-1945* (London, 1988)

Hutchinson, J., 'Irish nationalism' in Boyce, D.G. and O'Day, A. (ed.), *The making of modern Irish history; revisionism and the revisionist controversy* (London, 1996)

Inglis, K., *Churches and the working classes in Victorian England* (London, 1963)

Jackson, A., *The Ulster party: Irish unionists in the house of commons, 1884-1911* (Oxford, 1989)

—— 'Irish unionism' in Boyce, D.G. and O'Day, A. (ed.), *The making of modern Irish history; revisionism and the revisionist controversy* (London, 1996)

—— 'Unionist politics and Protestant society in Edwardian Ireland' in *The Historical Journal*, vol. 33, no. 4 (1990), pp 839-66.

Jackson, J., *Community and conflict: a study of French-English relations in Ontario* (Toronto, 1975)

Jones, E., *A social geography of Belfast* (Oxford, 1960)

—— 'Late Victorian Belfast, 1850-1900' in Beckett and Glasscock (ed.), *Belfast: the origin and growth of an industrial city*

Jordan, A., *Who cared? Charity in Victorian and Edwardian Belfast* (Belfast, 1993)

Kennedy, L., 'The rural economy, 1820-1914' in Kennedy, L. and Ollerenshaw, P. (ed.), *An economic history of Ulster, 1820-1940* (Manchester, 1985)

Kennedy, L. and Olarenshaw, P. (ed.), *An economic history of Ulster, 1820-1940* (Manchester, 1985)

Killen, W., *Memoirs of John Edgar* (Belfast, 1869)

Larkin, E., 'The devotional revolution in Ireland, 1850-75' in *American Historical Review*, lxxvii (1972), pp 625-52.

Loughlin, J., *Ulster unionism and British national identity since 1885* (London, 1995)

Lyons, F.S.L., 'Fenianism, 1867-1916' in Moody, T.W. (ed.), *The Fenian movement*

Malcolm, A., *Sanitary state of Belfast* (Belfast, 1852)

Malcolm, E., *Ireland sober, Ireland free: drink and temperance in nineteenth century Ireland* (Dublin, 1986)

Mandle, W.F., *The Gaelic Athletic Association and Irish Nationalist politics, 1884-1924* (London, 1987)

McAteer, G., *Down the Falls* (Belfast, 1983)

Macauley, A., *Dr William Crolly, archbishop of Armagh, 1835-49* (Dublin, 1994)

—— *Patrick Dorrian: bishop of Down and Connor, 1865-85* (Dublin, 1987)

Maguire, W., *Belfast* (Staffordshire, 1993)

Malcolm, A., *The sanitary state of Belfast* (Belfast, 1852)

McAteer, G., *Down the Falls* (Belfast, 1983)

McClelland, A., *William Johnston of Ballykilbeg* (Lurgan, 1990)

McCracken, J.L., 'Early Victorian Belfast' in Beckett and Glasscock (ed.), *Belfast: the origin and growth of an industrial city*

McDonagh, O., *O'Connell: the life of Daniel O'Connell, 1775-1847* (London, 1991)

Miller, D., *Queen's rebels: Ulster loyalism in historical perspective* (Dublin, 1978)

Monaghan, J., 'A social and economic history of Belfast, 1801-1825', PhD thesis, Queen's University Belfast, 1940.

Moody, T.W., *The Fenian movement* (Cork, 1968)

—— 'The Fenian movement in Irish history' in Moody, T.W. (ed.), *The Fenian movement*

Morgan, Rev. J., *Recollections of my life and times* (Belfast, 1874)

Morris, R.J., 'Inequality, social structure and the market in Belfast and Glasgow, 1830-1914' in Connolly, S.J., Houston, R.A. and Morris, R.J. (ed.), *Conflict, identity and economic development, Ireland and Scotland, 1600-1939* (Preston, Lancs., 1995)

Nolan, K., *The politics of repeal* (London, 1965)

Newsinger, J., *Fenianism in mid-Victorian Britain* (London, 1994)

O'Donnell, P., *The Irish faction fighters of the nineteenth century* (Dublin, 1975)

O'Hanlon, Rev. W., *Walks among the poor of Belfast* (Wakefield, 1971)

Ollerenshaw, P., 'Industry, 1820-1914' in Kennedy, L. and Ollerenshaw, P. (ed.), *An economic history of Ulster, 1820-1940* (Manchester, 1985)

Patterson, H., *Class conflict and sectarianism: the Protestant working class and the Belfast labour movement, 1868-1920* (Belfast, 1980)

Phoenix, E., *Northern nationalism: nationalist politics, partition and the Catholic minority in Northern Ireland* (Belfast, 1994)

Purdon, C., *The longevity of flax mill and factory operatives* (Belfast, 1875)

—— *The sanitary state of the Belfast factory district* (Belfast, 1877)

Rafferty, O., *Catholicism in Ulster 1603-1983* (London, 1994)

Robinson, P., *The plantation of Ulster* (Belfast, 1994)

Rogers, P., 'Father Hugh O'Donnell: parish priest of Belfast 1772-1812' in Cronne, H., Moody, T.W. and Quinn, D. (ed.), *Essays in British and Irish history in honour of James Eadie Todd* (London, 1949)

—— *St Peter's pro-cathedral, Belfast 1866-1966* (Belfast, 1967)

Roney, F., *Frank Roney: Irish rebel and Californian labour leader* (Berkeley, 1931)

Rude, G., *The crowd in history: a study of popular disturbances in France and England, 1730-1848* (London, 1981)

Savage, D., 'The origins of the UUP, 1885-6' in *Irish Historical Studies*, xii, no. 47 (March 1961), pp 185-208

Senior, H., *Orangeism in Britain and Ireland 1795-1836* (London, 1966)

Sibbett, R., *Orangeism in Ireland and throughout the empire* (Belfast, 1914)

—— *For Christ and crown: the story of a mission* (Belfast, 1926)

Slater, G., 'Belfast politics, 1798-1868', DPhil thesis, University of Ulster, 1982.

Stevenson, J., *Popular disturbances in England, 1700-1870* (London, 1979)

Stewart, A.T.Q., *The Ulster crisis* (London, 1967)

—— *The narrow ground: aspects of Ulster, 1609-1969* (Belfast, 1986)

Tilly, C., Tilly, L. and Tilly, R., *The rebellious century, 1830-1930* (London, 1975)

Thompson, E.P., 'Time, work discipline and industrial capitalism' in *Past and Present*, no. 38 (Dec. 1967), pp 56-97

—— 'The moral economy of the English crowd in the eighteenth century' in *Past and Present*, no. 50 (Feb. 1971), pp 76-136

Thompson, P., 'Voices from within' in Dyos, H. and Wolff, M. (ed.), *The Victorian city* (London, 1973)

Townsend, C., *Political violence in Ireland: government and resistance since 1848* (Oxford, 1983)

Vaughan, W.E. (ed.), *A new history of Ireland*, vol. 5 (Oxford, 1989)

Walker, B., 'Party organisation in Ulster, 1865-92: registration agents and their activities' in Roebuck, P. (ed.), *Plantation to partition: essays in Ulster history in honour of J.L. McCracken* (Belfast, 1981)

—— *Ulster politics: the formative years, 1868-86* (Belfast, 1989)

Whyte, J., *Interpreting Northern Ireland* (Oxford, 1990)

Wright, F., *Two lands on one soil: Ulster politics before home rule* (Dublin, 1996)

Index